CONSTRUCTIVIST, CRITICAL, AND INTEGRATIVE APPROACHES TO COUPLES COUNSELING

Couples counseling is distinct from individual and family therapy and, while ideas from these other formats may be overlapping, applying theoretical concepts to couples has distinctive challenges. *Constructivist, Critical, and Integrative Approaches to Couples Counseling* is unique in that it addresses how to conceptualize various theories around a single case. By discussing only one case, the reader is more readily able to compare and contrast the theoretical ideas of each theory, as well as the pragmatics of techniques. Five theories are discussed around four consistent parts: history, theory of problem formation, theory of problem resolution, and case transcript. This book follows the same format as its companion *Behavioral, Humanistic-Existential, and Psychodynamic Approaches to Couples Counseling*.

Michael D. Reiter, PhD, LMFT, is Professor in the Department of Family Therapy at Nova Southeastern University.

Ronald J. Chenail, PhD, is Associate Provost and Professor in the Department of Family Therapy at Nova Southeastern University. He is the current Editor of *Journal of Divorce and Remarriage*. He also served as Editor-in-Chief of the *Journal of Marital and Family Therapy*, the flagship research journal of the American Association for Marriage and Family Therapy (AAMFT).

CONSTRUCTIVIST, CRITICAL, AND INTEGRATIVE APPROACHES TO COUPLES COUNSELING

*Edited by Michael D. Reiter
and Ronald J. Chenail*

Routledge
Taylor & Francis Group

NEW YORK AND LONDON

First published 2017
by Routledge
711 Third Avenue, New York, NY 10017

and by Routledge
2 Park Square, Milton Park, Abingdon, Oxon, OX14 4RN

Routledge is an imprint of the Taylor & Francis Group, an informa business

Library of Congress Cataloging in Publication Data
Names: Reiter, Michael D., editor. | Chenail, Ronald J., editor.
Title: Constructivist, critical, and integrative approaches to couples counseling / edited by Michael D. Reiter & Ronald J. Chenail.
Description: New York, NY : Routledge, 2017. |
Includes bibliographical references and index.
Identifiers: LCCN 2016030492 | ISBN 9781138233973 (hardback : alk. paper) | ISBN 9781138233980 (pbk. : alk. paper) | ISBN 9781315308319 (ebook)
Subjects: | MESH: Couples Therapy–methods | Marital Therapy–methods | Counseling–methods
Classification: LCC RC488.5 | NLM WM 430.5.M3 | DDC 616.89/1562–dc23
LC record available at https://lccn.loc.gov/2016030492

ISBN: 978-1-138-23397-3 (hbk)
ISBN: 978-1-138-23398-0 (pbk)
ISBN: 978-1-315-30831-9 (ebk)

Typeset in Bembo
by Out of House Publishing

MDR: To Patricia and Salvador Minuchin—two people who came together to become an amazing couple and who helped countless couples and families through their work.

RJC: To Paula—this is our first book and first year of marriage—may we have many more of both.

CONTENTS

ABOUT THE EDITORS

Michael D. Reiter, PhD, LMFT, is a licensed Marriage and Family Therapist, Clinical Fellow of the American Association of Family Therapists (AAMFT), and a state and AAMFT Approved Supervisor. Currently, Michael is Professor of Family Therapy at Nova Southeastern University. He has written four textbooks on therapy and family therapy and has written many journal articles and book chapters on Solution-Focused Brief Therapy. Michael was able to obtain training from Insoo Kim Berg and Steve de Shazer, the founders of Solution-Focused Brief Therapy, and has provided Solution-Focused Brief Therapy trainings and conference presentations nationally and internationally.

Ronald J. Chenail, PhD, is Associate Provost and Professor of Family Therapy at Nova Southeastern University (NSU). Since 1990, he has published over 120 publications including five books and given over 180 formal academic presentations at conferences and meetings. He also served as Editor-in-Chief of the *Journal of Marital and Family Therapy* (*JMFT*), the flagship research journal of the American Association for Marriage and Family Therapy (AAMFT). In addition, he is an editorial board member of *Qualitative Research in Psychology*, *American Journal of Family Therapy*, *Contemporary Family Therapy*, *Qualitative Social Work*, *Counselling, Psychotherapy, and Health*, *JMFT*, and *Sistemas Familiares*.

ABOUT THE CHAPTER CONTRIBUTORS

Sheila Addison, LMFT, is a Visiting Assistant Professor in the Clinical Counseling program at Alliant International University San Francisco, and a clinician in private practice in Berkeley, California. Her clinical and scholarly work focuses on the needs of gender and sexual minorities, culturally competent mental health training, training therapists to work with the sexual concerns of diverse clients, culturally informed couple therapy using Emotionally Focused Therapy, and introducing the principles of Size Acceptance and Health at Every Size® to mental health clinicians. She has recently published an article on intersectional therapy with queer couples in *Family Process* as well as chapters in *Multicultural Couple Therapy* and *Clinical Casebook of Couple Therapy*. She currently serves as the President-Elect for the Association for Family Therapy of Northern California as well as a Board Member for TransLifeline, the first crisis hotline for transgender and gender-queer people.

James L. Furrow, PhD, is the Evelyn and Frank Freed Professor of Marital and Family Therapy at the Fuller Graduate School of Psychology, Pasadena, California. His research and writing focus on Emotionally Focused Therapy with couples and families, including *The EFT Casebook: New Directions in Couple Treatment*, *Becoming an EFT Therapist: The Workbook*, and *Emotionally Focused Couple Therapy for Dummies*. Jim is a certified EFT therapist, supervisor, and Executive Director of the Los Angeles Center for EFT.

Nicholas Lee, PhD is an Assistant Professor of counseling psychology at Radford University, Radford, Virginia. He is a certified EFT therapist and has been practicing EFT with couples for almost a decade. He lives in southwest Virginia with his wife and young daughter.

Megan J. Murphy, LMFT, is an AAMFT Clinical Fellow and Approved Supervisor, and Director of the Marriage and Family Therapy Master's Program at Purdue University Calumet. She has published in the *Journal of Marital and Family Therapy*, *Journal of Homosexuality*, *Journal of Feminist Family Therapy*, *American Journal of Family Therapy*, *Journal of Counseling Psychology*, *Journal of Family Psychology*, and *Contemporary Family Therapy*. Her research interests include power in relationships, supervision and training, diversity, feminist issues, ethics and decision-making, and LGBT issues. She serves as a Commissioner for the Commission on Accreditation for Marriage and Family Therapy Education (COAMFTE), and is a frequent presenter at both the American Association for Marriage and Family Therapy Annual Conference and the National Council on Family Relations Annual Conference.

Hannah S. Myung, MS, MA, is a doctoral student in clinical psychology at Fuller Graduate School of Psychology and research fellow for the Travis Research Institute. She practices therapy at Fuller Psychological and Family Services.

Catalina Perdomo is a Master's student at Our Lady of the Lake University in the Family, Couple, and Individual Psychotherapy program in combination with the certificate for Psychological Services for Spanish Speaking Populations. She recently became a fellow through the Minority Fellowship Program-Youth through the AAMFT. Catalina is a second-generation Colombian-American, whose bilinguality in Spanish and English has forced her to navigate between a variety of linguistic realities. When not in school, Catalina enjoys photography and spending time outdoors with her heeler mix Leila.

marcela polanco was born in Bogotá, Colombia, land of her Muisca ancestors. As a mestiza, cisgender woman, and immigrant in the US, she serves as an Assistant Professor at Our Lady of the Lake University in San Antonio/Yanaguana, Texas. She is the director of the Master's in Family, Couple and Individual Psychotherapy and the bilingual Certificate in Psychological Services for Spanish Speaking Populations. She also serves as international faculty of the Dulwich Centre in Adelaide, Australia and the Master's in Narrative Therapy of Universidad Extremadura in Spain. Her work is inspired by principles of solidarity, knowledge fair trade, cultural integrity, and rights to humanity.

Tirzah Shelton is an Our Lady of the Lake University doctoral student studying counseling psychology in San Antonio, Texas. Tirzah grew up in Beloit, Wisconsin and is currently residing in San Antonio, Texas. Tirzah's interests are to find ways to incorporate an embodied experience in work with families to open possibilities to explore the impact of systems of power.

PREFACE

This book was born from our work as family therapy teachers, supervisors, therapists, and researchers. In working with students, we saw that they usually tended to have an individualistic orientation and that learning to think systemically and relationally could sometimes be difficult for them. Further, we realized that in many family therapy graduate programs, students are taught family therapy approaches in many different classes, but may only have one course in couples therapy. While we see family therapy and couple therapy as siblings—since they both are predicated on understanding problems from a relational perspective—we also know that many couples therapy approaches are not given the exposure they deserve.

In thinking about how to present many of the most utilized and significant contemporary couples approaches, we wanted readers to not only understand the key concepts, but most importantly learn how to apply the ideas to an actual case. We found in many handbooks and case study collectives of couples therapy, there may have been a wide range of approaches presented; however, each chapter presented worked with distinct and different cases. While the reader may be able to learn about the model, the distinctions between models may not come through as well as they might. This is why we decided to have one case that is used in every chapter. This way, the reader is able to compare and contrast how the various models conceptualize why the same couple is having difficulties (the theory of problem formation) and what the therapist might do with the couple in therapy (the theory of problem resolution). This format of presentation of various models using a single case was utilized in my (Michael D. Reiter) previous book, *Case conceptualization in family therapy* (Reiter, 2014). Based on the positive responses from students and readers of that book, we again utilized this same format. This book has a companion (Reiter & Chenail, 2017), each book presenting five different couples theories and using the same case. This way, you can compare and contrast models in that book and across books. This current book explores what we are classifying as constructivist, critical, and integrative approaches. The companion book highlights behavioral, humanistic-existential, and psychodynamic approaches.

We want to thank a few people who helped out in various areas of making this book come together: Daisy Ceja, Stefano Fanfoni, Zillah Hodgkins, Clint Lambert, and Melissa Rosen for genogram and chapter reviews; Christopher Burnett, our friend and colleague, who let us use one of his amazing photographs for the cover of the book. This book would not have been possible without the contributions of all of the chapter authors: Sheila Addison, James Furrow, Nicholas Lee, Megan Murphy, Hannah Myung, Terence Patterson, Catalina Perdomo, marcela polanco, and Tirzah Shelton. We would also like to thank Elizabeth Graber, Associate Editor at Routledge, who helped us bring this book to fruition.

References

Reiter, M. D. (2014). *Case conceptualization in family therapy*. Upper Saddle River, NJ: Pearson.
Reiter, M. D., & Chenail, R. J. (Eds.). (2017). *Behavioral, humanistic-existential, and psychodynamic approaches to couples counseling*. New York: Routledge.

1

COUNSELING COUPLES

Michael D. Reiter

This book is a companion to *Behavioral, Humanistic-Existential, and Psychodynamic Approaches to Couples Counseling* (Reiter & Chenail, 2017) and focuses on the constructivist, critical, and integrative approaches to working with couples. Regardless of approach, couples counselors need to understand the various dynamics of couples, such as formation, history, and diversity (see Reiter, 2017). These dynamics filter into the case conceptualization, to provide a more encompassing view of the couple, why they are currently having difficulties, and potential pathways toward change.

Case Conceptualization

Case conceptualization has become a core competency in most of the counseling/therapy fields. Yet, what is a case conceptualization? Berman (2010) explained, "The goals of case conceptualization are to provide a clear, theoretical explanation for *what the client is like* as well as theoretical hypotheses for *why the client is like this*" (p. xi). Sperry and Sperry (2012) defined case conceptualization as such:

> Case conceptualization is a method and clinical strategy for obtaining and organizing information about a client, understanding and explaining the client's situation and maladaptive patterns, guiding and focusing treatment, anticipating challenges and roadblocks, and preparing for successful termination.
>
> *(p. 4)*

We can look at a case conceptualization in two primary areas. The first is that it allows the therapist to develop a ***theory of problem formation***. Regardless of the presenting symptom or the client configuration (i.e. individual, couple or family), the case conceptualization provides an understanding of how the problem developed and how it is maintained. The second area of a case conceptualization is that it promotes a *theory of problem resolution*. Based on the specific approach being used to make the case conceptualization, the therapist will develop an understanding of possible pathways to change. These will be the various interventions that might be used to help move the client toward therapeutic goals.

Perhaps the biggest decision to make when first meeting with a client (and in this book we are using "client" to refer to whoever comes into therapy, whether an individual, a couple, or a family, but a couple in our case), is deciding what type of case conceptualization to make. The two primary choices are to develop a symptom-based or a theory-based conceptualization.

Symptom-based conceptualizations give priority to "the problem" and center treatment around the symptom presented by the client. For instance, if a couple came in with the complaint that one of the dyad had engaged in a sexual affair, the therapist would explore the research around affairs and develop an understanding of how/why affairs happen and what treatment approach might be best suited for that issue.

Theory-based conceptualizations give the therapeutic model primacy rather than the problem. The problem would be seen as a symptom of some other underlying issue (for instance, an affair—or any other presenting problem—may be seen as a result of maladaptive thoughts). Given that most therapists go into a session with a primary theoretical orientation (even if that orientation is what we might call an integrative approach), this book takes a theory-based look at case conceptualizations.

Some authors make a distinction between a case conceptualization and a treatment plan. For them, the case conceptualization provides the theory of problem formation while the treatment plan explains the theory of problem resolution. For us, a treatment plan is included in what we consider to be a case conceptualization. Depending on your work context, the treatment plan may be informal (i.e. your thoughts about what you might do with the client) or in agency settings more formal (i.e. an explanation of the problem, the treatment goal, and the specific interventions to be used, which may need to be listed and signed off on a form for managed care purposes). Since most therapists operate from a theory-based conceptualization, this book is designed to provide an in-depth overview of the primary theories of couples counseling.

Developing a case conceptualization is a skill that is learned over time through deliberate practice (Sperry & Carlson, 2014). For instance, beginning therapists may need to do an assessment interview and then, with input from their supervisor, develop their understanding of why the client is having difficulties and what pathways toward change might be relevant. In juxtaposition, more senior therapists are able to develop their case conceptualization in the therapy room while they are engaging the client in the initial interview. The more thorough an understanding of one's primary theoretical model, the more quickly the therapist can develop the case conceptualization and begin working toward change.

The Importance of Theory

Over the last 20 years, the importance of common factors across models has gained significant focus (Lambert, 1992; Sprenkle & Blow, 2004; Wampold, 2001). Perhaps the viewpoint most expounded upon is that of Michael Lambert, who conducted a meta-analysis of outcome studies of the effectiveness of psychotherapy. Lambert determined that there are four common factors of therapy: client factors; therapeutic relationship; hope/placebo effect; and therapeutic model. Miller, Duncan, and Hubble (1997) hold that these four elements constitute a unifying language of psychotherapy.

Client factors tend to account for 40 percent of change. This area pertains to what clients bring with them to therapy—their strengths and resources. It might be their sense of resiliency, perseverance, sense of humor, etc. These extratherapeutic factors put focus on the client's motivation, perception of the therapist, the therapeutic process, past therapy and interpersonal relationships and experiences, and the client's stage of readiness for change (Prochaska, DiClemente, & Norcross, 1992).

The therapeutic relationship accounts for 30 percent of change. This is how the client connects and relates to the therapist. The better the quality of the relationship, the higher chance that positive change will occur for the client. This area is perhaps more difficult to utilize in couple counseling because of the multiple relationships in play. In couple counseling, there are four relationships occurring at once in the therapy room. The first is that between the two members of the couple, second between one partner and the therapist, third is between the other partner and the therapist and then the fourth is between the couple (as a dyad) and the therapist.

Hope/placebo effects account for 15 percent of client change. The more that clients hope and believe that therapy will be useful, the more likely it is for the client to change. The client's level of hope is intertwined with the therapist's expectation and hope for the client to change. That is, when the therapist truly believes that the work he/she is doing with the client will lead to positive outcomes, the greater possibility that therapy will end with positive gains. Yet, hope is not an isolated aspect of the therapeutic encounter. The therapist's hope is usually grounded in a belief that whatever model they use will most likely be helpful for that particular client.

The last area is **the therapeutic model**, which accounts for roughly 15 percent of change. As we know, one model is not more effective than another model, however, effectively utilizing a model is what is important instead of going into a session and floating around without a direction and purpose. When therapists do not operate from a model of therapy (and again, we include integrative therapy as a model), they tend to grasp for various interventions that may not make sense for them or fit for the client. The therapist may begin to feel desperate and not attain a level of expectancy for change for the client. This, in turn, may be sensed by the client and lead to lower levels of hope and expectancy from the client.

These four factors are not separate, but are interrelated. Based on a therapist's therapeutic model, the therapist will enter into a particular therapeutic relationship (although there are differences in therapists even within the same model). The therapist's theory also helps to inform how the therapist will focus on the various client factors that are present. Lastly, the more a therapist has a thorough and working understanding of a particular model, the more competent the therapist will be in that approach and the more the therapist will believe that model will be useful and effective for the client. The therapist's competency in that specific approach as well as hope for client change will help motivate the client to be hopeful and expectant for change. This book primarily explores the common factor of the therapeutic model while also bringing forth how therapists from that model may utilize the already occurring strengths and resources of clients and increase their hope and expectancy all via a distinct therapeutic relationship.

Effectiveness of Couples Counseling

Perhaps one of the first things to determine before investing in reading about the various models of couples counseling is to see whether engaging in couples counseling is effective. Fortunately, the answer to this question is "Yes!" Couples counseling is more effective than no therapy (Christensen & Heavey, 1999; Jacobson & Addis, 1993; Sexton, Robbins, Hollimon, Mease, & Mayorga, 2003; Shadish & Baldwin, 2003; Sparks & Duncan, 2010). Further, the positive results of therapy seem to remain in place or increase for at least two years after therapy ends (Lundblad & Hansson, 2006). Gurman and Fraenkel (2002) explained, "No other collective methods of psychosocial intervention have demonstrated a superior capacity to effect clinically meaningful change in as many spheres of human experience as the couple therapies, and many have not yet even shown a comparable capacity" (p. 248). However, not all couples find beneficial results. Approximately 25 to 30 percent of couples do not show gains from therapy (Snyder & Halford, 2012). This may be due to the timing of therapy (i.e. how long they experienced the problem before coming to therapy), differing agendas by each member of the couple, or a lack of fit between the couple and the therapist.

Shadish and Baldwin (2003), who conducted a meta-analysis about marriage and family therapy effectiveness, found that marriage therapy tended to be more effective than family therapy, but they attributed some of this to family therapists sometimes dealing with more difficult problems. Another finding they explained was that different interventions and models tend to lead to the same results. However, as we discussed, having a secure footing in one or more models is quite important. Davis, Lebow, and Sprenkle (2012) explain this issue, "This could explain why most tested couple therapy models are effective, but none significantly more than another—because they all do an adequate job of involving the right change mechanisms at the right times" (p. 38).

While some couples do not attain improvements in therapy, most do. Hampson, Prince, and Beavers (1999) found that 83 percent of the couples in their study made some significant gains. Further, couples who attended at least three sessions made 92.1 percent gains of at least some degree. However, not all couples find positive results (Jacobson & Addis, 1993; Snyder, Castellani, & Whisman, 2006).

Previously we presented a view of the common factors of therapy. However, these factors may not include others that pertain specifically when working with couples. Davis et al. (2012) presented several common factors that are unique to couple therapy, which included conceptualizing difficulties in relational terms, disrupting dysfunctional relational patterns, an expanded direct treatment system, and an expanded therapeutic alliance (i.e. the therapist's relationship with partner A, the therapist's relationship with partner B, the alliance between partners A and B, and the alliance between therapist, partner A, and partner B).

One potential common factor in couples counseling (as well as individual, family, or group therapy) is that of **feedback** (Halford et al., 2012; Sparks & Duncan, 2010). Anker, Duncan, and Sparks (2009) found that when couples are able to provide the therapist with feedback on their perceived progress they have improvements four times that of those who do not. One reason for this is that when therapists receive feedback from clients at the end of each session they can make corrections in their approach (Pepping, Halford, & Doss, 2015). While progress feedback is an important aspect of therapy, there may be additional challenges when utilizing it with couples. For instance, the therapist will need to integrate the feedback given by each partner, as they may disagree with one another.

Although not considered common factors, Benson, McGinn, and Christensen (2012) presented five common principles of couples counseling. These are: "(a) altering the couple's view of the presenting problem to be more objective, contextualized, and dyadic; (b) decreasing emotion-driven, dysfunctional behavior; (c) eliciting emotion-based, avoided, private behavior; (d) increasing constructive communication patterns; and (e) emphasizing strengths and reinforcing gains" (p. 25). These authors suggest that these principles become relevant at various times during the course of therapy, with earlier principles more applicable earlier in the process. These principles can be seen, in various ways, in all of the approaches presented in this book.

While we are presenting distinctive models of couples counseling, we understand that many couples therapists may engage in a type of therapy that is more integrative. There are different types of integration, such as assimilative, transtheoretical, and pluralistic (Snyder & Balderrama-Durbin, 2012). These authors suggest that "couples may benefit most from a treatment strategy drawing from both conceptual and technical innovations from diverse theoretical models relevant to different components of a couple's struggles" (p. 14). However, in order to engage in effective integration, the therapist must have a thorough understanding of the various models that he or she is attempting to integrate.

Whatever model of therapy is chosen—be it one of the models presented in this book, a model not presented here, or an integrated model—perhaps what may be more important is the skill and being of the therapist (Blow, Sprenkle, & Davis, 2007). These authors advocate that therapists have a thorough understanding of several models to be able to fit what they do to the who and what of the client system. Gurman (2011) concurred, stating that one of the overlooked aspects of couple therapy efficacy is the therapist himself/herself.

Not only is who the therapist is (his/her personality, familiarity with the model(s) being utilized, skills, etc.), but the person of the client is perhaps just as important. The client may be viewed as a common factor in therapy (Bohart & Tallman, 2010) wherein the client's active pursuit of self-agency is a key component toward effective change in therapy. For instance, Hampson et al. (1999) found that whether a couple had children and whether it was a first marriage or not impacted therapeutic outcome. More specifically, couples who did not have children tended to do best in therapy, then remarried couples with no children, first marriage couples with no children, first marriage couples with children and then remarried couples with children. Age of the partners in the couple may also be a factor as partners who are younger may experience more positive gains than couples who are older (Vansteenwegen, 1996).

The partners in a couple also have their own views and perceptions of what is helpful and unhelpful in couples therapy. Some helpful aspects of couples counseling include having choices in the mode of working in counseling; having a trustworthy therapist; and being able to develop new ideas about the couple relationship and how each partner might interact with the other (Bowman & Fine, 2000).

Book Organization

This book is organized to allow you to compare and contrast five of the most popular couples counseling theories by developing a case conceptualization of the same couple through each of these approaches. Chapter 2 presents a couple that was used by each of the chapter authors to conceptualize based on their specific approach. This fictionalized couple is a conglomeration of many couples that we (MR & RJC) have worked with throughout our careers.

We believe that people learn best when they can compare and contrast ideas. As such, we have organized this book so that you can understand five different models of couples counseling via a recurrent case. Chapter 2 presents a fictional case—an amalgamation of the many couples we have worked with in our careers—that will then be referenced in the remaining theoretical chapters.

Each of the theory chapters is organized similarly, with four main sections. The first is a brief history of the model. This is followed by a section on the theory of problem formation. In this section, the chapter authors explain how the model views why couples have difficulties. This is done through exploring the case of David and Natalie presented in Chapter 2. The third section explores the theory of problem resolution—how that model understands change. The last section provides a mock first session with explanation for why the therapist made certain interventions. Chapter 7 takes a different perspective where an intersectional framework is used to better understand how issues of race, gender, sexuality, and other aspects of people impact a couple and can be explored in therapy when conducting couples counseling. For this chapter, the common case has been modified to help exemplify those ideas. We provide the same case and format for five other approaches in a separate book (Reiter & Chenail, 2017).

References

Anker, M. G., Duncan, B. L., & Sparks, J. A. (2009). Using client feedback to improve couple therapy outcomes: A randomized clinical trial in a naturalistic setting. *Journal of Consulting and Clinical Psychology, 77*(4), 693–704.

Benson, L. A., McGinn, M. M., & Christensen, A. (2012). Common principles of couple therapy. *Behavior Therapy, 43*(1), 25–35.

Berman, P. S. (2010). *Case conceptualization and treatment planning* (2nd ed.). Thousand Oaks, CA: SAGE Publications.

Blow, A. J., Sprenkle, D. H., & Davis, S. D. (2007). Is who delivers the treatment more important than the treatment itself? The role of the therapist in common factors. *Journal of Marital and Family Therapy, 33*(3), 298–317.

Bohart, A. C., & Tallman, K. (2010). Clients: The neglected common factor in psychotherapy. In B. L. Duncan, S. D. Miller, B. E. Wampold, & M. A. Hubble (Eds.), *The heart and soul of change: Delivering what works in therapy* (2nd ed., pp. 83–111). Washington, DC: American Psychological Association.

Bowman, L., & Fine, M. (2000). Client perceptions of couples therapy: Helpful and unhelpful aspects. *The American Journal of Family Therapy, 28*(4), 295–310.

Christensen, A., & Heavey, C. L. (1999). Interventions for couples. *Annual Review of Psychology, 50*, 165–190.

Davis, S. D., Lebow, J. L., & Sprenkle, D. H. (2012). Common factors of change in couple therapy. *Behavior Therapy, 43*(1), 36–48.

Gurman, A. S. (2011). Couple therapy research and the practice of couple therapy: Can we talk? *Family Process, 50*(3), 280–292.

Gurman, A. S., & Fraenkel, P. (2002). The history of couple therapy: A millennial review. *Family Process, 41*(2), 199–260.

Halford, W. K., Hayes, S., Christensen, A., Lambert, M., Baucom, D. H., & Atkins, D. (2012). Towards making progress feedback an effective common factor in couple therapy. *Behavior Therapy, 43*(1), 49–60.

Hampson, R. B., Prince, C. V., & Beavers, W. R. (1999). Marital therapy: Qualities of couples who fare better or worse in treatment. *Journal of Marital and Family Therapy, 25*(4), 411–424.

Jacobson, N. S., & Addis, M. E. (1993). Research on couples and couple therapy: What do we know? Where are we going? *Journal of Consulting and Clinical Psychology*, *61*(1), 85–93.

Lambert, M. (1992). Psychotherapy outcome research: Implications for integrative and eclectic counselors. In J. C. Norcross & M. R. Goldfried (Eds.), *Handbook of psychotherapy integration* (pp. 94–129). New York, NY: Wiley.

Lundblad, A.-M., & Hansson, K. (2006). Couples therapy: Effectiveness of treatment and long-term follow-up. *Journal of Family Therapy*, *28*(2), 136–152.

Miller, S. D., Duncan, B. L., & Hubble, M. A. (1997). *Escape from Babel*. New York, NY: W. W. Norton & Company.

Pepping, C. A., Halford, W. K., & Doss, B. D. (2015). Can we predict failure in couple therapy early enough to enhance outcome? *Behaviour Research and Therapy*, *65*, 60–66.

Prochaska, J. O., DiClemente, C. C., & Norcross, J. (1992). In search of how people change. *American Psychologist*, *47*, 1101–1114.

Reiter, M. D. (2017). Couples counseling. In M. D. Reiter & R. J. Chenail (Eds.), *Behavioral, humanistic-existential, and psychodynamic approaches to couples counseling*. New York, NY: Routledge.

Reiter, M. D., & Chenail, R. J. (Eds.). (2017). *Behavioral, humanistic-existential, and psychodynamic approaches to couples counseling*. New York, NY: Routledge.

Sexton, T. L., Robbins, M. S., Hollimon, A. S., Mease, A. L., & Mayorga, C. C. (2003). Efficacy, effectiveness, and change mechanisms in couple and family therapy. In T. L. Sexton, G. R. Weeks, & M. S. Robbins (Eds.), *Handbook of family therapy* (pp. 229–261). New York, NY: Brunner-Routledge.

Shadish, W. R., & Baldwin, S. A. (2003). Meta-analysis of MFT interventions. *Journal of Marital and Family Therapy*, *29*(4), 547–570.

Snyder, D. K., & Balderrama-Durbin, C. (2012). Integrative approaches to couple therapy: Implications for clinical practice and research. *Behavior Therapy*, *43*(1), 13–24.

Snyder, D. K., Castellani, A. M., & Whisman, M. A. (2006). Current status and future directions in couple therapy. *Annual Review of Psychology*, *57*, 317–344.

Snyder, D. K., & Halford, W. K. (2012). Evidence-based couple therapy: Current status and future directions. *Journal of Family Therapy*, *34*(3), 229–249.

Sparks, J. A., & Duncan, B. L. (2010). Common factors in couple and family therapy: Must all have prizes? In B. L. Duncan, S. D. Miller, B. E. Wampold, & M. A. Hubble (Eds.), *The heart and soul of change: Delivering what works in therapy* (2nd ed., pp. 357–391). Washington, DC: American Psychological Association.

Sperry, L., & Carlson, J. (2014). *How master therapists work*. New York, NY: Routledge.

Sperry, L., & Sperry, J. (2012). *Case conceptualization: Mastering this competency with ease and confidence*. New York, NY: Routledge.

Sprenkle, D. H., & Blow, A. J. (2004). Common factors and our sacred models. *Journal of Marital and Family Therapy*, *30*, 113–129.

Vansteenwegen, A. (1996). Who benefits from couple therapy? A comparison of successful and failed couples. *Journal of Sex & Marital Therapy*, *22*(1), 63–67.

Wampold, B. E. (2001). *The great psychotherapy debate: Models, methods, and findings*. Mahwah, NJ: Lawrence Erlbaum Associates.

2

THE CASE

David and Natalie Johnson

Michael D. Reiter

Presenting Problem

David and Natalie Johnson (28 and 30 years old, respectively) made an appointment for couples therapy after Natalie discovered that David had been having an internet affair for the past six months. She happened to look in the history section of David's laptop and found a lot of personal messages between David and a woman named Devyn. In reading the messages, Natalie was heartbroken to read David saying that he wanted to divorce Natalie and move across the country to live with Devyn.

When she first confronted him with the affair, David denied it. She then made him open up his email folder and bring up the emails. He then explained that, yes, he had been conversing with the woman, but that it wasn't anything serious and he was just saying those things to her to get Devyn to continue talking with him. The following is the conversation they had during this argument:

Natalie: What is going on between you and this Devyn woman?
David: Nothing.
Natalie: Then why all the emails saying that you love her?
David: What are you talking about?
Natalie: David, I've seen the emails. Don't play stupid.
David: Okay, I am talking to someone, but it's not what you think.
Natalie: It's not that you love her, don't love me, and are going to divorce me and move in with her?
David: I might have said something like that, but I didn't mean it. I just said it to keep talking with her. It was just something fun to do. You know, kind of like catfishing.

Natalie: David, I'm not an idiot. If you want to be with her, then admit it and leave. But if you want any chance with me, then you better start telling me the truth.

David: Okay, okay. Look, you know things between you and me haven't been great recently. When's the last time we had sex, huh?

Natalie: And you think that's my fault?

David: You think it's mine?

Natalie: I'm not the one that's an alcoholic!

David: I forgot; you're perfect.

Natalie: I'm not perfect, but I'm not having an affair with someone on the internet. Have you ever met her?

David: No. It's only been via email.

Natalie: You never Skyped her? And don't bullshit me.

David: Fine, we video chatted.

Natalie: And did you talk naked and have sex online.

David: What does it matter? Do you think you've done everything to make this marriage work?

Natalie: I haven't led anyone else on.

David: But you've thought about divorce, right?

Natalie: I have, but I wanted to try to make things work out first. Do you?

David: Of course, otherwise I would have left already.

This conversation led the couple to agree to go for couples counseling to give the relationship one last chance before they contacted lawyers for a divorce. They had never gone for any type of individual or couples counseling before.

In terms of prior relationships, David is much more experienced than Natalie. David has had several long-term serious relationships, the longest of which was a two-year relationship he had during college. Natalie's longest relationship was for five months. She had several boyfriends in college, all of which cheated on her.

History of the Couple

David and Natalie Johnson have been married for three years. They met two years previously via an online dating website. David was 25 at the time while Natalie was 27. They talked to each other via online text chats for approximately three months before they agreed to talk on the telephone. While they were getting to know each other, David also was in conversations with several other women from the dating site. Only once did he meet up with one of these women, who lived in New York City, but the meeting did not go well.

After their first telephone conversation, Natalie and David started talking to each other several times per week. Natalie lived in Texas while David came from Maine. At the time of meeting, David was fully employed as a high school teacher. Natalie had established herself as a realtor in Texas.

After finding that their conversations were very fulfilling, the couple arranged for their first meeting five months after first contacting each other on the internet. David flew down to Texas and spent four days with Natalie. The two got along very well and sexually consummated their romantic relationship. For the next year David and Natalie visited each other at least once a month, flying back and forth from Texas to Maine or Maine to Texas. David did more of the traveling during this time.

The couple talked about being together and where they would live. Natalie thought it was much easier for her to stay in Texas as the real estate market was a lot larger than in the smaller town where David came from in Maine. During this time David applied for teaching jobs in Texas and eventually got one in the neighboring school district to where Natalie lived, however, he had to wait until the following school year to begin. In July of 2012 he packed up all of his belongings and drove across the country to move in with Natalie.

For the first year of their relationship David and Natalie both felt very much in love with one another. They shared an enjoyment of going out to restaurants, both having similar palates for food. They also enjoyed going to the movies, sitting at cafes drinking coffee and talking, as well as watching Dallas Cowboys games together. They had made Friday night "date-night" and had gone to new restaurants, theater shows, and other interesting activities. At the time, they each believed they had an active and enjoyable sex life.

During their second year together, they both noticed differences starting to emerge in the relationship. They began to argue more about small (i.e. where to go for dinner, which movie to see) and big things (i.e. whether, and if so when, to have a child). Natalie wanted to begin having a family right away while David wanted to wait until he found a better job. Natalie's argument was that she did not want to be an older mother and that she was already approaching 30. David stated that he wanted for them to have more time as a couple, although he began spending more nights out with friends at sports bars and sporting events.

In this past third year of their marriage, they have been finding themselves drifting apart from each other. David has gained weight over the three years of their marriage to where he is now 5 foot 8 and weighs 215 pounds. He also has increased his smoking of cigarettes from one every few days to now one pack a day. Natalie, while overweight herself, has become quite concerned about David's health and attempts to get him to be healthier. Earlier in the year, she attempted to get him to stop smoking. The conversation is below:

Natalie: David, are you going to have another cigarette now?
David: Perhaps. Why?
Natalie: Because I don't want you smoking in the house anymore. It makes everything stink.
David: You know, it's my house too.

> *Natalie:* I know. But we both need to keep the house clean. And cigarette smoke not only makes the house smell, but I have to breathe it if it's in the air.
>
> *David:* Fine, then I'll go out on the patio.
>
> *Natalie:* That's better. But I still don't want you to smoke.
>
> *David:* Why not? It's my body not yours.
>
> *Natalie:* But I want you to be healthy.
>
> *David:* I am healthy.
>
> *Natalie:* You've been gaining weight, and now you're smoking even more.
>
> *David:* What about you? You're overweight.
>
> *Natalie:* I know. We both need to get in better shape.
>
> *David:* Yeah, it would be nice if you lost weight.
>
> *Natalie:* David, don't be mean.
>
> *David:* I'm not being mean. Just truthful. I'm going outside to smoke.

Currently, the couple has not engaged in any sexual activity for seven months. At times, after they have argued, David has slept in the guest bedroom.

David's Family-of-Origin

David is the third child of three from Dana and Sheila. His siblings are his sisters Susan and Regina. Dana and Sheila met while they were both working together at a bank in Portland, Maine. Dana was a bank manager and Sheila a teller. They married two years after first meeting, when Dana was 27 and Sheila 24. After one year of marriage they had their first daughter, Susan. One year later, their second daughter, Regina, was born.

Sheila had only wanted two children, but Dana very much wanted a son. After many conversations, Sheila agreed to have another child, but warned Dana that this was the last, whether it was male or female. Three years after Regina was born, Sheila conceived and gave birth to David. When he was nine, Dana and Sheila divorced. Sheila has dated occasionally, but not seriously. Dana married Barbara in 2000.

David and his older sister, Regina, have not talked for the past six years. This was after many years of Regina's drinking and David telling her how irresponsible she was; especially as a mother. David is also somewhat distant from his father, Dana. Since the divorce of his parents, David has only talked with his father occasionally, mainly on holidays and birthdays. One of the reasons for this is that David tends not to initiate interaction, expecting his father to make the connection.

While he was growing up, David was on the shorter side. He was also not the most athletic kid in his class and was a little pudgy. Dana had been an athlete in high school, primarily playing varsity baseball. Dana had tried to force David into playing baseball, but David was usually one of the worst players on the field. This was a disappointment for Dana.

David's oldest sister, Susan, is close with their mother, Sheila. She is married to Alfredo, the only marriage for both of them. Ten years ago Susan had gotten pregnant but then had a miscarriage. This impacted her emotionally and physically. It was a tough situation for her, which brought Susan and her mother, Sheila, closer together. The doctors also told her that she would not be able to conceive another child. Susan and Alfredo then decided to adopt and eventually adopted a newborn from China, who they named Jordyn. Susan is very close to her daughter, Jordyn.

David's sister Regina is 31 and has been in recovery for the last three years. When she was 19 she gave birth to her daughter, Anna. Her boyfriend at the time, Don, left when he found out she was pregnant and would not get an abortion. When Anna was born, Regina was drinking and drugging and Sheila took over primary caretaking duties. Instead of getting help and cleaning up her life, Regina took this time to party even harder than she had been. She was arrested once for DUI and would ask Susan and David for money. Six years ago, at a family function, Regina had gotten drunk and began to berate David. He was also drunk at the time and their argument actually came to physical blows. David was arrested, but released on bond and put on probation. After that incident he refused to speak to Regina again. That event, though, led Regina to begin a program of active recovery and she went into a treatment center and joined Alcoholics Anonymous. She has been clean and sober and in recovery for over five years. She currently has full custody of Anna.

Natalie's Family-of-Origin

Natalie is the oldest of two children to Fred and Laura. Her brother, Scott, is three years younger. When Scott was two years old her parents divorced. Two years later her mother, Laura, married Nicholas. Together, they gave birth to Natalie's sister, Robyn, 10 years younger.

Scott is currently 27 years old and is married to Michele, which is his second marriage. He was married to Norma for one year, during which they had their daughter, Emma. Scott and Norma had met in college and married once Norma had become pregnant. However, during her pregnancy the couple had become contemptuous of one another and six months after Emma was born they divorced. Norma has full custody of Emma, with Scott spending time with Emma approximately once a week. Scott and Norma have frequent conflict, especially around the area of money. Two years ago Scott married Michele.

Natalie's younger sister, Robyn, is 20 years old and is going to college at a university in Oregon. When Fred and Laura divorced, Natalie and Scott lived with their mother. When Natalie was 10, her sister Robyn was born. Natalie played a parental role in taking care of her.

Natalie does not have a close relationship with her father, Fred. She was five years old when her parents divorced and seven when her mother remarried to Nicholas. However, she has not had a close relationship with either Fred or

Nicholas. Natalie felt that Nicholas attempted too hard to be her "father" and throughout her childhood, and especially during adolescence, she had a love/hate relationship with him. Once the divorce occurred, Fred backed out of the children's lives, and spent sporadic time with Natalie and Scott. During early adulthood, Natalie made an attempt to reconnect with Fred, but found that while he cared for her, he didn't initiate much interactions. This infuriated Natalie as she believed that it is the parent's responsibility to initiate and maintain connections. Figure 2.1 presents a genogram of the couple.

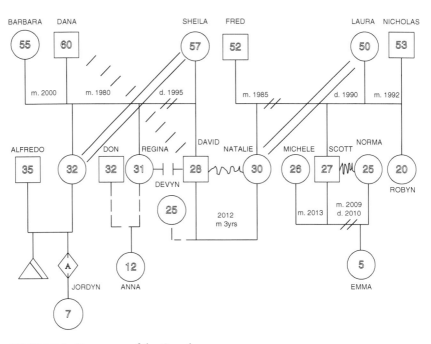

FIGURE 2.1 Genogram of the Couple.

3

EMOTIONALLY FOCUSED COUPLE THERAPY

James L. Furrow, Nicholas Lee, and Hannah S. Myung

History of the Model

Emotionally Focused Couple Therapy (EFT; Greenberg & Johnson, 1988; Johnson, 2004) is an integrative approach in the treatment of couple distress. It is among a few couple treatments that have established empirical support for effectiveness in treating couple distress (Chambless & Ollendick, 2001; Lebow, Chambers, Christensen, & Johnson, 2012). EFT was given its name to emphasize the pivotal role that emotions play in the organization of interactional patterns and experiences in intimate relationships (Johnson, 2004).

EFT was initially established in the 1980s when behavioral interventions for couple treatment were continually being developed and studied. The behavioral approach was known to be the most widely researched and recognized for its efficacious treatment in couple distress (Baucom, Shoham, Mueser, Daiuto, & Stickle, 1998). The behavioral interventions rooted in social learning theory and behavioral principles aimed to facilitate positive interactions through communication training, problem-solving, and behavioral exchanges and contracts in which the therapist mainly took on a coaching role (Jacobson & Margolin, 1979). Relationships were conceptualized more in terms of relational transactions and "quid pro quo" interactions. The beginning formulation of EFT sought to address the lack of validated couple treatments with more focus on humanistic approaches rather than behavioral interventions.

In their initial outcome studies, Susan Johnson and Les Greenberg (1985a, 1985b) observed therapy sessions of distressed couples working to repair their relationships. Their work drew from humanistic-experiential views (Gendlin, 1974; Perls, Hefferline, & Goodman, 1951; Rogers, 1951) and systemic theories, including structural family therapy (Minuchin & Fishman, 1981), which supported a framework that guided their observations and understandings that focused more on process rather than in the individual. Their humanistic-experiential emphasis gave attention to how partners process and construct their experiences and the systemic approach focused on each partner's responses in the context of inter-actions. The integration of the humanistic-experiential and systemic approaches allowed for a clearly delineated couple therapy model that engaged a couple's intrapersonal experiences and interpersonal patterns (Johnson, 2004).

Furthermore, Johnson included **attachment theory** (Bowlby, 1969, 1973a, 1973b) in her observations of couple dynamics and questioned viewing relation-ships as only rational bargains arguing instead that relationships could be better understood as affectional bonds (Johnson, 1986). Attachment theory eventually became a primary framework for conceptualizing patterns of relationship dis-tress and also a map to relationship reparation (Johnson, 2004). From an attach-ment perspective, couple distress is understood in the context of insecure bonds and separation. As partners experience prolonged periods of distress, the sense of attachment security is threatened and attachment-related fears are triggered.

Attachment-related affect plays a significant role in the organization of attach-ment responses. Negative affect that is continually experienced results in predict-able behaviors that are characterized by avoidant and anxious responses. Over time, partners eventually become stuck in insecure patterns of responding and relationship repair becomes difficult as partners become more prone to rigid ways of relating to the other and experiencing the self.

The attachment framework serves as a map for the couple therapist by focus-ing on the couple's attachment insecurities and highlighting attachment longings and needs for closeness and security. The attachment approach guides therapists in helping partners access, resynthesize, and restructure emotional bonds and interactions.

In summary, Johnson and colleagues (1999) suggested four treatment assump-tions characteristic of emotion and adult attachment in healthy couple rela-tionships. First, intimacy is best understood as an attachment bond in romantic relationships. Second, common patterns of couple conflict often interrupt part-ners' abilities to form and sustain secure attachment. Third, engaging emotional experience is critical to transforming intrapersonal and interpersonal dynamics. Fourth, emotional responses must be addressed in therapy to change a couple's negative interactional patterns. Also, a couple's ability to express attachment needs and desires is adaptive and facilitates intimacy (Johnson, 2004).

Empirical Support and Process Research

Research using clinical trials and process based studies are a hallmark of the EFT approach. EFT meets the highest criteria for **evidence-based practice** with extant research demonstrating absolute, relative, and contextual efficacy (Sexton, Gordon, Gurman, Lebow, Holtzworth-Munroe, & Johnson, 2011). For example,

Johnson and colleagues (1999) conducted a meta-analysis of the primary RCT studies and reported an effect size of 1.31, which is stronger than .90 commonly reported for couple therapy in general (e.g. Dunn & Schwebel, 1995). Couples receiving EFT showed significant decreases in marital distress with over half (70–73%) of the couples demonstrating treatment recovery. Findings from other meta-analyses describe EFT as an efficacious treatment for couple distress (Byrne, Carr, & Clark, 2004; Dunn & Schwebel, 1995; Johnson et al., 1999; Shadish & Baldwin, 2003; Wood, Crane, Schaalje, & Law, 2005). In Shadish and Baldwin's (2003) review of couple and family therapy meta-analyses, EFT was classified as a meta-analytically supported treatment.

In addition to findings from EFT clinical trial research, findings from EFT process research show support for the model's theory of change, reveal therapy factors predictive of successful outcomes, and inform clinicians in treating couple distress. In Johnson and Greenberg's (1988) initial process-outcome study, couples who appeared to benefit from EFT had significantly higher levels of emotional experiencing and affiliative responses than couples who did not show improvement. Similarly, higher levels of emotional experiencing and increases in affiliative interactions were observed in more resolved couples receiving EFT in a study with couples facing chronic illness (Couture-Lalande, Greenman, Naaman, & Johnson, 2007) and couples with attachment injuries (Makinen & Johnson, 2006; Zuccarini, Johnson, Dalgleish, & Makinen, 2013).

Researchers have also identified specific therapist interventions that correspond to successful treatment outcomes. Zuccarini et al. (2013) identified interventions associated with successful resolutions of attachment injuries. Similarly, Bradley and Furrow (2004) identified EFT therapist interventions and process themes in successful blamer softening change events. Furrow and colleagues (2012) found that therapist emotional presence and engagement predicted increased levels of client emotional experiencing necessary in the process of successful softening. Blamer softening is a significant change event in EFT that is predictive of increases in relationship satisfaction (Dalgleish, Johnson, Burgess Moser, LaFontaine, Wiebe, & Tasca, 2015) and has been identified in couples showing improvement (Burgess Moser et al., 2016; Johnson & Greenberg, 1988). The combination of outcome and process research studies have furthered the validation of the efficacy of the model and a deeper understanding of its process of change.

Treatment Applications

Furthermore, EFT has empirical support for treating various clinical issues including depression (Dessaulles, Johnson, & Denton, 2003) and low sexual desire (Macphee, Johnson, & Van Der Veer, 1995). Outcome research showing support for EFT in addressing attachment injuries (Makinen & Johnson, 2006) has demonstrated treatment effects remaining stable at a three-year follow-up (Halchuk, Makinen, & Johnson, 2010). It has also received support for reducing couple distress for couples with chronically ill children (Walker, Johnson, Manion, & Cloutier, 1996) with improvements observed at two-year follow-up (Cloutier, Manion, Walker, & Johnson, 2002).

Throughout the years, EFT has expanded its applicability to different populations including same-sex couples (Josephson, 2003), older couples (Bradley & Palmer, 2003), remarried couples (Furrow & Palmer, 2007, 2011), and families (Johnson, Maddeaux, & Blouin, 1998). A practical understanding of attachment theory and EFT has been made accessible for the general population through Johnson's (2008) book, *Hold me tight*, which has been translated into 20 different languages and has been implemented in workshops, psychoeducational settings, and relationship enrichment programs. In *Love sense* (Johnson, 2013), her most recent book for the general public, she provides a scientific understanding of emotional bonding and offers practical advice for partners in managing and strengthening secure attachment bonds. The focus of this chapter will be on exploring the application of EFT with couples.

Treatment Limitations

EFT is particularly appropriate for working with couples because its application of attachment theory for understanding and intervening in adult intimate relationships. However, it is worth mentioning the contraindications for EFT when working with couples. EFT has been developed mainly for partners who are working towards improving their relationship and would like to be together (Johnson, 2015). The model is not suitable for couples who clearly wish to separate, couples who are already separated and are ambivalent in working towards reconciliation, and couples where one or both partners are involved in an extramarital affair (Johnson, 2004, 2015). Therapists should assess and help clarify the needs and goals for the couple and make appropriate recommendations as deemed necessary, which may include individual work for those who are separating (Johnson, 2004, 2015). Also, the therapist should assess for areas that are threatening the couple's sense of safety in the relationship including ongoing abuse. The abused partner's experiences and expressions of vulnerability can be detrimental and place the partner at a higher risk for harm in an abusive context (Johnson, 2004). In such cases, it may be better to refer the abusive partner to individual or group therapy to address the issues and offer EFT after this process when the couple establishes a sense of safety appropriate for couple therapy (Johnson, 2004).

The following sections examine the EFT approach to problem formulation and problem resolution using the case of the Johnsons. Examples are provided to demonstrate how an EFT therapist might conceptualize this couple's distress and intervene over the course of treatment. Reference is made throughout to the discovery of David's affair and its implications for the course of treatment. The first session example and course of treatment assume that the couple is committed to working on their relationship and any active concern about a third party has been resolved.

Theory of Problem Formulation

In EFT, each partner's emotional experience provides a reliable guide from relational distress to a more intimate relationship. The EFT therapist focuses on each partner's emotional responses that drive partners further apart. These negative interactional patterns reinforce increasingly defended positions and keep partners in a cycle defined by a dance of distance and distress (Johnson, 1998). Emotions animate each partner's actions and reactions as the couple struggles to regain their connection. Attachment theory provides the therapist a map for the behaviors and motivations that make a couple's negative pattern predictable, understandable, and ultimately changeable.

Negative Interactional Patterns

The EFT therapist focuses on emotion as both a source of distress and a resource for its resolution. The reasons for a couple's conflict are secondary to powerful negative emotional patterns that create self-absorbing negative affect states (Johnson, 2004). Couples who are caught in cycles of escalating distress may have chronic disagreements, but it is each partner's inability to regulate the negative affect states that puts their relationship at risk for dissolution (Gottman, 1994). These insidious patterns develop over time as couples navigate around issues of vulnerability and fears mount as partners increasingly manage their needs on their own rather than as a couple. As conflict and crisis increase, these patterns take prominence and cascade couples toward greater isolation and emotional disengagement (Gottman, 1998). The process of EFT engages partners through these rigid interactions and transforms these cycles by accessing, expanding, and engaging the underlying attachment-related emotions and needs that are the basis of a more secure emotional bond (Johnson, 1999).

Systemically, EFT conceptualizes couple distress as an interactional pattern composed of partners' **secondary emotional responses** (Johnson, 1998; 2004). These secondary responses are informed by more vulnerable primary emotions of hurt, sadness, and fear that are reinforced by the painful interactions of the couple. Often without awareness, partners persist in behaviors (e.g. secondary emotions) that are motivated out of a need for the relationship and closeness with his or her partner (e.g. primary emotions). Together each partner's responses to these negative experiences form more rigid positions (e.g. pursuit, withdraw). As partners seek to regain their emotional balance in reaction to underlying concerns, the withdrawing partner quickly retreats in the face of the critical response of a more pursuing partner, which engages more pursuit from that partner and consequently greater withdrawal. Understanding the couple's positions and pattern begins with an understanding of this critical recognition of primary and secondary emotion.

The Johnsons enter therapy following a crisis of commitment in their relationship. Natalie's discovery of David's involvement in an internet affair surfaced immediate and long-standing issues of trust, commitment, and emotional engagement. They acknowledge a growing distance between them and their interaction in session pointing to Natalie's protest and frustration and David's more rational and minimizing tendencies. While the affair clearly casts partners into the role of the offender and the injured, it is clear in their interaction that David's efforts to avoid Natalie's anxious confrontation tells a broader story of the couple's struggle to find intimacy.

Attachment Bonds

Johnson (1986) recognized that what was at stake in couple distress was more than the social exchange of partners' personal interest but an enduring emotional bond. Following attachment theory (Bowlby, 1969) and its application to romantic love (Hazan & Shaver, 1987), Johnson proposed that EFT offers much more than an explanation of couple conflict but a theory of love (Johnson, 2013). Attachment theory not only provides the EFT therapist with a comprehensive approach to the couple's patterns of distress, but also the motivation underlying each partner's drive to connect and grow.

Primary motivation of couples seeking help in therapy is not simply the reduction of conflict but the need to renew and restore their intimacy as a couple. Research on couple conflict and its treatment have tended to focus on resolving conflict and negative relationship problems (Fincham, Stanley, & Beach, 2007) while couple therapies have lacked a systematic theory of intimacy (Roberts, 1992). Johnson (1986) initially proposed that relationships were built on emotional bonds and not simply a series of negotiated bargains between partners. Attachment theory (Bowlby, 1969) and its application to adult relationships (Hazan & Shaver, 1987) provide the EFT therapist with an overarching theory for the motivation and functions of romantic love where a couple's bond is best understood as an emotional tie that governs the relationship and one's experience in that relationship.

For the Johnsons, questioning the future of their relationship is both a reflection of the affair but also of a deeper more extensive experience of a lost felt connection in their relationship. The affair complicates the couple's ability to re-establish this bond and the traumatic nature of this relationship injury sends the couple reeling toward questions of divorce. Adults in more secure relationships are better able to express their needs and respond to those of their partners, especially when these needs are experienced in the context of vulnerability (Simpson, Rholes, & Phillips, 1996). The results of a more secure style are evident in couples reporting a more intimate, satisfying, and trusting relationship (Collins & Read, 1990). For Bowlby

(1988), the ability to maintain contact with one's attachment figure is essential to survival, and these relational needs are integral to wellbeing from the cradle to the grave. Through EFT couples are able to move to more effective dependence, which results in more coherent expressions of self and personal autonomy (Dalgleish et al., 2015).

Attachment theory provides the EFT therapist a map for understanding distressed partner's predictable responses. Using an attachment lens the EFT therapist can focus on relational insecurities, longings and needs that organize partner's actions (Johnson, 2015). At the heart of the relationship is an emotional tie which defines the importance of the other (e.g. attachment figure) and the relationship itself (i.e. attachment bond). The experience of insecurity and separation distress in a romantic relationship takes precedence in one's actions and experience (Johnson, 1999). Attachment theory enables the therapist to conjecture about the meaning and motivation underlying partner's responses. **Primary emotions** are understood as attachment-related emotions informed by a human need for social bonds and in a romantic relationship, the bond with one's partner is of ultimate importance.

A partner's behaviors in a distressed relationship can be understood as attempts to manage the inability to effectively respond to a threatened attachment bond. The patterns of anxious pursuit and avoidant withdrawal become predictable responses for couples where partners are no longer emotionally responsive and accessible. As these patterns persist, efforts to respond and repair are met with increasing disengagement. Building on Bowlby's (1988) observations of parent and child relationships, Johnson (2004) recognized that patterns of separation distress in couples follow a similar predictable sequence where a partner's angry protest over the experience of distress often gives way to anxious efforts to regain closeness and when these remain unsuccessful partners withdraw into depression and despair.

The level of despair is painfully clear at this point in the Johnsons' relationship. Questions of divorce are a reflection of the enduring pain and distance that neither Natalie nor David have been able to address. The affair renews Natalie's protest and, in predictable response, David's minimization and distance. The focal issue for the couple is the infidelity, yet the way the couple responds to this threat is indicative of a long-term pattern of demand and distance.

Couples caught in these vicious cycles of insecurity increasingly rely on less effective means of coping or relationship survival (e.g. fight, flight, freeze). The loss of emotional connection with an attachment figure can trigger "**primal panic**" which is a primary emotional system associated with social loss and a primary source of psychic pain (Panksepp, 1998, 2009). The impact and routine experience of fear reduces the couple's ability to make their way back to the secure relationship they desire and need. Fear blocks the couple's efforts to express their basic needs for contact, care, and comfort, and as a result couples rely on secondary strategies to manage the increasing insecurity in their relationship. The therapist's understanding of these blocks normalizes the struggle that the Johnsons face in connecting, especially after an affair. The discovery and disclosure of an affair is disorganizing for a couple. The level of distress is a source and a result of the ways each partner responds, often in automatic ways, to the threats experienced in the relationship.

Emotions play a central role in the organization and expression of attachment-related dynamics for couples. Each partner's response to distress in the moment is influenced by his or her attachment histories that impact the appraisal, interpretation, and response to an emotionally threatening interaction (Johnson & Whiffen, 1999). Partners with more insecure attachment styles are more likely to experience negative views of self (e.g. fear of rejection) or negative views of others (e.g. fear of abandonment). In response, these insecure styles result in a range of reactive behaviors including anxious and clinging responses demanding reassurance to distancing avoidant responses (Bartholomew & Horrowitz, 1991; Pietromonaco & Barrett, 2000). Through the lens of attachment, the actions of pursuit and withdraw can be further understood in the context of the significance of the relationship. The more anxious pursuing partner tends toward amplifying the anxiety of felt insecurity, while the more avoidant partner is more likely to deny or minimize this anxiety (Johnson & Whiffen, 1999). Partners' attachment strategies are evident in the secondary emotional responses that fuel the couple's negative interactional pattern and perpetuate the couple's felt insecurity.

Natalie's relationship history that has ended with partners who cheated may inform fears of abandonment and rejection. Her vigilance in response to David's affair makes sense in the context of infidelity in particular, but may also be consistent with her typical anxious responses to felt insecurity (Mikulincer, Shaver, & Pereg, 2003). Likewise, David's response in minimizing the importance of Devyn and the affair is understandable as an effort to avoid the crisis-related distress, but it is also indicative of a pattern of avoidance that is consistent with his pattern of relationships and his own struggle with addiction (Flores, 2004). David's minimization of the importance of the affair fits with his more avoidant attachment. Johnson and Zuccarini (2010) suggest that more avoidant partners are less emotionally connected to their partners and in David's case his minimization of the importance of the relationship may fit his experience. Natalie may find little solace in David's qualification, still the therapist's validation and recognition of David's disconnected experience is important to framing the impact of his avoidant tendencies on his experience of intimacy.

Change in these patterns results from new experiences, new information, and new interactions. The process of EFT provides partners with new experiences of the couple's problematic pattern through accessing, processing, and engaging the attachment-related affect underlying the more reactive roles that dominate even their best moments of trying to connect. The attachment strategies endure in the presence of experiences that confirm the felt insecurity (Shaver & Hazan, 1993). From an EFT perspective, **emotion** is seen as "an organizing force in working models rather than an outcome of them" (Johnson, 2009, p. 266) and these models are revised through emotional communication (Davila, Karney, & Bradbury, 1999).

Therefore, change in a couple's relationship results from new experiences that disconfirm past fears and expectations and inform models of self and other (Johnson & Whiffen, 1999). Johnson (2009) suggests that EFT offers a **corrective emotional experience** that provides partners with new experience and new meaning to what has become a familiar and expected outcome (e.g. negative pattern) and these changes through experience and meaning promise new possibilities for the relationship. She states that "when both partners then send clear and more coherent emotional signals and so create a closer and more attuned interpersonal dance, they literally are able to shape a new and transformative emotional world for each other" (p. 279).

For David and Natalie, the process of healing their relationship assumes more than recovery from an affair, although addressing this attachment injury will be critical to their progress. In EFT, the therapist focuses on the fundamental attachment dynamics of their emotional bond. For the Johnsons, this will require forming a new connection organized by the shared engagement of attachment-related emotions and needs in an accessible and responsive way. They must change their dance.

Attachment theory also guides the EFT response to reconciling breeches of trust between partners. These events, referred to as "**attachment injuries**" may involve incidents of abandonment or betrayal often occurring in a time of significant need. Attachment injuries result in a specific impasse that blocks partner's ability to renew and restore safety and trust in the relationship (Johnson, Makinen, & Millikin, 2001; Makinen & Johnson, 2006). Insecurity is heightened because one's attachment figure is equally sought as a solution to hurt and a source of pain (Johnson, 2005). Often an injured partner experiences trauma-like symptoms including hypervigilance, intrusive thoughts, and flashbacks that may overwhelm the offending partner, triggering that partner's defensive reaction, which furthers the couple's struggle to repair and begin a process of healing (Makinen & Ediger, 2011; Snyder, Baucom, & Gordon, 2007). Several studies support the efficacy and process of the eight-step attachment injury resolution model (AIRM) (Halchuk, Makinen, & Johnson, 2010; Makinen & Johnson, 2006; Zuccarini, Johnson, Dalgleish, & Makinen, 2013). In related research, EFT has shown effectiveness with couples impacted by trauma-related experiences (Dalton, Greenman, Classen, & Johnson, 2013).

The combination of the prominence of Natalie's hurt and anxious demands are reinforced by David's lack of responsiveness to her concern. The intensity of Natalie's concerns increases the likelihood that David will find himself overwhelmed by the combination of his own shame and the intensity of Natalie's expectations to make the relationship safe again (Johnson, 2005). While reconciling the Johnsons, attachment injury is a key focus in the EFT treatment. The therapist must maintain a focus on the long-standing relationship dynamics that inform the couple's history, but also their own approach to dealing with the infidelity (MacIntosh, Hall, & Johnson, 2007).

Problem Resolution

EFT helps partners access and expand their emotional experience, especially softer and more vulnerable emotions. Once shared, these emotions provide new patterns of engagement that are characterized by new levels of responsiveness and accessibility (Johnson, 2004). There are three primary change events: conflict de-escalation, withdrawer re-engagement, and blamer softening. These change events mark major shifts in the resolution of couple distress. The EFT process of change is composed of three stages that are illustrated in nine specific steps, originally identified by Greenberg and Johnson (1988). The change process is illustrated below with descriptions of each step and how they might apply to the treatment of the Johnsons.

Stage 1: Cycle De-escalation

The focus of Stage 1 is a de-escalation of the couple's negative interaction cycle which is evident when partners share in identifying their pattern and make it their common problem. This shift results in greater relationship flexibility and openness. Partners are less likely to use negative attributions and use reactive behaviors associated with anxious pursuit and avoidant withdrawal. Their shared openness is a reflection of the security experienced in the treatment itself and as a result partners are more likely to explore and risk more emotional engagement. As Johnson (2004) notes, this initial shift is a "first-order" change as partners modify their actions to move away from their conflict cycle, but neither partner moves toward a new position of engagement in the relationship.

Step 1: Assessment. Creating an alliance and identifying the relational conflict issues between spouses from an attachment perspective.

Step 2: Identify the negative interactional cycle that maintains attachment insecurity and distress.

In Steps 1 and 2, the EFT therapist establishes a working alliance with the couple and begins to track their relationship pattern. As an experiential therapy, EFT actively attunes to the experience of each partner, providing acceptance and validation of their unique perceptions and emotions. From an attachment perspective the therapist's alliance with each partner provides a secure base to begin to explore their relationship, especially in the here-and-now of the therapy conversation. Therapist responses validate client experience from a genuine non-blaming stance. Throughout the process of EFT, the therapist is actively monitoring the alliance providing an ongoing responsive and accessible support to each partner.

The alliance is established through eliciting and processing each partner's experience of the problem and through carefully tracking the unfolding negative interaction pattern.

The process of tracking specific "**stuck moments**" or arguments that typify the couple's felt distress enables the therapist to break down the actions and emotions associated with this unfolding pattern. A therapist's empathic reflection and validation helps partners to identify and express their feelings and thoughts that are often lost in the fury and confusion of an escalating negative pattern. This slows the process and enables the therapist to focus on the most poignant emotions that arise as partners begin to re-experience these difficult moments. These secondary responses are typical of a partner's attachment strategy, either escalating attachment-related anxiety (e.g. angry protest) or dampening anxiety through avoidant withdrawal (e.g. intellectualizing, numbing out).

In working with the Johnsons, the therapist would isolate a difficult moment that the couple recognized as typical of their presenting problem, such as Natalie's frustration with David when seeking his reassurance about his commitment and her importance. The therapist would begin to track and reflect both Natalie and David's experience as they "re-live" this past argument in the moment. In this process the therapist would provide empathic reflections and validation of Natalie's frustration in "not getting through" and her anger at feeling dismissed by David. In turn, the therapist would make sense together with David of his own hidden frustration at Natalie's worrying and chronic disappointment with his efforts. As the therapist walks through the rising tension between them in EFT the therapist begins to focus on the experience that is also present within them, namely Natalie's fear and pain in not mattering to David and his feelings of sadness that he is a chronic disappointment and often criticized for not doing enough in the relationship.

Step 3: Accessing the primary/unacknowledged emotions underlying each partner's interactional positions and attachment needs.

In Step 3, focus is given to staying with primary emotional responses so that each partner can begin to access and expand the underlying emotions that drive their reactive positions. The therapist uses empathic conjectures and questions to elicit the salient emotions associated with attachment-related needs and fears. For example, the therapist may reflect and intensify the focus on Natalie's fears of being invisible and unwanted by David, normalizing the desperation of these feelings and connecting this sense of panic to her critical responses and accusations.

Primary emotions come alive in the present moment and through the secure alliance these primary emotions are expanded and processed. In EFT these emotional experiences are not simply labeled but developed as a means for bringing focus to the attachment-related dynamics underlying each partner's reactive positions. So, as Natalie recounts her exasperation with David's intellectualizing, the therapist can track David physically turning away from the conversation. In noticing David's immediate response, the therapist using evocative questions can bring his present experience to the foreground. **Evocative questions** focus a client's attention to here-and-now experience. This enables partners to better engage his or her "present moment" and focus on emotions that are most relevant to these experiences (Johnson, 2004). "It's hard to hear these things she is saying, and the way they come across? What's happening inside you now as you turn away?" The therapist tracks and reflects immediate responses as "action tendencies" associated with felt emotion that partners can be guided toward.

The vulnerability experienced in the partner's primary emotion promotes a new awareness of what is at stake in a couple's conflict cycle. David's hurt is evidence of Natalie's importance to him and his rejected efforts to provide care support a further sign that he is ineffective, leading to his withdrawal in shame. Listening to the other's experience of the genuine hurt, sadness, and fear creates a new picture of the familiar postures of a distancing withdrawer and a demanding pursuer. The therapist uses an attachment lens to reframe the meaning and motivations associated with these felt emotions that have become real in session. Accessing and expanding these emotions helps to communicate the fears and longings both partners share for a different relationship.

Step 4: Reframing the problem in terms of the negative cycle, the underlying emotions, and attachment needs.

In Step 4, the therapist summarizes the interactional cycle with greater detail, including the predictable positions partners take along with the experience of each partner's underlying emotional experience. The therapist reframes the patterns as a relationship problem that has come between both partners and this obstacle is keeping them from what they want and need. Often the therapist reframes the cycle by summarizing the pattern as it has played out in this specific circumstance, enabling the therapist to emphasize what a partner does (i.e. secondary responses) and also what is going on in those moments at a deeper level (i.e. primary emotions).

The therapist shifts the focus from David's defensive withdrawal and Natalie's anxious control to the ways these take prominence in an escalating pattern of insecurity. David relies on a cool analytic distance to weather the intensity of Natalie's protests and intellectually manages the pain of her disappointment. Natalie's fear leads to desperation when she feels David pulling away and seeks to control a situation that increasingly feels out of her control. Together their efforts to connect and respond to the vulnerability they feel is lost in the escalating negativity of their cycle.

Cycles are often framed as an invader or an enemy, which has the effect of externalizing a predictable dynamic in their relationship and inviting partners to face this obstacle together. The negative attributions and polarizations associated with their conflict cycle lose their necessity as partners gain clarity about their experience and that of their partner. No longer alone in a fight for their needs, the couple can come together against the cycle that so easily entangles and defeats them. **Cycle de-escalation** results in a decrease in the couple's reactive pattern as each partner is better able to see and experience the ways in which their individual ways of responding (e.g. withdrawal, pursuit) feed into a perpetual cycle that works against what they seek as a couple.

A primary challenge facing the Johnsons is the recovery from an affair. The consequences of an affair vary by couple and the nature of the infidelity. In EFT, some couples will work through lesser violations in the context of Stage 1. For others the impact of the affair itself is tantamount to a fundamental breach of trust. These couples may work through aspects of the injury and achieve de-escalation, but the risk and vulnerability required in Stage 2 may interrupt a couple's progress until the "attachment injury" is fully addressed through the AIRM model (Johnson, 2005). In the case of the Johnsons, the affair is likely to result in an attachment injury given the extent and emotional nature of the affair, David's deception, and its discovery by Natalie.

Stage 2: Restructuring Positions

Stage 2 in EFT is focused on two change events that are each focused on a partner moving into a new level of emotional engagement. In **withdrawer re-engagement**, a previously withdrawn partner asserts his or her interests in the relationship with greater openness and accessibility to the other. This change event typically precedes the softening of the more demanding pursuing partner. The engaged withdrawer is more emotionally available and capable of responding to the needs and fears underlying a pursuer's anxious demands. In **blamer softening**, the more critical partner is able to reach to the other with his or her attachment-related fears and needs (Johnson & Greenberg, 1988). The softening represents a shift in control and closeness leading to new levels of shared vulnerability that when exchanged by both partners results in a bonding event; this, in turn, offers healing to past hurts and injuries and a new definition of the relationship itself (Johnson, 1999).

Step 5: Promoting identification with disowned needs and aspects of self and integrating these into relationship interactions.

The Stage 2 process follows the same three steps for withdrawer re-engagement and blamer softening. In Step 5, the therapist gives more attention to each individual focusing on accessing, expanding, and deepening the underlying emotions associated with that partner's position (e.g. withdrawer, pursuer). As the focus shifts into deeper emotional experiences and the history of anxious or avoidant attachment strategies, the therapist facilitates new experience and meaning associated with views of self (e.g. "I am unloveable") and views of other (e.g. "You might leave me"). These attachment schemas are poignant expressions of implicit attachment fears and longings, which inform the actions and experiences couples encounter in separation distress (Johnson & Whiffen, 1999). The therapist actively processes these new experiences and meanings while fostering the engagement and acceptance of this emerging experience with the other partner.

Typically, in Stage 2 the therapist shifts focus to the more withdrawing partner with the goal of re-engaging that partner's expression of attachment-related needs and desires with his or her partner. The therapist deepens the withdrawer's attachment-related experience through expanding and deepening the primary emotions associated with that partner's withdrawal. Through evocative interventions the therapist uses heightening and empathic conjectures to focus and prime security-related affect associated with one's need for care and comfort particularly in the face of felt vulnerability. Recent process research studies highlight the importance of high levels of in-session emotional experiencing especially given a withdrawing partner's tendency to easily exit their primary emotional experience (Lee, 2015; Rheem, 2011). In this respect, withdrawers need support to gradually enter into their primary, attachment-related affect. The therapist may have to cycle back, using more evocative questions and heightening interventions, to fully process and make poignant the withdrawer's in-session emotional experiencing.

David's pattern of withdrawal has a long history. In reflecting on his difficulty staying with the intensity of Natalie's frustrations and pain, the therapist helps David make contact with his own sense of helplessness and frustration in responding to Natalie's concerns. Staying with this experience the therapist repeatedly heightens his uncertainty and invites David to focus on his more vulnerable longings he feels in those moments. The therapist stays focused on these emerging feelings in session as the process unfolds encouraging David to take ownership for his withdrawal and the fears that drive his effort to cover his vulnerability. Through empathic conjectures and validation, the therapist helps David identify his attachment-related fears and longings to engage with Natalie differently in these moments.

As David articulates his attachment needs and longings he expands a new sense of self and clarity about who he wants to be in this relationship. As this process unfolds, the therapist would use this clarity by inviting David to share this directly with Natalie. The therapist invites the enactment using a proxy voice, "Could you turn to her now and share this part of you that says, 'I don't want to hide what I need, I don't want to avoid the hard things anymore and I want a place we can talk about my fears too, without taking control or telling me off.' Could you turn to her now and share this in your own words?"

Step 6: Promoting acceptance of the partner's new construction of the relationship and new interactional behavior.

In Step 6, witnessing the partner's emerging primary emotion and vulnerability often draws the listening partner toward greater care and connection. The power of deeper expressions of attachment affect is organizing and clarifying. David's sharing invites Natalie into a deeper level of understanding, which the therapist seeks to make explicit through evoking its impact, acknowledging the listening partner's acceptance, and then acting on this acceptance through sharing this with the other. However, this response is not automatic, and new expressions of vulnerability by a withdrawn partner may prompt feelings of distrust from the pursuing partner.

In situations where the partner struggles to accept their partner's newfound vulnerability, the therapist validates the struggle to trust these new emotional revelations. The therapist uses their alliance to validate the partner's distrust, which itself can be reframed and organized around the listening partner's need and longing for a vulnerability that is trustworthy and real. In doing so, the therapist holds hope that a new trusting connection is possible when partners begin to share at this level, even if time is needed to develop trust and consistency. This is particularly true in situations involving attachment injuries, where a concrete breach of trust must be resolved for the couple to move forward. The process of Steps 5 and 6 work together enabling partners to risk deeper expressions of attachment-related affect and new meaning and promoting acceptance through processing the impact of these new shared experiences.

Step 7: Facilitating the expression of specific needs and wants and creating emotional engagement. The key change events, withdrawer reengagement and blamer softening, are completed in Step 7. The result of these changes is a prototypical bonding event for the couple.

Step 7 culminates the process of restructuring positions as partners move toward one another enacting the expression of their attachment needs for security and care. As attachment-related fears and needs are crystallized in the context of that partner's experience, the therapist uses enactments to prompt the couple to share and respond to the essential needs that define their connection. **Enactments** in EFT involve the therapist directing partners to turn toward each other and share from their experience. The chief goal of an enactment may involve intensifying an individual's emotional experience or fostering a deeper emotional connection as a couple (Johnson et al., 2005). As such, Step 7 enacts attachment security where partners successfully risk, receive, and respond to one another's attachment bids which each feared expressing in the context of their history of distress (Johnson & Greenberg, 1988).

David hides his insecurity from Natalie for fear she will reject him if she were to really see his need for her support and comfort. Bowlby (1988) argued that the experience of fear can block humans from making bids for attachment. Ironically, these blocks obscure the attachment-related signals that coordinate proximity seeking in more secure relationships (Hazan & Shaver, 1987). As David is able to share his fears with Natalie, the therapist focuses David's attention on his unexpressed attachment needs (i.e. what he needs from Natalie in these moments). The therapist heightens his fear and invites an enactment again that is focused on his immediate needs. For example, the therapist might say in this moment of fear, "David, as you look at Natalie right now, and you see she is here for you, what do you need most from her in this moment? Can you ask her right now?" The therapist's more directive stance provides a resource for David to risk a new level of engagement. David could respond to Natalie, "I need you to believe me. I need you to believe in me. I want us to work, but I need you to support me, to be on my side, and not just criticize and disrespect me. I need you to give me the benefit of the doubt, and believe I do love you."

In the above examples we illustrate the process of David's withdrawer re-engagement, which sets the stage for working toward Natalie's blamer softening. Softening events predict successful treatment outcomes in EFT (Burgess Moser et al., 2016; Johnson & Greenberg, 1998). Blamer softening is perhaps the most challenging change event for the therapist (Johnson & Talitman, 1997) and has prompted further research on the process itself (Bradley & Furrow, 2004, 2007). For Natalie, the process of reaching toward David with her attachment may prove challenging because of the affair. As the therapist begins the Stage 2 process, the block in Natalie's ability to risk more vulnerable emotions with David may be justified by her experience of the "attachment injury." Consequently, the therapist would identify the injury and shift focus to the AIRM, which provides a specific focus on resolving violations of trust at the heart of the relationship (Makinen & Johnson, 2006; Zuccarini et al., 2013).

Stage 3: Consolidation

Step 8: Facilitating the emergence of new solutions to old relationship problems.
Step 9: Consolidating new positions and new cycles of attachment behavior.

The final stage of EFT focuses on consolidation of the progress of the couple to regain a secure connection in their relationship. Couples revisit persistent conflicts often rooted in differences in background, values, or preferences (e.g. money, parenting, family relationships) from new positions of accessibility, responsiveness, and emotional engagement (Johnson, 2008). Past issues may trigger their negative pattern, and in Step 8 the therapist helps the couple identify their previous work moving away from the reactive cycle to new positions of security. The therapist returns the focus to the underlying themes and experiences previously worked through in Stage 2 and enables the couple to face these persistent concerns with the resources they have in their secure connection. David's interactions with his sister Regina and her impact on the couple is one area where Natalie and David could get triggered. Though David's relationship with Regina has improved following her recovery, David still keeps his distance with Regina and Natalie is often drawn into David's family-of-origin issues. These tensions then play out in Natalie's relationship. The EFT therapist would help the couple use their renewed security to face these tensions together and identify how his sister can often trigger their cycle.

In Step 9 the couple has renewed confidence in what they have accomplished. Couples are able to reflect on changes they have made as the therapist heightens these differences and the narrative the couple now share. The therapist focuses on the couple's successes and positive examples where they have been responsive and accessible to one another. **Attachment rituals** are discussed as an opportunity for the couple to take intentional steps to invest in the secure bond they have renewed (Johnson et al., 2005). For David and Natalie, this may mean finding an activity that signals reassurance for Natalie and appreciation for David. This can be as simple as sharing written notes with one another or setting aside a specific time where the focus is on the needs and hopes they share.

Case Transcript

The following case vignette highlights several crucial elements of EFT practice including: (a) delineating a negative conflict cycle, (b) accessing primary emotional responses underlying the cycle, (c) using enactments to shape new interaction, and (d) reframing the negative cycle as the enemy in the couple's relationship and a barrier to attachment security. These components represent the first four steps associated with the EFT treatment model. It is important to note, however, while each of these steps builds on the previous step, the in-session process is more recursive than sequential. An effort has been made to highlight this aspect of clinical practice in the transcript.

As previously stated, the impact of an affair on a couple's felt sense of security will be a salient feature throughout the course of treatment. Early on in the treatment process the EFT therapist often utilizes the same techniques germane to most models of couple therapy including stopping all communication with the affair partner, increasing transparency regarding daily activities and any unplanned interactions with the affair partner (e.g. affair partner is a co-worker), enhancing self-soothing and coping skills, and establishing each partner's commitment to work on the relationship. The following case vignette picks up with David and Natalie after (a) all communication has ceased with the affair partner, (b) both David and Natalie have affirmed their commitment to work on the relationship, and (c) Natalie is able to regulate her affect regarding the affair enough such that she can both discuss the impact of the affair and their general relationship history in-session.

Therapist: I'm wondering if you can begin to help me understand a bit more about your marriage before David's online relationship with this woman. I want to get a sense of how the two of you related to one another, what your communication was like, and how each of you felt about the relationship.

Here the therapist begins the assessment process indicative of Step 2 in EFT. That is, the therapist wants to begin to construct an understanding of how each partner experiences the relationship. The therapist assumes that the long-standing relationship concerns leading to a lack of intimacy also play prominently within the context of the affair.

Natalie: I would say the first year of our relationship was really good. Wouldn't you say (*to David*)?

David: Yes. I would agree. It felt good and natural. It wasn't work. We really enjoyed being around one another. It's not the same anymore. We hardly do any of the things we used to, like going to football games or having date nights.

Natalie: (*Interrupting*) And whose fault is that? Are you blaming me for the lack of date nights? You never ask me out anymore!

David: (*Sighs*) I'm not blaming you. I'm just saying we don't spend time together anymore and when we do it's not the same. Besides, you look at me like I'm a complete stranger most of the time… or like you are always disgusted with me.

Therapist: I hear you both saying there used to be a strong connection, but over time this has slowly dwindled. Tell more about what it's been like to have this strong connection slowly go away over the last couple of years?

The therapist uses an evocative question centered on the deterioration of intimacy and closeness within the relationship. This helps to temporarily de-escalate the interaction between them from going further into blame and defensiveness.

Natalie: It's been awful. It's like he doesn't care about us anymore. And then this whole online relationship thing happened. I'm constantly checking his browsing history… his phone… his Facebook…

Therapist: Natalie that sounds like such a difficult place to be in. I hear you saying that you are unsure of where you stand with David… that you used to know, but your closeness has eroded over time and then the affair happened. Am I getting that right?

Natalie: Yeah… it's so infuriating! I try to talk with him about it, but he always has some excuse as to why I'm overreacting…

David: (*Defensively*) Look, I just want to get past all of this and move on. How can we do that when you are constantly asking me if I talked to her today… or wanting to look at my phone?

Natalie: (*To the therapist*) You see… I try to talk to him, but he doesn't want to talk. He gets so defensive.

David: (*Defending*) That's because you attack me and start pointing out all of things that are wrong with me!

Natalie: (*Protesting*) I'm just trying to talk with you. We don't talk anymore! We don't talk about this at all.

David: (*Contemptuously*) Why would I want to talk with you when you just pick at me? Besides, this is how it always seems to go, especially lately.

Therapist: Is this what happens to you at home? The two of you sort of get stuck in this cycle of interaction where you (*to Natalie*) try to come to David with your concerns and you are met with a "let's just move on and get over it" kind of response? It's like you get the message from David that your concerns are not important to him? And part of what you do then is get very upset and try to manage your concerns by looking at his online activity or checking his phone?

> *The therapist introduces the notion of the negative pattern of interaction—called* **the cycle**—*as the primary problem in the relationship. The therapist first highlights the attachment-related message Natalie receives from David (i.e. your concerns aren't important to me) and how this relates to her secondary emotional response of anger and subsequent behavior.*

Natalie: Exactly…

Therapist: And David, it seems like you don't really see Natalie as afraid of where she stands with you. What you hear is all the things that are wrong about you. All the things she doesn't like. When this happens I get the sense that you get defensive and push back on Natalie… it's like you try to say to her, "We can't go forward if you keep bringing up the past."

> *The therapist completes the reflection by adding in key components of David's secondary emotional response (i.e. upset) and behavior (i.e. gets defensive).*

David: That seems right… or sometimes I just don't care to say anything at all.

Therapist: I see… the two of you get caught in this pattern where you are both left feeling quite disconnected from one another. Natalie you end up feeling pushed away, uncared for and David you end up feeling picked at… am I getting that right?

David: Yes. I feel like I am the screw-up. It really doesn't matter if I try.

Natalie: It seems like our arguments are always the same. It doesn't matter what we fight about… it could be about the affair or anything really. He ends up shutting me out and I end up alone in the bedroom, feeling sad and lonely.

Therapist: And over time this pattern has eroded all that love and connection each of you felt was so strong in the beginning (*both Natalie and David nod*). Would it be okay if I ask each of you a bit more about this pattern?

> *The therapist is reframing the cycle as the real enemy to the couple's sense of felt security in the relationship. This is indicative of Step 4 in the EFT treatment process.*

David: Sure…

Natalie: I suppose so…

Therapist: Natalie, tell me more about that feeling of sadness you get after an argument with David. A second ago you said that after an argument you often end up in the bedroom, alone, and feeling sad. Can you help me understand your sadness more?

> *The therapist is using an evocative question to further explore Natalie's sense of sadness. This is indicative of Step 3 in the treatment process. Within EFT theory, sadness is conceptualized as a primary emotion that carries an adaptive action tendency. Moreover, Natalie's sadness often goes unacknowledged by David. By drawing attention to her sadness and processing it experientially, the therapist can then shape a new interaction between Natalie and David that makes space for her attachment-related emotions.*

Natalie: I don't know… It's hard to describe. It's just this strong feeling of dread I get after we fight. I often just sit upstairs in the bedroom and cry (*pausing then looking away she continues*). I am all alone.

Therapist: That's a painful place for you…

> *The therapist gently reflects Natalie's primary emotional experience (i.e. pain), inviting her to explore it more.*

Natalie: Yes. It really hurts when he pushes me away and shuts me out (*tears begin to well in her eyes*).

Therapist: Yes. It does hurt when the person we desperately want to be close with pushes us away. Natalie, what happens inside for you right now as we talk? I see tears in your eyes. It's like you're touching on some of that pain right now.

> *The therapist validates and acknowledges the attachment salience of her sadness (wanting to be close, yet pushed away) and then draws attention to how her primary emotion is emerging within the here-and-now moment.*

Natalie: I never thought we would end up here. It hurts so much and I don't know what to do anymore (*begins crying*).

Therapist: It hurts when you feel pushed away. It hurts when it seems like the connection that once was has gone away.

Natalie: Yes.

Therapist: Natalie, I'm wondering if you are ever able to talk with David about this hurt and pain you carry around? I get that you sometimes come to him when you are angry and upset... say about the affair, but I'm wondering if he knows about this part of you? The part of you that is really hurting... and alone.

> *The therapist invites Natalie to experientially imagine and reflect upon sharing her sadness with David. Attention is drawn to how the conflict pattern inhibits the expression of her primary emotional sadness. The therapist is setting the stage for an enactment whereby Natalie turns and directly shares her sadness with David. Before doing so, however, the therapist wants to check in with David to gauge his level of responsiveness to Natalie's emerging emotional experience.*

Natalie: I don't know. I'm not sure he really wants to know this stuff...

Therapist: David, what is it like for you right now as you hear Natalie talk about this pain she carries around on the inside? Can you look at her for a second? What happens inside for you as you see her pain right now?

> *The therapist draws David's attention to Natalie's sadness that stems from feeling dismissed by him, especially pertaining to the affair and her concerns. The therapist then uses an evocative question, inviting David to share his reaction to her hurt. According to attachment theory, primary emotional cues have the potential to pull a comforting response from partners. The therapist wants to capitalize on this and assist David in being more emotionally accessible and responsive to Natalie.*

David: I knew she was hurt, but I didn't know she felt this strongly about it. To me she just seems mad all the time, not hurt. She attacks every chance she gets.

Therapist: You know, David, that makes a lot of sense. You are used to seeing Natalie as angry with you, or upset at your behavior, so I can understand why this might be a bit new. What is it like for you right now as she touches on this pain that she feels... how when you say things like, "We just need to move on from this," it hurts so much?

> *The therapist is drawing attention to how David's dismissal of Natalie's concerns creates not only her sharp angry responses (secondary emotion), but also result in pain and sadness (primary, attachment-related emotion).*

David: I don't know. It's hard to see her as anything but mad. Look, I know what I did is awful, but we can't keep dwelling in the past or we aren't going to be able to move forward.

Therapist: It's hard to talk about this isn't it, David? It makes sense to me why it would be hard to talk about the ways in which your wife feels a lot of pain and anger because of your online relationship with another woman.

The therapist validates David's secondary emotional response and defensiveness. It is important to validate secondary responses and associated behavior to then move into processing primary emotions underlying those responses.

David: I guess over time lots of walls have come up between us. I do push her away. I'm not sure what to do anymore and that is the natural thing for me to do. I kind of freeze—not knowing what I should do. I never knew she was hurting like this. I didn't realize I was hurting her like this. She always seems so angry.

Therapist: That makes sense to me… I hear that. David, I wonder if you can share that with Natalie right now? What she usually sees is someone who has walled himself off. I wonder if you could do something different right now and let her know how her pain impacts you?

The therapist coordinates an enactment between David and Natalie. The therapist places specific emphasis on how the cycle often prevents this type of sharing and encourages them to have a different experience with one another.

David: It makes me sad to see you hurt this way… to know I've let you down like this. I know I can shut down and wall myself off, or tune you out. I know I've really hurt you… it's hard for me talk about it all the time.

Therapist: Thank you, David, for sharing how Natalie's pain impacts you in this moment. I imagine that was a big step for you… Natalie, I want to check in with you. What's it like to hear David share this with you now?

The therapist validates David's work in the moment and turns to process the experience of having David share from a place of vulnerability with Natalie.

Natalie: It's good to hear. We don't talk like this often. We usually just fight and go our separate ways.

Therapist: Yes, the two of you get stuck in this nasty cycle and it prevents you from being able to really hear and support one another.

The therapist continues to reframe the cycle as the enemy of the relationship.

Natalie: Yes. It's nice to hear that he cares about how I feel and sees that it really hurts me when he shuts me out.

Therapist: Natalie, can you begin to share that with David right now? In your own words, could you help him understand how painful it is for you when he shuts you out and "walls off" as he put it?

> *Now that the therapist has checked in with David and gauged his level of in-session responsiveness, an enactment is established whereby Natalie directly expresses her pain and hurt with David.*

Natalie: I think so… (*to David*). It's really painful when you shut me out. I know I don't always approach you in the best way, but it's so hard for me when I feel like I can't get to you or you just tell me to get over it. I need you to try and hang in there with me and not be so quick to close me out.

David: I'll try my best. It's hard for me too…

Therapist: That was really great you two. You are working so hard right now to try and do something other than the typical nasty cycle.

Natalie: Thanks… it's hard…

David: Yeah… It's definitely not easy.

Therapist: That's right… in time I think the two of you can team up against this cycle. David, we've heard a bit from Natalie about what seems to be happening for her under the surface during times of conflict. I'm wondering if you could also help me understand a bit more about what's going on for you? You said a second ago that it can be a painful place for you when you hear how you've disappointed Natalie. What is going on inside for you in those moments?

> *The therapist begins to explicate David's primary emotional experience much like what was just done with Natalie. This is indicative of Step 3 in the EFT treatment process.*

David: I'm not sure what to say…

Therapist: Take your time and try to find what fits best for you.

David: It's like I get hot all of sudden, then just want to escape.

Therapist: You get hot all of sudden…

David: Yeah… I'm not sure I know how to control it. I just feel hot when she is criticizing me. It could be anything really.

Therapist: I see. So this hot feeling, it happens quite quickly, then you shut down? I wonder if this is what Natalie is describing when she says she loses you emotionally.

David: Yeah. The only thing I want to do in that moment is stop the argument. Sometimes I get defensive and push back; other times I just walk away.

Therapist: David, what is going on inside for you the moment after you just walk away?

The therapist uses an evocative question to assist David in elaborating more fully about his emotional experience during a conflict with Natalie. Note how the therapist did not ask David, "What are you thinking at that moment?" Instead, the therapist draws attention to David's internal emotional experience.

David: I don't know… I'm pretty angry at that point. Frustrated…

Therapist: Yes, that makes sense. It would be very frustrating to get tangled in this argument and want it to end…

David: Yeah…

Therapist: So I get there's a part of you that gets angry and frustrated, but I'm wondering if there is another part of you? Like you said before… a part that feels a bit poked at perhaps? A part that feels a bit hurt?

Here the therapist uses an empathic conjecture and interpretation intervention to (a) highlight David's secondary emotional experience (his anger) and (b) conjecture about his possible primary emotional experience. At times, clients may struggle to identify their primary, attachment-related emotions. When this happens the therapist uses an **empathic conjecture** *to help the client move to the leading edge of her or his emotional experience. The therapist provides an empathic reflection on the one hand and then proposes an alternate, more vulnerable experience on the other. Often these conjectures are framed in attachment-related language to focus each partner on the relational poignancy of this experience. As a result, clients gain a deeper more profound experience of their primary emotional experience.*

David: I guess so. I mean it's hard being criticized all the time, especially when I know I messed up. It wears on me.

Therapist: Yes, it wears one down, doesn't it? Can you say more about that part of you? The part that feels worn down; the part that feels a bit hurt?

David: I grew up being picked on you know?

Therapist: Yes, I recall you said something about that.

David: Yeah… I wasn't the most athletic in school; or the best student; and, I got made fun of for it. I learned early on to deal with my emotions by either getting really mad or just shutting down.

Therapist: David, I'm wondering if it's actually quite painful for you when Natalie comes to share her concerns? It's like you hear someone who is disappointed in you. And that is a familiar feeling from your past.

The therapist utilizes another empathic conjecture to help David elaborate further on his emotional experience. The therapist "guesses" that David might be feeling some hurt and/or pain stemming from his wife's complaints about him. A good empathic conjecture is tentative and allows the client to "try on" the emotional experience to see if it fits.

David: Yeah…

Therapist: What's it like for you to feel like your wife is disappointed in you?

David: It's awful.

Therapist: Yes… can you say more about that?

> *The therapist uses an evocative question to ask David to elaborate further on his experience.*

David: I don't like feeling like I'm disappointing my wife. It's a terrible feeling in the pit of my stomach.

Therapist: In the pit of your stomach? (*David nods*) Tell me, David, are you feeling that now?

David: A little bit. It's tight right here (*rubs his hand over his stomach area*).

Therapist: Stay with it for a moment. I want you to check in with that part of you that feels tight. If you can, I would like you to try and speak from that knot in your stomach.

> *The therapist uses heightening to help David stay with his primary emotion and expand it in-session.*

David: Okay I'll try… I just feel tense; the same way I feel when we argue.

Therapist: I'm wondering if this is what you mean when you say you go hot David? It's like some part of you gets angry and irritated when Natalie brings up her concerns. I also hear there is another part of you; a part that feels small and disappointed. It's a familiar feeling for you… one that you experienced growing up.

David: Yeah… I feel like a disappointment to Natalie.

Therapist: Those are powerful words David. You feel like a disappointment to Natalie.

David: Yeah… I do.

Therapist: David, I'm wondering if you have ever shared this with Natalie? Have you ever told her, "It's hard for me to talk about the affair because I know I screwed up, I let you down, and I feel like such a disappointment in your eyes. I just want to move past it as quickly as I can."

> *The therapist invites David to experientially imagine sharing his pain and vulnerability with Natalie.*

David: No. I don't think I've ever shared it quite like that.

Therapist: Could you begin to share that with Natalie now in your own words?

> *The therapist coordinates an enactment whereby David directly expresses primary emotional experience (feeling like a disappointment) with Natalie.*

David: I'll try. (*To Natalie*) It's really hard for me to talk about this.

Natalie: I know it is.

David: I feel like I constantly disappoint you; that I'm letting you down. So rather than have another argument about it I try to shut it down.

Natalie: I didn't know you felt that way.

David: I don't want to be a disappointment to you. That's why I feel like I have to defend myself all the time. It's like I'm trying to prove to you I'm not that guy anymore.

Therapist: Natalie, what's it like for you as David begins to open up about this place he goes to that says, "I feel like such a disappointment?"

Natalie: I don't like it. I don't want him to feel that way. I just want to talk and try to make us better.

Therapist: You know what strikes me about our meeting today is how this pattern has gotten a hold of your relationship in a powerful way. Natalie, you desperately want to address the issues within your relationship. So you go to David and try to talk with him about what is concerning you. Only David, you don't hear it as concerns. You experience Natalie as criticizing you, which leads you to a place of feeling like a disappointment. Rather than sharing that with her you become angry and defensive... telling her it's time to move on. And Natalie, when David shuts your concerns down like that you are left feeling lonely and hurt. Am I getting this right? (*Both David and Natalie nod*) I wonder if we can make addressing this cycle a primary goal of our subsequent sessions? You both did something different today; you had a different type of interaction. I want to support the two of you in teaming up against this cycle so you can hear one another's concerns and find ways to support each other.

> *The therapist summarizes the entirety of the conflict pattern highlighting (a) each partner's behavior, (b) the behavior's relative impact on the other, (c) the primary emotional experience underlying the conflict pattern, and (d) how the negative cycle of interaction is a common enemy the couple can team up to fight against.*

References

Bartholomew, K., & Horowitz, L. M. (1991). Attachment styles among young adults: A test of a four category mode. *Journal of Personality and Social Psychology, 61*, 226–244. http://dx.doi.org/10.1037/0022-3514.61.2.226.

Baucom, D. H., Shoham, V., Mueser, K. T., Daiuto, A. D., & Stickle, T. R. (1998). Empirically supported couple and family interventions for marital distress and adult mental health problems. *Journal of Consulting and Clinical Psychology, 66*, 53–88. doi:10.1037/0022-006X.66.1.53.

Bowlby, J. (1969). *Attachment and loss: Vol. 1. Attachment.* New York, NY: Basic Books.

Bowlby, J. (1973a). Affectional bonds: Their nature and origin. In R. Weiss (Ed.), *Loneliness: The experience of emotional and social isolation* (pp. 38–52). Cambridge, MA: MIT Press.

Bowlby, J. (1973b). *Attachment and loss: Vol. 2. Separation.* New York, NY: Basic Books.

Bowlby, J. (1988). *A secure base: Parent-child attachment and healthy human development.* New York, NY: Basic Books.

Bradley, B., & Furrow, J. L. (2004). Toward a mini-theory of the blamer softening event: Tracking the moment-by-moment process. *Journal of Marital and Family Therapy, 30*(2), 233–246. doi:10.1111/j.1752-0606.2004.tb01236.x.

Bradley, B., & Furrow, J. L. (2007). Inside blamer softening: Maps and missteps. *Journal of Systemic Therapies, 26,* 25–43. doi:10.1521/jsyt.2007.26.4.25.

Bradley, J. M., & Palmer, G. (2003). Attachment in later life: Implications for intervention with older adults. In S. M. Johnson & V. E. Whiffen (Eds.), *Attachment processes in couple and family therapy* (pp. 281–299). New York, NY: Guilford Press.

Burgess Moser, Johnson, S. M., Dalgleish, T. L., Lafontaine, M., Wiebe, S. A., & Tasca, G. A. (2016). Changes in relationship-specific attachment in emotionally focused couple therapy. *Journal of Marital and Family Therapy, 42*(2), 231–245. doi:10.1111/jmft.12139.

Byrne, M., Carr, A., & Clark, M. (2004). The efficacy of behavioral couples therapy and emotionally focused therapy for couple distress. *Contemporary Family Therapy, 26,* 361–387. doi:10.1007/s10591-004-0642-9.

Chambless, D. L., & Ollendick, T. H. (2001). Empirically supported psychological interventions: Controversies and evidence. *Annual Review of Psychology, 52,* 685–716. doi:10.1146/annurev.psych.52.1.685.

Cloutier, P. F., Manion, I. G., Walker, J. G., & Johnson, S. M. (2002). Emotionally focused interventions for couples with chronically ill children: A 2-year follow-up. *Journal of Marital and Family Therapy, 28,* 391–398. doi:10.1111/j.1752-0606.2002.tb00364.x.

Collins, N. L., & Read, S. J. (1990). Adult attachment, working models, and relationship quality in dating couples. *Journal of Personality and Social Psychology, 58,* 644–663. http://dx.doi.org/10.1037/0022-3514.58.4.644.

Couture-Lalande, M. E., Greenman, P. S., Naaman, S., & Johnson, S. M. (2007). Emotionally focused therapy (EFT) for couples with a female partner who suffers from breast cancer: An exploratory study. *Psycho-Oncology, 1,* 257–264. doi: 10.1007/s11839-007-0048-7.

Dalgleish, T. L., Johnson, S. M., Burgess Moser, M., Lafontaine, M. F., Wiebe, S. A., & Tasca, G. A. (2015). Predicting change in marital satisfaction throughout emotionally focused couple therapy. *Journal of Marital and Family Therapy, 41,* 276–291. doi:10.1111/jmft.12077.

Dalgleish, T. L., Johnson, S. M., Burgess Moser, M., Wiebe, S. A., & Tasca, G. A. (2015). Predicting key change events in emotionally focused couple therapy. *Journal of Marital and Family Therapy, 41,* 260–275. doi:10.1111/jmft.12101.

Dalton, E. J., Greenman, P. S., Classen, C. C., & Johnson, S. M. (2013). Nurturing connections in the aftermath of childhood trauma: A randomized controlled trial of emotionally focused couple therapy for female survivors of childhood abuse. *Couple and Family Psychology: Research and Practice, 2*(3), 209–221. doi:10.1037/a0032772.

Davila, J., Karney, B., & Bradbury, T. N. (1999). Attachment change processes in the early years of marriage. *Journal of Personality and Social Psychology, 76,* 783–802. http://dx.doi.org/10.1037/0022-3514.76.5.783.

Dessaulles, A., Johnson, S. M., & Denton, W. H. (2003). Emotion-focused therapy for couples in the treatment of depression: A pilot study. *The American Journal of Family Therapy, 31,* 345–353. doi:1080/01926180390232266.

Dunn, R. L., & Schwebel, A. I. (1995). Meta-analytic review of marital therapy outcome research. *Journal of Family Psychology, 9,* 58–68. http://dx.doi.org/10.1037/0893-3200.9.1.58.

Fincham, F. D., Stanley, S. M., & Beach, S. R. H. (2007). Transformative processes in marriage: An analysis of emerging trends. *Journal of Marriage and Family*, *69*, 275–292. doi:10.1111/j.1741-3737.2007.00362.x.

Flores, P. J. (2004). *Addiction as an attachment disorder*. Lanham, MD: Jason Aronson, Inc.

Furrow, J. L., Edwards, S. A., Choi, Y., & Bradley, B. (2012). Therapist presence in emotionally focused couple therapy blamer softening events: Promoting change through emotional experience. *Journal of Marital and Family Therapy*, *38*(1), 39–49. doi:10.1111/j.1752-0606.2012.00293.x.

Furrow, J. L., & Palmer, G. (2007). EFFT and blended families: Building bonds from the inside out. *Journal of Systemic Therapies*, *26*, 44–58. doi:10.1521/jsyt.2007.26.4.44.

Furrow, J. L., & Palmer, G. (2011). Emotionally focused therapy for remarried couples: Making new connections and facing competing attachments. In J. L. Furrow, S. M. Johnson, & B. A. Bradley (Eds.), *The emotionally focused casebook: New direction in treating couples* (pp. 271–294). New York, NY: Routledge.

Gendlin, E. T. (1974). Client-centered and experiential psychotherapy. In D. A. Wexler & L. N. Rice (Eds.), *Innovations in client-centered therapy* (pp. 211–246). New York, NY: Wiley.

Gottman, J. M. (1994). *What predicts divorce? The relationship between marital processes and marital outcomes*. Hillsdale, NJ: Lawrence Erlbaum Associates.

Gottman, J. M. (1998). Psychology and the study of the marital processes. *Annual Review of Psychology*, *49*, 169–197. doi:10.1146/annurev.psych.49.1.169.

Greenberg, L. S., & Johnson, S. M. (1988). *Emotionally focused therapy for couples*. New York, NY: Guilford Press.

Halchuk, R. E., Makinen, J. A., & Johnson, S. M. (2010). Resolving attachment injuries in couples using emotionally focused therapy: A three-year follow-up. *Journal of Couple & Relationship Therapy*, *9*, 31–47. doi:10.1080/15332690903473069.

Hazan, C., & Shaver, P. (1987). Romantic love conceptualized as an attachment process. *Journal of Personality and Social Psychology*, *52*, 511–524. http://dx.doi.org/10.1037/0022-3514.52.3.511.

Jacobson, N. S., & Margolin, G. (1979). *Marital therapy: Strategies based on social learning and behavior exchange principles*. New York, NY: Brunner & Mazel.

Johnson, S. M. (1986). Bonds or bargains: Relationship paradigms and their significance for marital therapy. *Journal of Marital and Family Therapy*, *12*, 259–267. doi:10.1111/j.1752-0606.1986.tb00652.x.

Johnson, S. M. (1998). Listening to the music: Emotion as a natural part of systems theory. *The Journal of Systemic Therapies*, *17*(2), 1–17. Retrieved from http://psycnet.apa.org/psycinfo/1998-10088-001.

Johnson, S. M. (1999). Emotionally focused couple therapy: Straight to the heart. In J. M. Donovan (Ed.), *Short-term couple therapy* (pp. 13–42). New York, NY: Guilford Press.

Johnson, S. M. (2004). *The practice of emotionally focused couple therapy: Creating connection* (2nd ed.). New York, NY: Brunner-Routledge.

Johnson, S. M. (2005). An emotionally focused approach to infidelity. In F. Piercy (Ed.), *Handbook on treating infidelity* (pp. 17–29). New York, NY: Haworth Press.

Johnson, S. M. (2008). *Hold me tight: Seven conversations for a lifetime of love*. New York, NY: Little, Brown & Company.

Johnson, S. M. (2009). Extravagant emotion: Understanding and transforming love relationships in emotionally focused therapy. In D. Fosha, D. J. Siegel, & M. F. Solomon (Eds.), *The healing power of emotion: Affective neuroscience, development and clinical practice* (pp. 257–279). New York, NY: W.W. Norton & Company, Inc.

Johnson, S. M. (2013). *Love sense: The revolutionary new science of romantic relationships.* New York, NY: Little, Brown and Company.

Johnson, S. M. (2015). Emotionally focused couple therapy. In A. S. Gurman, J. L. Lebow, & D. K. Snyder (Eds.), *Clinical handbook of couple therapy* (5th ed., pp. 97–128). New York, NY: The Guilford Press.

Johnson, S. M., Bradley, B., Furrow, J., Lee, A., Palmer, G., Tilley, D. & Woolley, S. (2005). *Becoming an emotionally focused therapist: The workbook.* New York, NY: Routledge.

Johnson, S. M., & Greenberg, L. S. (1985a). Differential effects of experiential and problem-solving interventions in resolving marital conflict. *Journal of Consulting and Clinical Psychology, 53,* 175–184. doi:10.1037/0022-006X.53.2.175.

Johnson, S. M., & Greenberg, L. S. (1985b). Emotionally focused couples therapy: An outcome study. *Journal of Marital and Family Therapy, 11,* 313–317. doi:10.1111/j.1752-0606.1985.tb00624.x.

Johnson, S. M., & Greenberg, L. S. (1988). Relating process to outcome in marital therapy. *Journal of Marital and Family Therapy, 14,* 175–183. doi:10.1111/j.1752-0606.1988. tb00733.x.

Johnson, S. M., Hunsley, J., Greenberg, L., & Schindler, D. (1999). Emotionally focused couples therapy: Status and challenges. *Clinical Psychology: Science & Practice, 6,* 67–79. doi:10.1093/clipsy.6.1.67.

Johnson, S. M., Maddeaux, C., & Blouin, J. (1998). Emotionally focused family therapy for bulimia: Changing attachment patterns. *Psychotherapy: Theory, Research and Practice, 35,* 238–247. http://dx.doi.org/10.1037/h0087728.

Johnson, S. M., Makinen, J. A., & Millikin, J. (2001). Attachment injuries in couple relationships: A new perspective on impasses in couples therapy. *Journal of Marital and Family Therapy, 27,* 145–156. doi:10.1111/j.1752-0606.2001.tb01152.x.

Johnson, S. M., & Talitman, E. (2007). Predictors of success in emotionally focused marital therapy. *Journal of Marital and Family Therapy, 23,* 135–152. doi:10.1111/j.1752-0606.1997.tb00239.x.

Johnson, S. M., & Whiffen, V. (1999). Made to measure: Adapting Emotionally Focused Couple Therapy to partners' attachment styles. *Clinical Psychology: Science & Practice, 6,* 366–81. doi:10.1093/clipsy.6.4.366.

Johnson, S. M., & Zuccarini, D. (2010). Integrating sex and attachment in emotionally focused couple therapy. *Journal of Marital & Family Therapy, 36,* 431–445. doi:10.1111/j.1752-0606.2009.00155.x.

Josephson, G. J. (2003). Using an attachment-based intervention with same-sex couples. In S. M. Johnson & V. E. Whiffen (Eds.), *Attachment processes in couple and family therapy* (pp. 300–317). New York: Guilford Press.

Lebow, J. L., Chambers, A. L., Christensen, A., & Johnson, S. M. (2012). Research on the treatment of couple distress. *Journal of Marital and Family Therapy, 38,* 145–168. doi:10.1111/j.1752-0606.2011.00249.x.

Lee, N. L. (2015). *A task analysis of withdrawer re-engagement in emotionally focused couple therapy.* Unpublished doctoral dissertation, Ball State University, Muncie, IN.

MacIntosh, H. B., Hall, J., & Johnson, S. M. (2007). Forgive and forget: A comparison of emotionally focused and cognitive-behavioral models of forgiveness and intervention in the context of couple infidelity. In P. R. Peluso (Ed.), *Infidelity: A practitioner's guide to working with couples in crisis* (pp. 127–147): New York, NY: Routledge/Taylor & Francis Group.

MacPhee, D. C., Johnson, S. M., & Van Der Veer, M. C. (1995). Low sexual desire in women: The effects of marital therapy. *Journal of Sex & Marital Therapy, 21,* 159–182. doi:10.1080/00926239508404396.

Makinen, J. A., & Ediger, L. (2011). Rebuilding bonds after the traumatic impact of infidelity. In J. L. Furrow, S. M. Johnson, & B. A. Bradley (Eds.), *The emotionally focused casebook: New directions in treating couples* (pp. 247–268). New York, NY: Routledge.

Makinen, J. A., & Johnson, S. M. (2006). Resolving attachment injuries in couples using emotionally focused therapy: Steps toward forgiveness and reconciliation. *Journal of Consulting and Clinical Psychology, 74*, 1055–1064. http://dx.doi.org/10.1037/0022-006X.74.6.1055.

Mikulincer, M., Shaver, P. R., & Pereg, D. (2003). Attachment theory and affect regulation: The dynamics, development, and cognitive consequences of attachment-related strategies. *Motivation and Emotion, 27*, 77–102. http://dx.doi.org/10.1023/A:1024515519160.

Minuchin, S. M., & Fishman, H. C. (1981). *Family therapy techniques.* Cambridge, MA: Harvard University Press.

Panksepp, J. (1998). *Affective neuroscience: The foundations of human and animal emotions.* New York, NY: Oxford University Press.

Panksepp, J. (2009). Brain emotional systems and qualities of mental life: From animal models to implications for psychotherapeutics. In D. Fosha, D. J. Siegel, & M. F. Solomon (Eds.), *The healing power of emotion: Affective neuroscience, development and clinical practice* (pp. 1–26). New York, NY: W. W. Norton & Company, Inc.

Perls, F., Hefferline, R., & Goodman, P. (1951). *Gestalt therapy.* New York, NY: Julian Press.

Pietromonaco, P. R., & Barrett, L. F. (2000). Attachment theory as an organizing framework across diverse areas of psychology. *Review of General Psychology, 4*, 107–110. http://dx.doi.org/10.1037/1089-2680.4.2.107.

Rheem, K. M. (2011). *Analyzing the withdrawer re-engagement event in emotionally focused couple therapy: A preliminary task analysis.* Unpublished doctoral dissertation, Argosy University, Washington, DC.

Roberts, T. W. (1992). Sexual attraction and romantic love: Forgotten variables in marital therapy. *Journal of Marital and Family Therapy, 18*, 357–364. doi:10.1111/j.1752-0606.1992.tb00949.x.

Rogers, C. R. (1951). *Client-centered therapy.* Boston, MA: Houghton-Mifflin.

Sexton, T. L., Gordon, K. C., Gurman, A., Lebow, J., Holtzworth-Munroe, A., & Johnson, S. M. (2011). Guidelines for classifying evidence based treatment in couple and family therapy. *Family Process, 50*, 377–392. doi:10.1111/j.1545-5300.2011.01363.x.

Shadish, W. R., & Baldwin, S. A. (2003). Meta-analyses of MFT interventions. *Journal of Marital and Family Therapy, 29*, 547–570. doi:10.1111/j.1752-0606.2003.tb01694.x.

Shaver, P. R., & Hazan, C. (1993). Adult romantic attachment: Theory and evidence. In D. Perlman & W. Jones (Eds.), *Advances in personal relationships* (Vol. *4*, pp. 29–70). London, UK: Jessica Kingsley.

Simpson, J. A., Rholes, W. S., & Phillips, D. (1996). Conflict in close relationships: An attachment perspective. *Journal of Personality and Social Psychology, 71*, 899–914. http://dx.doi.org/10.1037/0022-3514.71.5.899.

Snyder, D. K., Baucom, D. H., & Gordon, K. C. (2007). *Getting past the affair: A program to help you cope, heal, and move on—together or apart.* New York, NY: Guilford Press.

Walker, J. G., Johnson, S., Manion, I., & Cloutier, P. (1996). Emotionally focused marital intervention for couples with chronically ill children. *Journal of Consulting and Clinical Psychology, 64*, 1029–1036. http://dx.doi.org/10.1037/0022-006X.64.5.1029.

Wood, N. D., Crane, D. R., Schaalje, G. B., & Law, D. D. (2005). What works for whom: A meta-analytic review of marital and couples therapy in reference to marital distress. *American Journal of Family Therapy*, *33*, 273–287. doi:10.1080/01926180590962147.

Zuccarini, D., Johnson, S. M., Dalgleish, T. L., & Makinen, J. A. (2013). Forgiveness and reconciliation in emotionally focused therapy for couples: The client change process and therapist interventions. *Journal of Marital and Family Therapy*, *39*, 148–162. doi:10.1111/j.1752-0606.2012.00287.x.

4

FEMINIST COUPLE THERAPY

Megan J. Murphy

History of the Model

Feminist therapy emerged in reaction to family therapy models that had failed to consider gender and power dimensions of family life. In 1978, Rachel Hare-Mustin wrote a pivotal article in *Family Process* outlining the need for a feminist approach to family therapy. She highlighted several parts of feminist therapy that would be further expounded on by women in the field, including challenging traditional gender roles, challenging the idea of a "normal" family, and challenging therapists to be aware of gender patterns in families that are detrimental to women. The themes she wrote about nearly 40 years ago are still relevant to families and therapy today.

Up until the late 1970s, family therapy models were developed by white males, which reflected their understandings and knowledge of the field, with the exception of Virginia Satir, who was the first female therapist to openly espouse empathy, connection, warmth, and emotions with her experiential approach to working with families (Satir, 1972). As conceptualized by founders of the field, one major advancement in terms of systems thinking was expanding the etiology of schizophrenia to the family instead of looking solely at individual causes (Bateson, Jackson, Haley, & Weakland, 1956). However, reflective of dominant discourses then and now, mothers were seen as responsible for the family, and so this advancement in the field underscored mother blaming, which is a criticism feminist therapists put forward about family therapy (Boss & Thorne, 1989).

Models of family therapy were also critiqued by feminists for ignoring **power**. Hierarchy was a part of both structural and strategic family therapies. Structural family therapists helped families reinforce the hierarchy between parents and children. Hierarchy was considered to be generational; structural family therapists did not address power in terms of gender. Strategic therapists also used the concept of hierarchy, yet again did not address gender or sex roles assigned to men and women via gender socialization (Walsh & Scheinkman, 1989).

Systems theory was quite a paradigm shift for the field of mental health when it first emerged in the 1950s (McGeorge, Carlson, & Wetchler, 2015). Prior to the advent of systems theory, individualistic views on mental health predominated. Systemic perspectives offered an expanded view of health and psychopathology, in a way that was perhaps more respectful than locating problems within a person. Terms such as reciprocity, circular causality, and feedback loops were meant to highlight the interactional nature of individuals and the family. This makes intuitive sense now, yet at the time it was revolutionary. However, the emphasis on circular causality did not leave room for consideration of power. If power was considered, it was seen as the exception, rather than the rule. Feminist therapists challenged this vision of systems on both levels—that power needed to be considered or interwoven into systems understandings, and that power was *always* present in systems; it was not only present when violence was occurring in families (Goodrich, 1991).

Hare-Mustin's (1978) article paved the way for women in the field to write about the centrality of gender and power as important dimensions for examination in family therapy. Goldner (1985) wrote about how gender was ignored in transgenerational approaches, and suggested ways that gender be considered along with generation when working with families. Other feminist therapists worked together to present at conferences, despite much resistance from men in the field (McGoldrick, Anderson, & Walsh, 1989). In the late 1980s, another publication, *The invisible web*, had a large impact on the field in terms of directly challenging therapists to incorporate gender into their work (Walters, Carter, Papp, & Silverstein, 1988). Around this time, issues greatly impacting women, such as battering, were also brought to the forefront (Hansen & Harway, 1993). Feminist therapists called for therapists to assess for domestic violence with all couples seen for therapy, given the high prevalence of violence in clinical couples (Avis, 1992; Bograd, 1992).

As much as these therapists and writers impacted the field with their revolutionary ideas, Black therapists pointed out family therapy was also oppressive to Black families, as they were largely coming from a white point of view (Hardy, 1989). Writers such as Boyd-Franklin wrote about how family therapy models could be used when working with Black families (Boyd-Franklin, 1987a). Boyd-Franklin (1987b) further began writing about therapy that attends to the specific needs of Black women. In about the mid 1990s, sexual orientation began to emerge as a topic that was overlooked, similar to how gender and race were ignored previously (Green, 1996; Laird, 1994; Leigh, 1995; Long, 1995). These changes in family therapy reflect feminism's larger shift from **2nd wave**—with a focus on women's empowerment, valuing women's perspectives, and ensuring that women are seen as equal to men—to **3rd wave feminisms**, which focus on challenging binaries typically associated with gender, race, sexual orientation, etc., as well as highlighting women's diverse experiences. The focus of this chapter is on 2nd wave feminism; an intersectionality approach to family therapy can be found in Chapter 7.

It is worth mentioning that there are many different forms of feminist therapy; feminist therapy is not a monolith. There are many overlapping concepts and approaches that are discussed in this chapter; however, there can be some differences, depending on the particular beliefs of the therapist. Carolyn Enns (1997) has published a book outlining many different kinds of feminist therapies, from liberal feminist therapy to cultural feminist therapy to women of color feminist therapy. Differences in feminist approaches lie on a number of dimensions. For example, a liberal feminist therapist would focus on encouraging couples to embrace egalitarian relationships, whereas a cultural feminist therapist would focus on valuing relationships and caring that are central to women's lives. Many of these themes are present in this chapter; yet all therapists are faced with the task of starting *somewhere*; some issues or topics have to be prioritized. Different feminist approaches would perhaps start somewhere different. As discussed below, therapy is reflective of the therapist and their own beliefs about families.

Theory of Problem Formation

At a larger level, feminists point to the prevalence of patriarchy in social systems as a major contributor to relational problems. **Patriarchy** refers to "social arrangements in which women's interests are subordinated to those of men" (Hare-Mustin, 1991, p. 63). As a result, society is structured so that men hold power in relation to women; for example, in government, heads of corporations, as head of households, who will be paid more for jobs, who are more likely to advance in jobs, etc. Language is male-centered; for many years, "he" was considered appropriate to refer to both men and women; likewise, terms such as mankind and humankind are known to refer to everyone. At first glance, one may wonder how this connects to couple relationships; although upon further exploration, relationships are permeated with effects of patriarchy. These effects of patriarchy play out in terms of power dynamics experienced by couples within their relationships (Luepnitz, 1988).

Despite our culture's embracing of equality, much research has shown that few couples are truly egalitarian (Knudson-Martin & Mahoney, 2009). For those couples who embrace and work toward egalitarianism in their relationship, a return to traditional gender roles is likely after the birth of a child. From the time we are in the womb to the present, men and women are directed in different paths, starting out perhaps innocuously in being identified with pink for girls and blue for boys. Much research has been done on how traditional gender roles shape available career and relationship options for men and women; these gender roles continue forward into adult romantic relationships. Feminist therapists see gender roles as restrictive of both men and women and their options for displaying a full range of behavior and emotions within relationships. For David and Natalie, we can see that David is more restricted in his communications about his marriage, whereas Natalie works hard to pull information from David about his thoughts and feelings.

Work and Home Domains

Being channeled into different directions, such as women being socialized to take on more caregiving occupations and roles, and men being socialized to take on more logical occupations and roles, may not in itself be harmful for relationships, except for the existence of power that is imbued in these different pathways for men and women. Men are likely to earn more money than their female partners; this is an example of patriarchy infiltrating romantic relationships. Because men are likely to earn more in their jobs, couples quite often decide to move in pursuit of the male's job, leaving the women in a position to find work in the location of her husband's job. Similarly, it makes much financial sense for women to drop out of the workforce or work part-time when the couple has a child. A vicious cycle ensues, in which women who stay home with children are not seen as interested in, prepared for, or up to the challenge of the working world. Myths about women being uninterested or unprepared for work are perpetuated, further keeping women in their place at home with their children. Some might suggest that a society that values children and women would pay livable wages to those who care for children, or at least offer reasonable and paid maternity leave. In Natalie and David's case, the couple decided for David to move from Maine to Texas to find employment; this runs counter to typical gender arrangements made in heterosexual relationship; however, David may have some resentment in giving up his job as a teacher in Maine to make a move in support of Natalie's career.

The workforce is still seen as men's domain, and the home is women's domain. This carries forward to and affects relationships in many ways. Women are considered responsible for household chores, such as cooking, dishes, laundry, dusting and cleaning, as well as caring for children. Traditional gender roles suggest that men are responsible for repairs, mowing the lawn, and upkeep with cars, in addition to being the breadwinner, responsible for supporting the family financially. Women are responsible for the **emotional labor**, such as scheduling doctor's appointments, handling the children's school issues, sending out holiday cards, smoothing things over in a relationship when there has been a fight, arranging for visits to family and friends, etc. For women, the list of things to do is never ending, even under the best of circumstances. Women who work outside the home are not exempt from being responsible for these household tasks. The **second shift** (Hochschild, 1989) refers to women working one shift outside the home (paid employment), and then coming home to do a second shift of unpaid work—dinner, dishes, homework, laundry, putting the children to bed, etc. The end result is utter exhaustion; and for relationships, this can mean the building of resentment, when men come home and expect to be waited on while they watch TV and/or read the newspaper. It can be difficult to determine gender arrangements regarding household work and emotional labor for Natalie and David; however, hints at these topics may be present. Natalie seems to be responsible for initiating discussion about problems in their marriage, which is an example of emotional labor. David has reached the point where he is spending more time with friends and out at bars, which may mask a lack of participation in household chores at home.

Motherhood and Career

Many women relish the opportunity to become a mother. Motherhood is often seen as the pinnacle of women's lives. Some feminists suggest that motherhood is not an inherent desire in women; instead, seeing women as being socialized to value mothering as central to their identity (Taffel, 1991). Women are taught to care for others, beginning in childhood when girls are given baby dolls as toys. Motherhood is simultaneously highly valued by women, but de-valued by society as in the aforementioned lack of laws in the United States supporting maternity leave. Moreover, women face biological limits to reproductive opportunities, which places further pressure on them to have children sooner in life. In addition, women on career paths are faced with dilemmas to either further their career or have children and cut back on their career or drop out of the work force altogether. To some extent, these challenges are socially constructed (Sangster & Lawson, 2014); women may have children after 35 or 40 with assistance from reproductive technology, or women may be able to have children *and* work with the help of a supportive partner, friends, and families. Regardless, the pressures women feel on these fronts combine to add to worries about when to have children, and with whom. The age difference, in addition to the gender difference, between Natalie and David contribute to marital problems related to decisions about having children. Natalie faces biological limitations to having children, whereas David does not; her position vis-à-vis David on this issue affords David more power in making this decision.

Domestic Violence

Feminist therapists raised the profile of domestic violence in relationships.

For many years, violence in marriage remained unspoken publicly, and certainly not considered in therapy. Even though some studies indicate that at least 50 percent of couples presenting for therapy have experienced at least one incident of domestic violence or sexual abuse, therapists remain reluctant to assess for or intervene in violent relationships (Avis, 1992). Therapists, who are trained in systems approaches, may not have an adequate understanding of power dynamics that are present in relationships; as a result, both partners can be seen as equally responsible for abuse in relationships. This line of thinking, when combined with women seen as responsible for the health and functioning of relationships, can further undermine women's sense of agency when violence is present in relationships. In the case scenario, it is possible that David has an issue with drinking—either past or present—since it came up during one of their arguments. In addition, several years ago, David was involved in a physical fight with his sister Regina, for which he was arrested and ultimately placed on probation. He was drinking during this fight. As is common in many domestic violence incidents, alcohol is present. Alcohol use may continue to be present in their relationship, as David frequently is out with friends at venues in which alcohol is readily available.

Gender Socialization

Gender socialization and gender role expectations impact couples, as they do individuals (Avis, 1991). Couples subconsciously bring gendered expectations into their relationships from their families-of-origin. Much is learned by watching parents on all of the possible gendered dimensions already discussed, and more. Children learn who is responsible for the emotional work in the relationship, how decisions are made, what is valued, as well as subtle indicators of power in relationships that may play themselves out in their current relationship. In addition to absorbing cultural messages about men and women from friends, school, television, and movies, David's family provided him with powerful information about the value and power of men, which supported what was learned from outside sources. The part of the case scenario that is very telling is the story of how David's parents decided to have a third child—the desire for a son by David's father, Dana. Feminist therapists may hypothesize that the value placed on having a son has implications for *all* of the relationships in the family, including between David and his sisters, and ultimately between David and Natalie. The usually implicit message is made explicit: boys are more valued than girls. In addition to the overt value on boys, the process by which the decision was made by his parents (or, more accurately, by Dana) can send a message to David that women are flexible and will bend for men's wants or desires.

Again, children learn by watching their parents about gender roles and expectations. How parents connect with each other, as well as how they interact with their children, can differ significantly by gender. David and Natalie both have distant relationships with their fathers; indeed, both fathers lack initiative in fostering relationships with their children, which is consistent with traditional gender roles. Both David and Natalie may have learned that men are not the stewards of relationships, but instead, women are, leaving both without skills to navigate healthy intimate relationships. Feminist therapists might anticipate this pattern of gendered behavior around nurturing relationships to continue with the next generation, should Natalie and David have children.

Sexual Relationships

Sexual intimacy is part of normal, healthy relationships. Yet sexual intimacy is not immune from gender socialization and gender expectations that impact romantic relationships. Men receive clear messages about sex—that they are in charge, they are entitled to have their sexual needs met, that their sexual pleasure comes first, that sex is over as soon as he climaxes (Hare-Mustin, 1994). Sex is seen by many men as an indicator of love and affection from their partners. Women, on the other hand, receive mixed messages about sex. These messages are brought forward into romantic relationships by *both* partners. Cultural messages place value on women being pure and virginal; they are not to have sex before marriage. This cultural ideal exists even in the face of overwhelming research that suggests that most women have premarital sex (Finer, 2007). Women who express interest in sex, initiate sex, or enjoy sex are still seen as sluts and whores—there is no negative label for men. Furthermore, men are seen as entitled to sex; there is a common cultural view that if men are not getting their sexual needs met within a marriage or relationship, then they are entitled to meet their needs outside of the relationship, regardless of the impact on their current relationship. Society's messages can have tremendous negative implications for couples. The incident that propels Natalie and David in for therapy is around an online affair. David expresses his displeasure with the marital relationship in terms of lack of sex; he could be seen as justifying his online dalliances because his sexual needs are not being met in the marriage. The difficulties with their relationship, sex life, and boundaries appear to have started at the beginning of their relationship, when David continued to talk with other women online; it does not appear that Natalie did the same. Feminist therapists would wonder about how it was decided—and by whom—that the relationship should or should not be exclusive. David's decision to continue talking with other women could be viewed as entitlement to "play the field," which is much more acceptable for men than it is for women.

Impacts on Men

The impacts of gender role socialization and power differences between men and women are clear for women and relationships; what may not be so clear are the impacts on men. Although men vary in the level they are impacted by gender role socialization, the vast majority of men subscribe to expectations of them as men, just as women do for women. In some ways, men are seen as having an even more rigid role defined for them in terms of **masculinity**—or what is acceptable behavior for men (Kimmel, 1997). Failing to meet social norms can have devastating effects on men and their intimate relationships. Feminist therapists examine the social context of all clients they work with, including men. Men tend to have a smaller social network than women, and have fewer close friends. It can be difficult for men to talk with any close friends they *do* have because men have been greatly socialized to avoid talking about relationships, particularly with other men. As a result, David may not have an outlet to be able to discuss his concerns; even though he has friends with whom he attends sports events, or frequents bars, it may be unlikely for him to be able to share his innermost concerns in such settings. Men enforce masculinity norms with other men. David may be publicly shamed if he brings up his concerns about his marriage; or he may be encouraged to seek out other women as a remedy to his ailing marriage.

Likewise, men are not taught to express emotions. Indeed, some men suffer from alexithymia, or difficulty expressing emotions (Levant, 2003). Over time, men are socialized to distance themselves from emotions, perhaps to the point of being unable to identify their own emotions, let alone express their emotions to others, such as an intimate partner. The shame associated with emotions can lead to utter paralysis when discussing relationship issues. Meanwhile, women are socialized to talk about emotions, which contributes to communication issues and frustration. We can see David's minimal answers when Natalie questions him about his online activities. He seems to take a cognitive-logical approach to his discussion with Natalie about her inquiries. Being able to communicate his concerns and feelings would likely strengthen their marriage.

Considering Context

Context is critical in feminist therapy. In this case, we see this couple living in Texas, after David moved from Maine to move in with Natalie. It appears as if David has made friends in Texas, as he goes out with them on occasion. Texas is very likely a different culture than the one David was used to in Maine. When moving to a new place, David may be asked how he came to Texas from Maine; if he answers that he moved to be with his female partner, he may be chided by his friends, depending on his friends' view of masculinity. This may be further compounded if he says he has moved into his female partner's house. Any comments by friends may exacerbate David's feeling of inadequacy as a man, which may then impact his relationship with Natalie. It appears as if David is looking for a better job; a career is often central to men's identity. At this point, it is not clear what would be "better" for David if he had another job—whether that is pay, hours, schedule, location, etc. Again, even though the current generation values egalitarianism, it still can be difficult for men to be paid less than their partners or spouses. Natalie could be making more money in real estate than David is as a teacher. Even if David is fine with making less money than Natalie, it may be brought to his attention by others, such as friends or family. That his father was a bank manager and his mother was a bank teller may foreshadow their responses to their son bringing in less money in their marriage. Stepping outside the traditional masculine role brings hefty emotional consequences for men, which may be linked to use of drinking as a coping mechanism.

If Natalie and David are like many couples, they have not learned how to make equitable decisions in their relationship. Instead, they are likely to figure out how to navigate large and small decisions as they go. Many couples are focused, of course, on the content of decisions – what will they decide? – as opposed to the process of decision-making. Common assumptions related to gender may go unquestioned, such as what is fair for both of us in deciding where to live? Do we value earning as much money as possible between the both of us, compared to living closer to family? How will we handle the bills if we decide to have a child together? What messages are we sending to our child with our decision about who stays home to be with the baby, if that is what we decide? Even if couples are aware of and able to communicate about these gendered values and expectations, the discussion itself is imbued with gender. Who is more likely to give in? Who is most likely to smooth things over for the sake of the relationship? Who might be better at raising facts to support a position? Do emotional arguments hold the same sway as logic? The process by which Natalie and David talk about decisions and issues in their marriage is crucial to the success of the discussion.

Caretaking

Women are seen as the caretakers of their family and relationships. Women are taught to value relationships, particularly male–female relationships and marriage, from a very young age. Messages women receive about relationships include: you are not valuable unless you are in a relationship; if you work hard enough or love someone enough, you can change them to be a suitable partner; you are not complete without a relationship; if a relationship ends, it is your fault; if you do not satisfy your male partner's sexual needs (which includes not being attractive enough), then he will find someone else who will be what he needs. As a result, women can work very hard at relationships, trying all angles to change herself and her partner to create the ideal relationship. She can compromise, put her needs aside, place herself last in terms of priorities, and shape herself to fit what she thinks her male partner wants. This includes overlooking transgressions, living with distrust, and ultimately doubting herself. In their initial discussion of David's online affair, Natalie indicates that there have been previous breaches of trust in their relationship in the past. She may overlook her own needs to the sake of the relationship. Meanwhile, David is not considering Natalie's needs or wants in the relationship. Rather, he is quite dismissive of her at times, and is dishonest in his communications with her.

Longtime demand-withdraw patterns can be devastating for relationships. Research shows that women tend to fulfill the demand role, whereas men fulfill the withdraw role, particularly in dissatisfied marriages (Gottman & Levenson, 1999). Men can see women's demands as nagging, and tune them out over time. Nevertheless, women keep trying to mend the relationship and work through issues. In the end, women are more likely to initiate divorce (Sayer, England,

Allison, & Kangas, 2011), and have mourned the loss of the marriage long before men realize that something is seriously wrong in the relationship. Men withdraw and tune women out to the detriment of their marriage. Men may present in therapy wanting desperately to work on their marriage, while their wives have already emotionally checked out, saying that they have tried to communicate difficulties to their husband for years, to no avail. When women reach the point of seeking divorce, they have made as many attempts as possible to work on the marriage, and also have overcome strong societal messages against ending a marriage. Yet research shows that men accepting influence of their wives is a key component to successful marriages (Gottman, 1999).

Women's Voice

Feminist therapists are particularly attuned to how women view themselves, and the lack of voice they have in their lives and relationships. Having one's view of reality constantly questioned and challenged can contribute to low self-esteem, and a diminishment of women's voices. A lack of value felt by women in their intimate relationships is seen as problematic, both for women and for their partners. It is difficult to give fully to a relationship if women are lacking in self-esteem. Over time, women can learn to ignore their intuition, even if that intuition signals something important to them. Natalie had discovered online messages between David and another woman. Even though she had evidence of these messages, David denied the existence of the messages at first. Depending on a woman's self-esteem and evidence on hand, she may question herself and her discoveries. Akin to denying is minimizing, followed by blaming, which are included in David's response to Natalie's initial discovery. The denials and shifting the blame are undoubtedly exhausting for Natalie, as she continues to seek recognition of her knowledge and experience within the relationship.

Theory of Problem Resolution

Feminist therapy is more of a framework or worldview for therapy; it does not follow a formulaic, step-by-step approach. Rather, the course of therapy is very much dependent on the therapist and the clients, as each is unique to the therapeutic relationship. Feminist therapy is a collaborative endeavor, with therapist and clients working together to set goals and decide upon the length and outcomes of therapy (Haddock, Zimmerman, & MacPhee, 2000; Whipple, 1996).

Therapist Role

Feminist therapists understand that what happens in the therapy room is often a reflection of larger socio-cultural-political contexts in which both therapist and clients reside. Aware of power dynamics embedded in all interactions, feminist therapists take time to understand themselves as persons of culture, as power brokers by virtue of their role as therapists, while examining the power they have (and do not have) within the therapy room (Adleman, 1990; Lerman & Rigby, 1990). Therefore, before therapy even commences, feminist therapists engage in **self-of-therapist work**, in which they work on developing an understanding of their experiences, values, and biases related to their clinical work. They have a well-developed understanding of their gendered experiences, both personal and professional, that undoubtedly contribute to the therapeutic relationship. Feminist therapists are aware of and acknowledge their role in upholding sexist, racist, homophobic, and classist discourses, and actively work to minimize their participation in these discourses, both in their personal life as well as in their clinical work and other professional activities. They are not immune to the deep impact societal and cultural messages have on everyone, including themselves.

As a result of continuous self-of-therapist work, feminist therapists work to be transparent with their clients, sharing with them their values and biases, which highlights the collaborative nature of therapy (Haddock et al., 2000). Being open and honest, and discussing values as they may relate to the issues couples bring in for therapy helps clients make informed decisions about participation in therapy. In a first session with Natalie and David, a therapist may share that she values egalitarian relationships; further, she may share why she believes this, how her values are tied to her ethnic, cultural, and/or religious background (for example), and/or how these values are based in current research.

Collaboration is a hallmark of feminist therapy; however, this does not mean that therapists do not take a stand on certain issues or ignore power dynamics (Enns, 1997). Rather, feminist therapists *do* take a stand; the main difference compared to other approaches is that they are transparent in how they take a stand, and engage in conversation with clients about their position. Similarly, they actively attend to the multiple levels of power dynamics that occur within couples' relationships, as well as within the therapist–client relationship.

Collaboration also means working together with clients, and refraining from taking an expert stance (Haddock et al., 2000). Although feminist therapists have clear beliefs—for example, that gender is a central construct in family relationships—they do not embrace the idea that they have answers for clients. A focus on process is key; helping couples to work together, in an egalitarian fashion, to determine solutions for their goals. In this way, collaboration does *not* mean "anything goes." The feminist therapist is an active participant in shifting dynamics in couples' relationships. Means to achieve this include raising difficult, challenging, or unique questions. In the end, clients are free to decide for themselves how to respond to questions, how they feel about their partner's answers, and how to proceed (or not) in their relationship.

Because feminist therapists consider gender to be a central organizing factor in couples' relationships, they are aware of and intervene in the process of therapy, as it relates to gender (Haddock et al., 2000). First, they are likely to discuss power dynamics between themselves and their clients. Preferring overt conversations, they may raise the topic of gender embedded in the therapeutic relationship. In working with heterosexual couples, if the therapist is a woman, she may talk with each member of the couple about how they might experience therapy provided by a woman. Further, the couple might be asked if they have any concerns, allowing for each partner to express any worries. By putting these issues out on the table, the therapist introduces the idea of gender as impactful in relationships, and opens the conversation to a topic that may be discussed further or returned to at some point in the future. In working with a woman therapist, Natalie may feel and talk about relief that another woman may understand her point of view. David may wonder if he will be "ganged up on" by two women; he may fear not being heard. Ideally, both clients would feel comfortable sharing how the therapist's gender may impact therapy. Feminist therapists also realize that these kinds of conversations may be quite "new" for couples, so they keep in mind that there may be underlying discomfort, even if both clients express comfort when discussing the therapist's gender.

Feminist therapists are extremely attentive to communication and power dynamics as they play out in the session. Research shows that therapists interrupt women clients three times more than men clients—this is true for both women and men therapists (Werner-Wilson, Price, Zimmerman, & Murphy, 1997). Therefore, it is necessary to monitor one's own interruptions of clients, as well as to intervene to allow for equal "air time" in session for both members of a couple. In addition to monitoring and changing these communication patterns, therapists themselves are mindful of who is defining reality—a form of power in relationships, and intervening when necessary. As with all therapists, feminist therapists will not allow name-calling or other overtly abusive or harmful statements in session; yet this applies as well to gendered statements used as put-downs. Feminist therapists would pause a discussion and highlight the harm that is inflicted when statements such as "she's just crazy" or "she's an emotional wreck" are made by partners or family members. These statements are usually made by the person in the relationship that has more power—men—and until then have gone unchecked by friends or family. The therapist uses her power as a therapist to define these statements as harmful to the partner and to the relationship.

Feminist therapists set ground rules and boundaries in session in many ways. Ideally, couples always show up for sessions, arrive on time, and arrive together. Yet boundaries must be established and maintained for eventualities in therapy, such as one partner not being able to attend a session, one partner arriving late, and inconsistent attendance. Boundaries around what is allowed to be said in session are necessary, including no name-calling, not arriving inebriated, no insulting comments, etc. The therapist shares this stance with the couple upfront, including the reasons for this boundary, and how it will be enforced. The therapist can say that they will interrupt the person if something hurtful was said, and the person will be asked to rephrase their statement in a healthier way, and that the therapist will help if needed.

Feminist therapists think carefully about seeing one or both partners individually, in the event that the other does not show for a session or does not continue with couples therapy. Because women are held accountable for relationship maintenance and success, and because women internalize this expectation and therefore work very hard to improve their relationships, therapists are cognizant of the impact of their treatment decisions on women in particular. Feminist therapists talk with women whose male partner is not in attendance, and share the risks and shortcomings of working with them individually, including that it is difficult to work on couples issues with just one person, and the (justified) worry that working with the woman alone will send the message to both her and her partner that she is solely responsible for making changes in the relationship. Given that feminist therapy is collaborative, this is a discussion held with the client, ultimately respecting her decision to whether to continue therapy individually or not.

Being aware of the political nature of therapy and the connections between what happens inside the therapy room to the larger socio-political landscape is crucial for feminist therapists (Singh & Burnes, 2011). They are always seeing connections between national policy, workplace politics, personal experiences, and client symptoms. In other words, one cannot simply "do therapy" and then go about living one's life, ignoring the common threads throughout that connect therapists to clients. As a result, feminist therapists are frequently engaged in some sort of **social activism**—working to make a difference in women's lives. This activism can take many different forms, such as mentoring underprivileged women who are attending college, being on academic committees involved with changing workplace policies that impact women, joining a protest against proposed legislation that threatens women's reproductive rights, or running for political office. Feminist therapists demonstrate that the personal is political.

Assessing for Domestic Violence

Given the assumption that patriarchy shapes intimate relationships, and patriarchy gives men more power over women in those relationships, which sets the stage for abuse, feminist therapists have a responsibility to assess for domestic violence, even if that is not the problem presented by couples. The vast majority of couples will not call in seeking therapy with violence as their main concern. Yet feminist therapists are aware of the great likelihood of violence as present in intimate relationships, and therefore routinely assesses for violence early on when working with couples. Within the first or second session, feminist therapists take time to meet separately with each member of the couple to hear about their concerns that bring them in to therapy, without worrying about what the partner will say. This time alone with each partner allows the therapist to assess for abuse, and to determine the safety of both members of the couple before proceeding with couples therapy. Neither Natalie nor David are likely to call for therapy saying that they have a concern about violence in their relationship (or gender dynamics, for that matter). Their presenting problems are likely to be communication issues and/or an internet affair. For many reasons, the couple is not likely to view their relationship as "abusive," which leaves it to the therapist to raise as a possibility, or to provide the frame for seeing certain statements or actions as abusive.

The importance of establishing safety is paramount when working with couples (Avis, 1992). Being aware of the power dynamics inherent to intimate relationships, feminist therapists see that one person may feel safe, whereas the other person may not, even if abuse is not present in the relationship. The consequences for ending the relationship are likely worse for women than for men, given that women earn less than men, and women are still overwhelmingly the parent with full-time custody of children. Making any change in therapy will disrupt current patterns in a relationship; attending to power issues will raise the stakes even more.

Power Issues

In terms of conceptualization, feminist therapists will look for connections between the clients' presenting problems and underlying power dynamics, as influenced by patriarchy and rigid gender roles (Goodrich, 2003). The connections made are unique to each couple and the way they discuss their concerns. Topics frequently presented in therapy at a first session include communication and conflict resolution, sexual concerns, finances, household chores, child care/parenting, difficulties with family, and making decisions. These issues are often interrelated and overlapping; for the purpose of this chapter, they will be discussed separately.

Communication and Conflict Resolution

In meeting with couples whose concern is communication, feminist therapists will give each partner a chance to talk about what they find problematic about their communication. As all therapists know, communication issues may indeed be communication issues, and/or the couple may actually be wanting to work on another more sensitive issue. Feminist therapists are listening to the clients' reports of their communication issues, and are picking up on cues such as who is able to define the problem, whose definition of the problem is most valued, what has been attempted as a solution and by whom, and who has most concern for the issue, all of which can be related to gendered power dynamics. Feminist therapists note who says what and when; who checks in with who to see if it is acceptable to introduce a topic, and who has the ability to be silent and not work toward a resolution when communicating. In addition, feminist therapists are also listening for other concerns related to or masked by the original communication concern. Communication can be a process of discussing a topic that has caused friction in the relationship, which again may be tied to gendered power. Even in the first session, feminist therapists are noticing these patterns and commenting on them, or asking questions. The therapist may comment on Natalie being unusually quiet while David talks about his nights out with his friends. In this way, the therapist is working to balance talk time between the couple, while also creating space for Natalie to say what is happening for her at the moment.

Sexual Concerns

Feminist therapists examine **sexual concerns** for connections to larger societal expectations as related to patriarchy, and then challenges those connections (Goodrich, 1991). Building a mutually satisfying and respectful sex life will be part of the therapist's goal when working with couples with sexual concerns. This may involve challenges to many assumptions that both men and women have about sex: that sex equals intercourse, sex concludes with the man's climax, women have to be physically perfect to please men sexually, men are entitled to sex when and where they want it, women's needs come second to men's needs, men are entitled to find other partners if their needs are not met, etc. Each of these assumptions is tied to men's dominance in relationships, and they powerfully shape expectations and satisfactions regarding sexual concerns. Feminist therapists help couples decide together how they want to define their sexual relationship in ways that reflect mutuality and respect.

Finances

Many feminist therapists advocate for asking each partner about income at the first session, thereby introducing a powerful shaper of relationship dynamics: who makes more money (Haddock et al., 2000). Asking directly about income alerts couples to the fact that the feminist therapist will raise uncomfortable topics related to power, out of a belief that income is a strong indicator of who holds power in the relationship. In addition, therapists will explore how money is spent, how bills are paid, and whether this arrangement is equitable and satisfactory to both parties. Attention to language is also important; for example, sometimes the woman is given an "allowance" if she is not working or if she makes substantially less money than her partner. The therapist may challenge this term, given its associations with what children are given from their parents. Furthermore, both partners' knowledge of the household finances may be explored. Too often, one partner is burdened or responsible for tracking all of the income and bills, whereas the other partner is blissfully unaware. There are differential gendered impacts; one may think that being unaware is ideal—for men, this may be an example of a task in which an already overburdened woman (with other household tasks) is responsible for; yet for a woman who is unaware, she may truly be disempowered in not knowing how her partner is spending the money, placing her at risk if the relationship dissolves. The handling of money is a very loaded topic, and the therapist raises this issue through questions about who is handling the money and how is that decided. Even though Natalie and David have not introduced money as a topic of main concern, feminist therapists would inquire about finances very early in the process of therapy.

Household Chores

It is quite common for women to mention the burden of **household chores** in therapy, even though again, this is not likely to be a presenting problem for most couples. However, the unending routine of chores can make women tired at best, and resentful at worst. Feminist therapists inquire about the division of household labor, specifically asking who does what chores, and highlighting how often each chore needs to be done, and what happens if it is not done. Therapists may prescribe that partners swap household duties for a week to evaluate fairness, if the lack of fairness is not apparent to both partners. It can be very difficult for some women to "let go of" the idea that the house needs to be clean; women are often socialized to have high standards of cleanliness. Women can be encouraged to lower their cleanliness standards, and allow men to participate more in household duties, even if his cleaning standards are lower than his partner's. Yet, feminist therapists challenge men who sabotage the re-balancing of household duties by ruining clothing or leaving dishes dirty after they are "cleaned." Power dynamics permeate household duties in these ways, and therapists challenge these dynamics.

Child Care/Parenting

As discussed earlier, for many women, being a mother is central to their identity. For men, being a father can be highly rewarding and enjoyable, yet it may not be as central to their identity; indeed, having a career is more highly valued in society, whereas being a mother is admired, but not valued. As a result, women either embrace or are expected to embrace the role of mother. Therapists can ask men to step up their role of father, which allows their partners time for much-needed rest. Silverstein (1996) argued, "One of the most significant impediments to equality for women in the *public* world is the failure of men to assume equal responsibility in the *private* world of family" (p. 5, italics in original). Feminist therapists believe it is crucial to help couples find more balance in terms of parenting, and hold men accountable for achieving this balance.

Closely related to child care is the equal division of leisure time. Therapists can ask couples to describe what leisure time means for them. Women's leisure time may involve activities with children; men's leisure time can involve time out with friends. Typically, men have much more leisure time than women. Therapists can highlight these differences, and ask men to take initiative to offer to watch the children while their partner spends her leisure time as she wishes. Feminist therapists also encourage women to spend time by themselves or with friends.

Difficulties with Family

Relationships with in-laws and family members can be a significant source of stress for couples. Therapists can highlight the expectations of women to make arrangements for family time; to handle conflict that comes up in families over spending holidays together, buying gifts, making time for birthdays, anniversaries, graduations, etc. Therapists can ask men to explicitly take on these tasks, and ask women to step back from these activities. The couple can be asked to make a list of all of the tasks associated with this type of emotional labor that need to be done, and evenly split them.

Making Decisions

Decision-making is embedded throughout many of the topical areas addressed above. The couple may have decided that the man is responsible for making decisions about finances, whereas the woman is responsible for the household and children. One could say that this is an equal form of decision-making, as each partner is in charge of a separate set of decisions; however, a feminist therapist would challenge this arrangement on grounds of unequal power. The arrangement is inequitable because the more meaningful decisions involve money, whereas the least powerful decisions involve the home. This arrangement is reflective of society's patriarchy. The therapist would also point out that these types of overall decision-making are unjust, and leaves both partners vulnerable in the event of divorce, or illness or death of one partner.

Empowerment

Another hallmark of feminist therapy is **empowerment** (Avis, 1991; Smith & Douglas, 1990). Women are consistently devalued in society, in both overt and covert ways, in multiple contexts. Feminist therapists who work with women clearly communicate the value of women. Their concerns are taken seriously. Their complaints are believed. Their perspectives are valued and asked to be expanded upon. Therapists working with couples facilitate women's partners to communicate this value to the women in their lives. Furthermore, women are asked to value themselves, to trust their instincts, to listen to what their gut is telling them, to trust in their knowledge and experiences. These sound like small interventions, yet when living in a patriarchal society, they are huge, and they certainly challenge the status quo. Therapists can prepare women for "change back" messages, as those in her life may not be prepared for the changes she is making on her own behalf. The therapist can empower Natalie by supporting her in challenging David about his online internet activities. Through this support, the therapist shows that her needs and concerns are valid.

Because women are highly socialized to care for others, a significant part of empowering women is helping them to care for themselves. Women who care for themselves are labeled "selfish," which can be a very hurtful accusation, and serves to keep women in their (subservient) place. When working with couples, therapists can talk about the harm imposed on women by being labeled "selfish," and help women embrace care of themselves. The men in women's lives can be coached to stand up for their partner if family or friends question her steps to care for herself. Using the metaphor of placing the oxygen mask on oneself before helping others (in the event of an emergency on an airplane) can be a concrete illustration to women of the importance of caring for self before caring for others. With regard to the case scenario, we know that David frequently spends time out with friends; a feminist therapist would ask Natalie what she does to take care of herself. If she is unable to identify ways she cares for herself, the therapist could brainstorm with her some hobbies or activities she would enjoy, or draw her attention to spending time with family or friends. She could also take time in solitary activities, such as reading, getting a massage, exercising, going for walks, painting, taking a class, etc.

Challenging Internalized Belief Systems

Both men and women in couples therapy can have their **internalized belief systems** challenged. Without further reflection, most of us do not think about where our beliefs come from, what we think about those beliefs, and the impact of those beliefs on our lives and relationships. Feminist therapists consider this central to therapy. Similar to narrative therapy (see Chapter 6), feminist therapists can help couples deconstruct taken-for-granted assumptions that are negatively impacting relationships. Natalie and David's conversation about smoking provides an example. Natalie has expressed concern with David's health, and the negative implications of that for him in terms of his own health. A therapist may validate her care for others (in this case, her husband), yet may challenge her to take care of herself. In caring for others, the spotlight is shifted away from maintaining one's own health to maintaining health of others. A feminist therapist would point out that this is a way to maintain and strengthen relationships, which is important, yet can be detrimental to self, because one is not considering one's own health. The feminist therapist would connect this idea to how all women are socialized to care for others—Natalie is not alone in engaging in this type of emotional labor. In her conversation with David, she says that the cigarette smoke makes the house smell, and that she ends up breathing it in as well. Here, Natalie is appealing to David's sense of **relational responsibility**—she is wanting him to consider his impact on others with his actions (Bergum & Dossetor, 2005). The therapist can validate this sense of relational responsibility that Natalie is requesting, and underscore the idea that women are often thinking of the needs of others. David argues that it is his body, he can decide what to do with it, that he can smoke if he wants. The therapist can emphasize that this is an individual discourse that men are socialized to subscribe to, yet it can be harmful to his relationship. The therapist can encourage David to embrace the impact he has on others as a result of his actions.

Going further, the therapist can connect these discourses—the individual discourse and the relational responsibility discourse—to the roles of men and women. Questions can be asked, such as: who benefits from these discourses? How are these discourses impacting the relationship? Who has participated in maintaining these discourses? What challenges have you been witness to regarding these discourses? Which discourse might be better for your relationship, and what makes you say that? There are opportunities to challenge internalized belief systems at every turn; all content concerns are ripe for deconstruction of gendered discourses.

Valuing Emotions and Empathy

Traditionally, emotions have been considered exclusively women's domain. The expression of emotions is considered a female trait, whereas men's realm was in the domain of logic. Feminist therapists challenge these rigid, traditional views for men and women, encouraging a wide range of emotional expression for both men and women.

Because of gender role socialization, women are taught to express emotions; and as a result, they may be more comfortable expressing sadness, joy, fear, and frustration. Yet feminist therapists also encourage expression of traditionally male emotions, such as anger, which is an emotion that is reflective of injustice and lack of fairness (Rampage, 2003). As much as women may want to (and do) express emotions, anger is often reserved for men; women who express anger may end up alienating their partners. Even the expression of emotion is tied with relational considerations—how will the partner receive these emotions, particularly if they are not acceptable for women. Feminist therapists address this issue and encourage women to be angry, if that is what they are feeling. In working with heterosexual couples, feminist therapists help men remain present and receptive to their partner's feelings, including anger.

It is crucial that men be able to respond to women's emotions. Feminist therapists encourage men to reflect and respond to women's feelings, providing much-needed validation. Helping men to understand that women's expression of emotions is not indicative of her wanting to end the relationships is important to helping men remain present, particularly if addressed early in a relationship (Rampage, 2003). Yet attending to and validating emotions, while helpful, is not enough; men are encouraged to see how they play a role in women's anger, frustration, and sadness. When these emotions are linked to lack of support with child care or household tasks, there are actions men can take to step up and alleviate the work load, which then helps their partners with a sense of "we-ness." Explicitly teaching men to not "flee" when women raise issues is vital to healthy romantic relationships.

Feminist therapists work with men to greatly expand their repertoire of emotions, above and beyond the socially acceptable expression of anger. The therapist helps explore this range of emotions, first labeling emotions for men, and then encouraging varied emotions, including mixed emotions (Levant, 2003). Men's partners play a supportive role, yet the therapist may need to intervene to keep this task as the man's responsibility, so that women do not take on responsibility for assisting men with their emotional expression.

When exploring emotions with both men and women, **social context** is drawn in for examination. Certain contexts may not be safe places for a full range of emotional expression for men as well as for women. Here, partners can be encouraged to provide a safe haven for emotions, when, for example, workplaces are not. Feminist therapists may explore multiple avenues for activism for their clients. For example, men can be encouraged to respond differently when a male co-worker expresses sadness or vulnerability, thereby modeling a different kind of relationship between men.

Ultimately, the couple and therapist may explore more radical interventions as a way of demonstrating support for the partners in a couple. This may mean examining pros and cons of finding different employment—employment that allows for more couple/family time or more support with caring for children, even if at lower pay. Feminist therapists empower couples to consider options that support egalitarian relationships, and perhaps eschew competitiveness, consumerism, and hierarchy supported by patriarchy.

Addressing Power Issues

One mainstay of feminist therapy is in addressing power issues and connecting the couple's concerns with power issues (Rampage, 2002). This may seem straightforward enough, yet the *process* of raising these issues can be challenging. It could be argued that all approaches to therapy involve connecting clients' presenting concerns with another way of seeing the world, whether through a solution-focused lens, a structural lens, or a psychodynamic lens. Feminist therapy is no different. However, in a sense, the stakes are higher—connecting presenting problems to power and privilege can be challenging for the therapist, because *real change* is involved, particularly for the partner who holds more power. As a result, the challenge is to raise power issues in ways that appeal to both partners, yet clearly upends the status quo.

One option is for the therapist to directly challenge power issues as they come up in therapy (Parker, 2003). This approach requires the therapist to be able to spot inequalities when they are raised by the couple in session. It is difficult to anticipate what may be said, yet the therapist needs to be on the lookout for hidden gender assumptions embedded within clients' statements or goals. Typically, a partner is not challenged until a solid therapeutic relationship has been established, and then the use of humor can be helpful, particularly when statements are made that are so contrary to the status quo that the couple has to take time to think before responding. In directly naming power issues, the therapist can situate the assumptions within a broader social context. Indeed, we are all gender socialized, so the therapist can remind the couple that it is not surprising that they hold the views they do. The therapist can then encourage the couple to decide for themselves whether they want to embrace a new way of being, and discuss the implications of their decisions on their relationship. No doubt, addressing power issues requires courage on the part of the therapist; yet the alternative is upholding the status quo of inequality in relationships (Parker, 2003).

Working with Men

A large part of feminist therapy involves helping men take responsibility for their part in the relationship. Maintenance of relationships, the burden of household work, and child care duties are traditionally considered women's domains. This exempts men from equally sharing in the work and rewards of relationships. Therapists assist men to step into mutual relationships in a way they had not previously considered. Framed against a backdrop of patriarchy in which both men and women lose, men are held accountable for their actions. Although this can be difficult for men at first, the rewards far outweigh the risks.

First is sharing emotions, particularly vulnerability. Feminist therapists encourage men to share their innermost thoughts and feelings with their partners, and that the relationship is a safe haven for expression of one's fears, concerns, and day-to-day struggles. Men are encouraged to talk about the burden of financially supporting the family, and the limits this expectation places on relationships and family time. Feminist therapists can encourage both partners to release men from this responsibility, and truly share in all aspects of family life, including bringing in money to support the family. In short, men and women can be challenged to let go of gendered expectations that limit their options for a full and healthy relationship.

Related to patriarchy and the sense of entitlement men feel as a result of the privileges associated with patriarchy, feminist therapists help make men aware of the privileges they hold and the impact these privileges has on both them and their partners (Brooks, 2003), including the privilege not to engage in discussion about household tasks; the privilege to be unaware of one making most of the significant decisions for the relationship; the privilege of not being aware of how dirty the house is and the message this sends to guests about his partner's housekeeping abilities; the privilege of not maintaining the relationship until it "suddenly" comes to an end, as a complete surprise. Feminist therapists point out the privileges that come for men by virtue of being men, and the negative impact this has on men, women, children (if present) and the relationship itself.

Core Values

Feminist therapists hold many **core values** in working with families. Further, feminists contend that all therapists hold values that impact clients, yet they are transparent in sharing these values with clients so that clients can decide for themselves if this therapist and therapeutic approach is a good fit for them.

Feminist therapists highly value equality between men and women. Both men and women are equally valued. They are equally capable of expressing emotions; they equally contribute to decision-making, household tasks, sharing themselves, and defining the boundaries of the relationship. Overall, there is a balance in the relationship, a give-and-take that is fair on a day-to-day basis as well as at macro-levels.

Family life is complicated. The reality is that both partners may not be able to make the same amount of money, or be able to spend exactly equal amounts of time on household tasks, or equally be responsible for facilitating family relationships. Here, the idea of **equity** is critical, that there is a sense of balance overall in the relationship. This equity is not guided by traditional gender norms, for those traditional gender norms unfairly advantage men at women's expense. Couples that have equitable divisions of labor actively discuss these issues and make decisions together, adjusting and maintaining flexibility as required by life. There is flexibility in gender arrangements; women are not relegated to cooking, cleaning, and doing laundry, while men wash the car and mow the lawn. Both members of the couple are aware of the different amounts of time and attention that go into tasks, and both are equally concerned about fairness in the relationship, and they work together to ensure that fairness continues in light of changes to their relationship, like having a child, moving across the country, or caring for older relatives.

True equity in a relationship means there is consistent mutuality, positive regard for the other, and an acknowledgement that the relationship exists within unequal power structures that favor men. The couple is active in setting up shared responsibility that is fair for both partners. They care for each other. They openly discuss challenges, while keeping in mind the patriarchy that presses on them individually and as a couple as they live their lives together. Feminist therapists help the couple to value interdependence and mutual reliance on the other that contributes to strong and healthier intimate relationships.

Consistent with the principle of collaboration, termination of the therapy is decided mutually by the therapist and the couple. Feminist therapists utilize the termination of the therapeutic relationship as an opportunity for clients to experience the ending of a relationship in a positive way (Good, Gilbert, & Scher, 1990)—with reflection on what was helpful or not, what the couple and the therapist has learned from the process, and how the couple might handle issues related to their original presenting problem. The therapist affirms the emotional experiences of both members of the couple at termination, including sadness, relief, accomplishment, and/or happiness. At the termination session, the therapist continues to help the partners support each other in displaying a wide range of emotions.

Case Transcript

Natalie calls to set up the first session. She says that she and her husband, David, are fighting and have drifted apart; they are seeking therapy as a last-ditch effort to save their marriage before they contact divorce lawyers.

> *Therapist:* Welcome Natalie and David, it's nice to meet you. Before we get started, I want to tell you a little bit about myself and the therapy services I provide. I consider myself to be a feminist therapist. That means that I value equality and mutual responsibility in relationships. I believe that we live in a patriarchal society that advantages men and disadvantages women in many ways, and that this can play out in our intimate relationship in ways that are harmful for women *and* men, and that make it harder for us to have healthy relationships. That being said, I also value transparency—that is, you have the right to know what I'm doing as your therapist and why I'm asking you about certain things. If you have any questions, you can stop us at any time and ask.
>
> *Here, the therapist begins therapy by being transparent about values and beliefs, and encourages a sense of collaboration by inviting the couple to stop and ask questions at any time.*

> *Natalie:* That sounds OK with me, although I've never heard of feminist therapy before.
> *David:* Does that mean this will be a male-bashing session?
> *Therapist:* Good question, David; this is not an uncommon question. Feminist therapy is about finding balance in relationships, and challenging everyone's taken-for-granted assumptions about how men and women "should" be in relationships. I will challenge both of you to think about things in your relationship in a different way, and will ask you to try new ways of being together as a couple. Ultimately, both of you decide how you want to build your relationship going forward. I see my role as one to challenge you both and support you both in your relationship, and to work collaboratively with you to achieve your goals. If either of you feels as if we are going in a direction that is not helpful for your relationship, let's talk about that.
> *David:* Well, I think that sounds reasonable. I'm willing to try.
> *Therapist:* Great. Natalie, you were the one to call in to say that you are having frequent fights and are drifting apart in your relationship, and that you both were interested in coming in for therapy at this time, is that right?

Natalie: Yes. I think the straw that broke the camel's back was when I caught David talking with another woman on the computer. I just thought "here we go again." I don't know how much more I can take of this. Not only that, but at first he denied it. I just don't feel like I can trust him anymore. I don't know what to believe.

David: (*to Natalie*) I'm here, aren't I?

Therapist: Hold on a minute, David, we'll get to you. Natalie said a lot in a short space here. David, does any of what Natalie said surprise you?

> *The therapist intervenes to redirect David to connect with and hopefully validate some part of what Natalie has said.*

David: Not really. I've heard this all before. I understand that she doesn't want me talking to someone else, I get that. But we haven't had sex in… I can't even count how many months it's been now. What's a guy supposed to do?

Therapist: Is there anything in what Natalie said just now that makes sense to you? That, on some level, makes you sad, given the woman that you met and fell in love with?

> *Here the therapist is continuing to ask David to connect with Natalie on some of her feelings, while also offering David the opportunity to identify with feelings other than distance and anger.*

David: I can understand the trust part a little bit. I think we both have done some things that have destroyed the trust in our relationship.

Therapist: Is there a part of you that wishes it could be different? A part of you that is sad about what has happened in your relationship?

David: I try not to think about it most times. I wish things could go back to the way they were. I do love her and I want this to work.

Therapist: Natalie, what have you heard David say here that is different from what you've heard before?

Natalie: I'm surprised to hear him sort of agree that there's a part of him that is sad about us. I get the impression that he doesn't give a shit half the time. Just hearing that he wants us to work gives me a bit of hope.

Therapist: (*to both*) It is important for you both to connect with each other during the difficult times as well as during the good times. We don't come with an instruction manual about how to talk through difficult topics. Natalie, you hearing some vulnerability from David can be very helpful to both of you in knowing what's going on emotionally in your relationship. David, sharing most of your vulnerabilities with Natalie can go a long way toward healing your relationship and working through difficult times. Often, men are taught just the opposite—to avoid vulnerability and instead to wear a mask of invulnerability.

The therapist is helping David express a range of emotions—aside from anger— while highlighting his vulnerability. In addition, the therapist connects social themes with how David is limited in expressing himself and his emotions; having to learn or re-learn how to express emotions is the therapist's way of showing that emotions are an important means for connecting in the relationship.

David: I never thought about it that way.

Natalie: Me neither. I always thought that that was part of David's personality— he can be quite distant and aloof, and downright mean at times.

David: Well, when you're holding out on me…

Therapist: David, you mentioned earlier that you were unhappy with your and Natalie's sex life, can you say more about that?

David: Sure. We haven't had sex in months. I feel like it's something that I need, and she denies sex when I ask for it.

Natalie: Sometimes that's true but I don't want to have sex with someone who is mean at times and is not present in other parts of our relationship.

Therapist: So it seems to me that you are not the only couple that struggles with this kind of dynamic in your sex life. We can learn messages about sex and our roles about sex that can be quite unhealthy for relationships. Earlier, David, I heard you say that, in a sense, you are entitled to have sex, and that if Natalie doesn't meet your sexual needs, you are within your rights to seek to have those needs met elsewhere. Where do you suppose you have learned those messages?

First, the therapist is normalizing the couple's struggles with their sex life, helping them to understand that they are not the only ones dealing with this sort of issue. Next, the therapist is connecting their difficulties with the larger social context by highlighting that their roles in relation to sex are learned; and indeed, these roles can be changed. With the question about learning messages, the therapist is suggesting that they can be un-learned or re-learned, that they are not resigned to continue in their rigid ideas about sex, and that David is responsible for making changes in the relationship.

Natalie: Well, it's all over in the movies and on TV. And I don't agree with it. I find it disrespectful and hurtful.

Therapist: You might be onto something there, Natalie. Let's see what David thinks about this.

David: I guess some of it does come from TV and movies. I'm not sure.

Therapist: How do you think this idea that men are entitled to sex affects your relationship with Natalie?

David: I know it [sex] helps me feel closer to her.

Therapist: How do you think it affects her?

David: I don't know. She probably doesn't always like that.

Natalie: I feel a constant pressure to be sexually ready, and that's a turn off. And then I feel guilty because I know that David feels closer to me after we have sex.

Therapist: Natalie, are there times when you initiate sex?

Natalie: Rarely, and lately, not at all of course.

> *The therapist is highlighting the imbalance in sexual relationships, at least in terms of initiation, and is starting to connect this with larger sociopolitical themes in which men feel entitled to sex.*

Therapist: So from what I'm hearing so far, Natalie, you are wanting a closer and exclusive relationship with David that involves mutuality and respect. It seems that being closer emotionally is part of what you are looking for. David, so far I have heard you say that you would like to feel closer to Natalie, and that may be related to your sex life, specifically the frequency of sex. Am I accurate so far on this?

David and Natalie: Yes.

Therapist: OK. We will talk more about goals you would like to work on while in therapy. First, there are some things I need to know about you as a couple and how you work together as a couple. How much do each of you earn?

Natalie: My income is pretty variable, depending on sales—I'm a realtor. I have worked hard to build up my reputation in the community. I earn about $75,000 per year, which is actually a decent amount. I definitely bring in more during the spring and summer months than the rest of the year.

Therapist: All right, David, what about you?

David: I am a high school teacher, and earn about $48,000 per year. I'm frustrated because it's a little below average for where I should be, given my experience. When I moved here from Maine, I took a pay cut because I had to establish myself in the school system here. I'm currently looking for another teaching job that pays better than the job I have now, although that might mean a longer drive to work if I move out of the district I'm in now.

Therapist: How do you see your incomes impacting your relationship?

David: I don't like how Natalie makes more than me. She never says anything to me about it, and we don't ever talk about it, but I feel like I should be the one to support her. I know things have changed these days but I can't help it, it's the way I was raised.

Natalie: I know he feels this way, he mentions it every so often. I tell him that I don't mind, we split the bills evenly and I pick up on some of the extras, like going out to dinner.

Therapist: David, you've been raised to take care of your partner, and for you that has meant bringing home more money than Natalie. When is this highlighted for you, or when are you reminded that you are making less than Natalie?

David: Sometimes it is those times when we are out for dinner, I want to be able to pay for us both. I just don't have the extra spending money. A part of me feels like I'm letting her down. Even though she says it's OK, I don't agree. Other times are when I'm out with friends. It's not the money, per se, it's that I moved here to be with her. They kid me about it. I laugh it off with them, but it strikes a nerve.

Therapist: It seems that they all have received messages about what it means to be a man, and that is tied not only to income but also to being able to take charge and make decisions in relationships. Yet that might differ from your and Natalie's ideas of what it means to be a man. What are the values that both of you would like to live by in terms of income and decision-making in your relationship?

> *Here, the therapist is connecting pressures that David feels to be the primary income earner and decision-maker in the relationship with larger messages about what it means to be a man. Further, she is asking when and where these ideas emerge. Finally, she is offering the couple the opportunity to decide for themselves how they want to construct their relationship based on values of their choosing.*

Therapist: We are coming to the close of the session. I want to thank you for coming in today. How did the session go for you?

Natalie: This was different from what I thought it would be, but it was helpful. I can see how we are going to move forward.

David: It sure was different than I expected. To be honest, I was a little nervous at the beginning when you said you were doing feminist therapy—I thought that I would be blamed for our problems. Instead, I felt supported yet challenged.

Therapist: Great, I appreciate both of you for speaking the truth, and for speaking from your heart. At the next session, I will meet with you separately, to get a chance to know each of you a bit more, and to explore safety as you experience it in your relationship. After meeting with you separately, we will then spend the last 10 minutes together to decide on a course of action. That may involve a few separate sessions, or it may involve continuing for you both to come in as a couple together. Do you have any questions for me?

Natalie and David: No.

Therapist: It was nice to meet you, and I'll see you again next week.

> *Feminist therapists encourage clients to reflect and comment on the therapeutic process; this is a demonstration of collaboration with clients. The therapist also sets the stage for seeing each partner individually at the second session, so as to assess for domestic violence.*

References

Adleman, J. (1990). Necessary risks and ethical constraints: Self-monitoring on values and biases. In H. Lerman & N. Porter (Eds.), *Feminist ethics in psychotherapy* (pp. 113–122). New York, NY: Springer.

Avis, J. M. (1991). Power politics in therapy with women. In T. J. Goodrich (Ed.), *Women and power: Perspectives for family therapy* (pp. 183–200). New York, NY: Norton.

Avis, J. M. (1992). Where are all the family therapists? Abuse and violence within families and family therapy's response. *Journal of Marital and Family Therapy, 18*(3), 225–232. doi: 10.1111/j.1752-0606.1992.tb00935.x.

Bateson, G., Jackson, D. D., Haley, J., & Weakland, J. H. (1956). Toward a theory of schizophrenia. *Behavioral Science, 1*(4), 251–264. doi: 10.1002/bs.3830010402.

Bergum, V., & Dossetor, J. (2005). *Relational ethics: The full meaning of respect.* Hagerstown, MD: University Publishing Group.

Bograd, M. (1992). Values in conflict: Challenges to family therapists' thinking. *Journal of Marital and Family Therapy, 18*(3), 245–256. doi: 10.1111/j.1752-0606.1992.tb00937.x.

Boss, P., & Thorne, B. (1989). Family sociology and family therapy: A feminist linkage. In M. McGoldrick, C. M. Anderson, & F. Walsh (Eds.), *Women in families: A framework for family therapy* (pp. 78–96). New York, NY: Norton.

Boyd-Franklin, N. (1987a). The contribution of family therapy models to the treatment of Black families. *Psychotherapy, 24*(3S), 621–629. doi: 10.1037/h0085760.

Boyd-Franklin, N. (1987b). Group therapy for Black women: A therapeutic support model. *American Journal of Orthopsychiatry, 57*(3), 394–401. doi: 10.1111/j.1939-0025.1987. tb03548.x.

Brooks, G. R. (2003). Helping men embrace equality. In L. B. Silverstein & T. J. Goodrich (Eds.), *Feminist family therapy: Empowerment in social context* (pp. 163–176). Washington, DC: American Psychological Association.

Enns, C. Z. (1997). *Feminist theories and feminist psychotherapies: Origins, themes, and variations.* New York, NY: Haworth.

Finer, L. B. (2007). Trends in premarital sex in the United States, 1954–2003. *Public Health Reports, 122*(1), 73–78.

Goldner, V. (1985). Feminism and family therapy. *Family Process, 24*(1), 31–47. doi: 10.1111/ j.1545-5300.1985.00031.x.

Good, G. E., Gilbert, L. A., & Scher, M. (1990). Gender aware therapy: A synthesis of feminist therapy and knowledge about gender. *Journal of Counseling & Development, 68*(4), 376–380. doi: 10.1002/j.1556-6676.1990.tb02514.x.

Goodrich, T. J. (1991). Women, power, and family therapy: What's wrong with this picture? In T. J. Goodrich (Ed.), *Women and power: Perspectives for family therapy* (pp. 3–35). New York, NY: Norton.

Goodrich, T. J. (2003). A feminist family therapist's work is never done. In L. B. Silverstein & T. J. Goodrich (Eds.), *Feminist family therapy: Empowerment in social context* (pp. 3–15). Washington, DC: American Psychological Association.

Gottman, J. M. (1999). *The marriage clinic: A scientifically based marital therapy.* New York, NY: Norton.

Gottman, J. M., & Levenson, R. W. (1999). Dysfunctional marital conflict: Women are being unfairly blamed. *Journal of Divorce & Remarriage, 31*(3–4), 1–17. doi: 10.1300/ J087v31n03_01.

Green, R. J. (1996). Why ask, why tell? Teaching and learning about lesbians and gays in family therapy. *Family Process, 35*(3), 389–400. doi: 10.1111/j.1545-5300.1996.00389.x.

Haddock, S. A., Zimmerman, T. S., & MacPhee, D. (2000). The power equity guide: Attending to gender in family therapy. *Journal of Marital and Family Therapy, 26*(2), 153–170. doi: 10.1111/j.1752-0606.2000.tb00286.x.

Hansen, M., & Harway, M. (1993). *Battering and family therapy: A feminist perspective.* Newbury Park, CA: SAGE Publications.

Hardy, K. V. (1989). The theoretical myth of sameness: A critical issue in family therapy training and treatment. *Journal of Psychotherapy and the Family, 6*(1–2), 17–33. doi: 10.1300/J287v06n01_02.

Hare-Mustin, R. T. (1978). A feminist approach to family therapy. *Family Process, 17,* 181–193. doi: 10.1111/j.1545-5300.1978.00181.x.

Hare-Mustin, R. T. (1991). Sex, lies, and headaches: The problem is power. In T. J. Goodrich (Ed.), *Women and power: Perspectives for family therapy* (pp. 63–85). New York, NY: Norton.

Hare-Mustin, R. T. (1994). Discourses in the mirrored room: A postmodern analysis of therapy. *Family Process, 33,* 19–35. doi: 10.1111/j.1545-5300.1994.00019.x.

Hochschild, A. R. (1989). *The second shift.* New York, NY: Avon Books.

Kimmel, M. S. (1997). Masculinity as homophobia: Fear, shame and silence in the construction of gender identity. In M. M. Gergen & S. N. Davis (Eds.), *Toward a new psychology of gender* (pp. 223–242). Florence, KY: Taylor & Francis.

Knudson-Martin, C., & Mahoney, A. R. (2009). The myth of equality. In C. Knudson-Martin & A. R. Mahoney (Eds.), *Couples, gender, and power: Creating change in intimate relationships* (pp. 43–61). New York, NY: Springer.

Laird, J. (1994). Lesbian families: A cultural perspective. In M. P. Mirkin (Ed.), *Women in context: Toward a feminist reconstruction of psychotherapy* (pp. 118–148). New York, NY: Guilford.

Leigh, L. A. (1995). The evolving treatment of gender, ethnicity, and sexual orientation in marital and family therapy. *Family Relations: An Interdisciplinary Journal, 44*(4), 359–367. doi: 10.2307/584991.

Lerman, H., & Rigby, D. N. (1990). Boundary violations: Misuse of the power of the therapist. In H. Lerman & N. Porter (Eds.), *Feminist ethics in psychotherapy* (pp. 51–59). New York, NY: Springer.

Levant, R. F. (2003). Treating male alexithymia. In L. B. Silverstein & T. J. Goodrich (Eds.), *Feminist family therapy: Empowerment in social context* (pp. 177–188). Washington, DC: American Psychological Association.

Long, J. K. (1995). Working with lesbians, gays, and bisexuals: Addressing heterosexism in supervision. *Family Process, 35*(3), 377–388. doi: 10.1111/j.1545-5300.1996.00377.x.

Luepnitz, D. A. (1988). *The family interpreted: Feminist theory in clinical practice.* New York, NY: Basic Books.

McGeorge, C. R., Carlson, T. S., & Wetchler, J. L. (2015). The history of marriage and family therapy. In J. L. Wetchler & L. L. Hecker (Eds.), *An introduction to marriage and family therapy* (2nd ed., pp. 3–42). New York, NY: Routledge.

McGoldrick, M., Anderson, C., & Walsh, F. (1989). Women in families and in family therapy. In M. McGoldrick, C. M. Anderson, & F. Walsh (Eds.), *Women in families: A framework for family therapy* (pp. 3–15). New York, NY: Norton.

Parker, L. (2003). Bringing power from the margins to the center. In L. B. Silverstein & T. J. Goodrich (Eds.), *Feminist family therapy: Empowerment in social context* (pp. 225–238). Washington, DC: American Psychological Association.

Rampage, C. (2002). Marriage in the 20th century: A feminist perspective. *Family Process*, *41*(2), 261–268.

Rampage, C. (2003). Gendered constraints to intimacy in heterosexual couples. In L. B. Silverstein & T. J. Goodrich (Eds.), *Feminist family therapy: Empowerment in social context* (pp. 199–210). Washington, DC: American Psychological Association.

Sangster, S. L., & Lawson, K. L. (2014). "Falling down the rabbit hole": The construction of infertility by news media. *Journal of Reproductive and Infant Psychology*, *32*(5), 486–496. doi: 10.1080/02646838.2014.962016.

Satir, V. (1972). *Peoplemaking*. Palo Alto, CA: Science and Behavior Books, Inc.

Sayer, L. C., England, P., Allison, P. D., & Kangas, N. (2011). She left, he left: How employment and satisfaction affect women's and men's decisions to leave marriages. *American Journal of Sociology*, *116*(6), 1982–2018. doi: 10.1086/658173.

Silverstein, L. B. (1996). Fathering is a feminist issue. *Psychology of Women Quarterly*, *20*(1), 3–35. doi: 10.1111/j.1471–6402.1996.tb00663.x.

Singh, A. A., & Burnes, T. R. (2011). Feminist therapy and street-level activism: Revisiting our roots and "acting up" in the next decade. *Women & Therapy*, *34*(1–2), 129–142. doi: 10.1080/02703149.2011.532457.

Smith, A. J., & Douglas, M. A. (1990). Empowerment as an ethical imperative. In H. Lerman & N. Porter (Eds.), *Feminist ethics in psychotherapy* (pp. 43–50). New York, NY: Springer.

Taffel, R. (1991). "Why is Daddy so grumpy?" In T. J. Goodrich (Ed.), *Women and power: Perspectives for family therapy* (pp. 257–262). New York, NY: Norton.

Walsh, F., & Scheinkman, M. (1989). (Fe)male: The hidden gender dimension in models of family therapy. In M. McGoldrick, C. M. Anderson, & F. Walsh (Eds.), *Women in families: A framework for family therapy* (pp. 16–41). New York, NY: Norton.

Walters, M., Carter, B., Papp, P., & Silverstein, O. (1988). *The invisible web: Gender patterns in family relationships*. New York, NY: Guilford.

Werner-Wilson, R. J., Price, S. J., Zimmerman, T. S., & Murphy, M. J. (1997). Client gender as a process variable in marriage and family therapy: Are women clients interrupted more than men clients? *Journal of Family Psychology*, *11*(3), 373–377. doi: 10.1037/0893-3200.11.3.373.

Whipple, V. (1996). Developing an identity as a feminist family therapist: Implications for training. *Journal of Marital and Family Therapy*, *22*(3), 381–396. doi: 10.1111/j.1752-0606.1996.tb00212.x.

5

SOLUTION-FOCUSED COUPLES THERAPY

Michael D. Reiter

History of the Model

Solution-Focused Brief Therapy (SFBT) is an approach for working with individuals, couples, families and groups that has roots in systemic therapies. The model was primarily developed by Steve de Shazer and Insoo Kim Berg in Milwaukee, Wisconsin, a husband and wife team who revolutionized the way that therapists address problems—by focusing not on people's problems but on their solutions. The roots of SFBT are housed within the therapeutic work of Milton H. Erickson, the philosophy of Gregory Bateson and the problem-focused practice of the Mental Research Institute's Brief Therapy (de Shazer, 1982; de Shazer et al., 2007).

The approach began in the late 1970s with Steve de Shazer, who had studied the hypnotic therapy of Milton Erickson as well as the problem-focused brief therapy of the group at the Mental Research Institute. de Shazer met Berg through John Weakland, one of the developers of the MRI Brief Therapy model. De Shazer and Berg married and moved to Milwaukee and eventually opened the Brief Family Therapy Center out of their home. Their initial work was to develop a family therapy clinic similar to the MRI and hold true to that model. However, they realized they were doing something quite different, and by a series of accidents and observations they shifted their thinking from the problem sequences that MRI pays attention to to the non-problem sequences, what came to be known as the solutions.

The foundational article by this group was entitled, "Brief therapy: Focused solution development" (de Shazer et al., 1986), which was a play on the MRI Brief therapy article, "Brief therapy: Focused problem resolution" (Weakland, Fisch, Watzlawick, & Bodin, 1974), which was published in the same journal 12 years previously. De Shazer et al.'s article gave homage to the MRI roots, as well as that of Erickson, Bateson, and Haley. However, at this time, the model was not yet called Solution-Focused Brief Therapy, but rather was titled Brief Therapy.

Throughout the 30 years of its existence, SFBT has grown and changed with the continuing formation of ideas and new techniques. This may be because many therapists, besides de Shazer and Berg, contributed to what was happening in the Brief Family Therapy Clinic in Milwaukee as well as experimenting with new techniques in a variety of different settings and contexts. Some of the original SFBT therapists broke off and developed their own similar approaches.

There is a distinction between solution-focused and solution-oriented therapies. The solution-oriented therapists, such as Michelle Weiner-Davis (1993), who was one of the original team members at the Brief Family Therapy Center, and Bill O'Hanlon (O'Hanlon & Hudson, 1994; O'Hanlon & O'Hanlon, 1999; O'Hanlon & Weiner-Davis, 1989) present many similar ideas, but with their own take on the approach. Each of these solution-oriented therapists enhanced the field, in particular with a focus on couples. O'Hanlon and O'Hanlon (1999) explained that intimacy in couples is a combination of two components: "The first is the ineffable chemistry of love and attraction or liking for a person, and the second is the constellation of actions that support or dissipate love and connection" (p. 247). Therapy utilized the second component, helping people to engage in those actions that for them help to maintain and promote their connection to one another.

Solution-focused therapy has been used in many different settings including schools, hospitals, social agencies, and therapy contexts, involving clients from a wide range of ethnic and social class backgrounds. This chapter will explore how the approach is utilized with couples (which is considered to be two romantic partners regardless of gender, marital status, age, race, or any other distinction). However, the foundation of the model does not change based on working with one, two, three, or more people.

One reason the solution-focused model is appropriate for work with couples is that it does not endeavor to take sides of one partner against another (Lipchik & Kubicki, 1996; Ziegler & Hiller, 2007). The reason for this is that by challenging a person's position may lead to that person becoming defensive and angry. Ziegler and Hiller discuss the necessity to join with both members of the couple as inclusive rapport. This is important since many times the two members of the couple will come in with quite distinct ideas of what is problematic in the relationship, who is causing it, what to do about it, and what goals they want. Thus, SFBT is a method in which the therapist joins with both parties equally, exploring what each of them wants from the relationship. In couples therapy, the solution-focused model has been used in the domestic violence field (Lipchik & Kubicki, 1996; Stith, McCollum, & Rosen, 2011). However, Stith et al. (2011) caution that when there are threats to safety or serious unresolved experiences from past violence, the therapist should consider techniques and interventions from other approaches.

SFBT has become an evidence-based psychotherapy. It has been found to be successful when working with couples in premarital counseling (Murray & Murray, 2004), couples groups (Nelson & Kelley, 2001), and to prevent divorce (Davoodi, Etemadi, Bahrami, Jafari, Amir, & Hosnije, 2012). The rest of this chapter will explain how Solution-Focused Brief Therapy conceptualizes how couples maintain problems and what the therapist and couple can do to move toward their solutions by utilizing the case of the Johnsons.

Theory of Problem Formation

Solution-focused therapy is a strengths-based approach that is predicated on looking toward the future—and what clients want—rather than the past and what clients do not want. As such, little time is spent exploring the concerns that bring clients to therapy, let alone trying to investigate the origins of those problems. This is because the solutions that will help clients attain their goals are not necessarily related to what happened to lead to the problems.

However, SFBT does have a view of why clients continue to have problems; they are too focused on what has not been working in their lives rather than what has been useful and productive. This view becomes encompassing to them so that they are not able to view their lives differently. Hoyt and Berg (2000) explained, "A 'problem' arises and a couple seeks therapy (intervention) when the partners view their situation in such a way that they do not have access to what is needed to achieve what they consider reasonable satisfaction" (p. 144). This can be seen for David and Natalie Johnson. They have been experiencing ways of relating that they each agree are problematic and place their focus on what the other person is doing that they do not appreciate. As such, they are failing to see their own resources that they have to develop a different way of being with one another.

Couples have a tendency to focus on what it is they do not want (usually from the partner) and pay so much attention to how they are trying to fix the problem rather than focusing on getting along together (Berg, 1988). However, the problems that bring people into therapy are not one time events, but happen repetitively; to the point where it is distressing for one or more people. This may be because they are misappropriating what to put in the foreground and the background of their experience. For instance, David and Natalie have been taking verbal shots at one another for the past year. These events have moved from a sporadic occurrence to monthly, weekly, and now daily patterns. When asked, Natalie might say that David is not affectionate or caring anymore and that he is letting himself go. This perception has moved into her foreground while David's other actions, such as cooking her dinner or agreeing to smoke outside (even if she wants him to not smoke at all, he was willing to not smoke in the house). Conversely, David is focusing on what he considers Natalie's nagging of him and her change in weight instead of her concern for him and his health and other positive actions that she is making.

SFBT has developed three rules that function as the foundation for the approach (Berg, 1994; de Shazer et al., 2007): 1) if it isn't broken, don't fix it; 2) if it isn't working, do something different; and 3) if it works, do more of it. People come to therapy because they do not adhere to these rules. In regards to the first rule, they try to change aspects of their relationship that have been working. David and Natalie had a long-standing Friday night "date night" where they would go out to dinner together. They seemed to get along better during these times; however, they tried to change these nights into family time.

Per the second solution-focused rule, people continue to try to solve their problem in the same way. They utilize the Western mantra—if at first it doesn't succeed, try try again. Unfortunately, this can be taken to extremes where the same failed solution attempt leads to continued problem or even an increase in the experience of the problem (Watzlawick, Weakland, & Fisch, 1974). Over a year ago, David and Natalie both realized there were issues in their marriage; however, they tried to solve it by not bringing it up and working on it. This led them to hold back some of their pain so that it built up into resentment. Even when they did let their anger and frustration out, it came across as an attack. While they both realized that what they were doing wasn't working, they did not switch their approach, but continued in their same failed solution attempts.

Lastly, clients become blind to rule number three, where they are not aware of things they have done that have worked and thus are not doing more of what has been useful for them in the past. Berg (1988) explained, "In every couple relationship, there are periods when the partners are reasonably comfortable with each other and getting along well. Most clients forget this at the point when they are upset enough to seek professional help" (p. 36). As a result, clients coming to therapy mainly fall into the opposite of rule number two: if it isn't working, do the same thing, but maybe to a greater extreme. This is where the Johnsons are at this point in time. They have forgotten what they actually did when their relationship was working in the way they wanted—particularly when David first moved to Texas. They may recall the feeling of being in love with one another; however, they are focusing instead on currently not having that sensation.

Complaints

SFBT is a post-structural approach (de Shazer & Berg, 1992) where problems—and solutions—are created in language. The meanings of actions and experiences are based on how people conceive and talk about them. This is founded on how we "language" what we call problems/complaints as well as goals/solutions.

Clients come to therapy with **complaints**. These are just everyday difficulties that clients have not been able to overcome and then are seen as "problems" (de Shazer, 1988a). When these difficulties happen, people define them as "problems" and attempt to change them; however, how they have attempted to solve the problem has not worked. In the case of couples, they will have disagreements, as all couples do during the course of their relationship. Yet, for some, the differences become arguments, which are notated as problems. The members of the couple then change how they view their problems. De Shazer explained, "Their description shifts from 'we have a fight now and then' to 'we are always fighting'" (p. 115). The Johnsons have experienced this change in languaging from where, a couple of years ago, they would exclaim, "We get along for the most part with an occasional spat," to now saying, "We're not on the same page at all."

The complaints that people have, which bring them to therapy, are maintained by their view that how they have attempted to solve these problems is the only rational and logical means they have available (de Shazer, 1985; de Shazer et al., 1986). They then enter into a process of doing more of the same; more change attempts that do not solve the problem, but instead either maintain it or make it worse. David tried to solve the problem of lack of intimacy with Natalie by making connections with other people—his drinking buddies and Devyn, another woman that he flirted with over the internet. Natalie has tried to solve the problem by pointing out where David is lacking in certain areas (i.e. health and connections). Each member of the couple believes that what they are doing is right and what the other person is doing is what is problematic.

Complaints have several elements, some of which are more prominent for some clients or less prominent for others. De Shazer (1985, p. 27) described these complaint elements to include:

1. a bit or sequence of behavior;
2. the meanings ascribed to the situation;
3. the frequency with which the complaint happens;
4. the physical location in which the complaint happens;
5. the degree to which the complaint is involuntary;
6. significant others involved in the complaint directly or indirectly;
7. the question of who or what is to blame;
8. environmental factors such as jobs, economic status, living space, etc.;
9. the physiological or feeling state involved;
10. the past;
11. dire predictions of the future; and
12. utopian expectations.

While both members of the couple may not agree on all of these elements, they usually have a high overlap. In exploring these elements, Natalie's complaints may be most focused on numbers 1, 2, 3, 5, 6, 7, 9, 10, and 11. She views David's smoking and computer interactions with Devyn (1) as showing his unfaithfulness to the marriage (2), especially since it has happened on many occasions (3). She believes that David (6) has the capability of not talking to other women (5). Although she might not be as affectionate to him as she once was, she views this as being because David has been distant and noninitiative (7). Natalie is feeling depressed over the last few months (9), wondering if she will continue to experience pains she had previously (10) and is thinking that the situation shows that the chances for the marriage are slim (11). David's complaints may target elements 1, 2, 3, 6, 7, and 11. He is paying attention to Natalie's comments to him (1) that he is viewing as attacking and nagging (2). For David, these sequences have been increasing in frequency over the last year (3) and are all Natalie's fault (6 & 7). Based on these verbal attacks, as he sees it, David does not expect the marriage to last that long (11).

Berg (1988) explained that couples tend to come to couples therapy because of their perceived disagreements in one or more areas (i.e. finances, roles, or parenting). Upon presenting in therapy, the couple usually languages these issues as communication problems. The therapist understands this presenting problem as a complaint of one partner not agreeing with the other partner. What happens is that a pattern occurs between them where one partner tries to convince the other that his/her position is correct while the other partner retains his/her position. The therapist's position is to view how both members' viewpoints are valid. Usually, the therapist can find the bridge between each position—both individuals want a different and better relationship with one another. Natalie and David both believe that they are in the right and the problems in the marriage are because of the other person. While they may view their own actions as not "the best" to fix things, they are attributing their behavior as a reaction to their partner's problematic actions. If asked for a short explanation of what the problem is in the marriage, David might say, "Natalie keeps harping on me" while Natalie might say, "David is not being faithful." The solution-focused therapist would attempt to find the **relational bridge** between the two—they are both seeking a way to be committed to a marriage that is emotionally sustaining for each of them.

Because problems are based on how a client is **languaging** a situation, complaints/problems persist because the person continues to language the situation in the same way; they are not able to shift the point of view to develop a new meaning or way of talking about the situation. What tends to happen with couples is that they continue to be "engaged in a problem or complaint-focused language game" (de Shazer & Berg, 1992, p. 78).

This is an important aspect as no event in itself has inherent meaning. As such, people label situations as symptoms and can label them as non-symptoms. De Shazer et al. (1986) explained this process, "That is, any behavior can be seen from a multitude of points of view, and the meaning the behavior (or sequence of behaviors) is given depends on the observer's construction or interpretation" (p. 209). When Natalie found out David was communicating with Devyn, she languaged this as him having "an affair." David attempted to language it as "just playing around." There were a multitude of possibilities the couple could describe their situation, such as "the end of the marriage," "a chance to reconnect," or "a redefinition of what it means to be married."

We have been talking about complaints/problems; however, solution-focused therapy has been accused of not focusing on people's problems. This is not quite the case as solution-focused therapists hear what clients do not want (their problems) while also hearing in that statement what they do want (their solutions) (de Shazer et al., 2007). When Natalie says that she is upset that David was having an affair with Devyn, she is also saying that she wants a romantic and monogamous marriage with him. Conversely, when David expresses his frustration with Natalie harping on him, he is saying that he wants her to look up to him more and respect him. The therapist, especially in the beginning of the first session, may hear what people do not want, but will also hear the underlying desires.

People have strengths that they sometimes are aware of and sometimes lose sight of during the course of their lives. For clients with complaints that bring them to therapy, they most likely are not utilizing their resources. Therapy aids them in utilizing their strengths to achieve a more satisfactory life (de Shazer et al., 1986).

Whatever complaint clients present are taken at face value—that these are the issues most prevalent for the client (Berg, 1988). As such, no further exploration of what the underlying root problem is need to occur. The therapist working with the Johnsons will not have to try to find out the "core" problem, as David and Natalie will explain what it is they do not like happening in the marriage—these are the problems the couple brings to therapy and when these things are no longer languaged as problems, therapy will have been successful.

Problem Talk and Solution Talk

Since complaints are based on how people language their experience, non-complaints are also housed within language. Therapists can focus on either of these areas; however, solution-focused therapists find that movement happens when people talk about what is working (**solution talk**) rather than what has not been working (**problem talk**).

Traditional solution-focused therapists do not intentionally avoid any problem talk, but join the clients where they are at, hearing their concerns, but also the unsaid of what they said—the nonproblem times (Reiter & Chenail, 2016). Other solution-focused therapists, particularly when working with couples, believe that therapists should avoid any problem talk (Connie, 2013). This relieves the therapist from having to try to defuse arguments during the session; the same arguments that have become the maladaptive patterns that led the couple to therapy in the first place.

As explained, couples engage in interaction patterns that they language into "problems"—these patterns are what they have been focusing on and are trying to solve; the failed solution attempts becoming part of the problem pattern (Berg, 1988). In placing their energies in looking at these problematic patterns the partners lose sight of the patterns they had previously languaged as good.

In working with the Johnsons, the solution-focused therapist will have to balance how much problem talk occurs and when to shift it to solution talk. If the therapist began the session asking, "What brings you in today" the couple will most likely focus on what they are doing that they do not like—this would be considered problem talk. To try to start the session on a more productive note, many solution-focused therapists might ask, "What would have to happen today that would let you know this session was useful." Here, the therapist begins the session with the possibility that the clients will explain what might be different—and more useful—in their lives.

However, clients tend to want to be heard; especially members in a couple who have been in serious conflict. Most likely, each person has the experience that their partner does not listen and hear their concerns. If the therapist did not acknowledge the complaints, the client may continue to have this frustrated experience. Thus, most solution-focused therapists do acknowledge the complaint, primarily as a means of joining the client. During this time, they also acknowledge the client's strengths and resources to begin the solution building process.

Client Relationship Types

Solution-focused therapists do not work with all clients in the same way. They will engage clients differently based on the relationship they have with them, as well as on the clients' motivation to be in therapy and move toward change. The assessment of which type of relationship therapists have with clients usually occurs during the first session, but therapists maintain an eye to this relationship throughout the course of therapy. These classifications of relationships include the visitor, complainant, and customer (Berg, 1994; Berg & Miller, 1992).

The **visitor-type relationship** occurs when the client does not express any concerns. Thus, they do not believe there is a need for them to do anything to change. Usually, they are coming to therapy because someone else wants them to be there—perhaps a spouse or the criminal justice system. Many times, these clients are labeled as "resistant" since they are not going along with other people's views of what they should do and what should happen for them. However, solution-focused therapists tend not to think in terms of resistance (de Shazer, 1984). Rather, they focus on "cooperating" and how the therapist can make a fit with the client. For the client who does not see a problem (or at least does not agree with their partner, the court, or probation system as to what the problem is), the therapist's job is to find out how the two might work together towards something that is significant for the client. This happens by the therapist joining the client's world view (Berg, 1994). Since both David and Natalie have concerns—regardless of who they think is responsible for them—neither would be considered a visitor.

The **complainant-type relationship** occurs when the client expresses a complaint, yet believes that for things to get better someone else needs to change. They are usually very good at providing the therapist with information about what is going wrong—the various patterns, behaviors, and situations that are problematic—along with who should change (mainly the other person in the couple). The complainant usually sees him/herself as a victim of some other person's actions. In working with someone who engages in a complainant-type relationship, the therapist acknowledges the person's helpful descriptions of the problem and may compliment the client on trying to get help for the couple/family. At the current time, David and Natalie are most likely complainants since they each have concerns but think that the other person is the main one to change. However, during the course of the session, the therapist might engage in a conversation with the couple in a way that helps shift them to become customers for change.

For the **customer–type relationship**, the client experiences a complaint and believes that if they change then the complaint can be overcome. This complaint may include another person, however, the person realizes that they play a function in the problem and that a change in them can lead to a change in the interaction. Customer-type relationships lead to a strong alliance between therapist and client as they both are committed to change. While neither Natalie or David are currently customers since they are very focused on what the other is doing wrong in the relationship, they each may be likely to quickly see what they can do to change to make the marriage more of what they want.

These distinctions of where clients are at in terms of change are important because the person in the room may not necessarily be the person who is most concerned about change happening (Berg, 1988). Further, in couples, they might not be on the same page or level as to what is wrong and what needs to change. However, Berg (1994) explained that some clients are "**hidden**" **customers**—people who come to therapy because someone else has issues with their actions that they do not agree with. Solution-focused therapists can, instead of trying to force them to agree to engage in therapy for the referred problem, work with them to be a "customer" for concerns that they have and want changed.

One concern in couples counseling is when one member attempts to use therapy as a threat over the other person (Berg, 1988). The threat may be that if the partner does not go to therapy they will divorce them or leave the relationship. Further, clients may try to use therapy to get the therapist to side with them against their partner. In either case, this client may not be a customer for change and the therapist would need to have a conversation with them to see whether they truly want change and how motivated they are to do something different themselves. While Natalie and David have talked about the possibility of therapy, it does not seem that either is using therapy as a weapon against their partner but are both open to the possibility that it will help their relationship.

Theory of Problem Resolution

SFBT is a systemic therapy, similar to many of the interactional approaches that make up couples and family therapy. Because the viewpoint is relational, based on patterned interactions, therapy can be done with an individual, a couple, or a family (as well as other configurations). Given this, de Shazer and Berg (1985) do not distinguish between working with both members of a couple or only one member since a change in one part of the system will lead to a change in the other part of the system—this is based on the notion of wholism (de Shazer, 1985). However, working with dyads, in this case couples, presents its own unique challenges such as a likely frustration with one another, history of their relationship with a private language (both verbal and nonverbal), and a heightened attunement to each other (De Jong & Berg, 2013).

Being a relational therapy, solution-focused therapists may work with only one member of a couple (Berg, 1988; de Shazer & Berg, 1985) or both members. However, when two people are present they tend to focus and talk on the level of individual personalities (De Jong & Berg, 2013). For instance, Natalie may call David as someone who has an "addictive personality" or David may say that Natalie is "overbearing."

De Shazer et al. (2007) explained that the "solutions" that are explored in therapy are interactional, including significant family members as well as other people in the client's relational field. When people do more of what works, they change how they engage others and thus how others interact with them. For the Johnsons, aspects of their solutions may be having their weekly date nights, calling or texting one another during the day, or cooking dinner for one another. Each of these solutions involves both members of the couple engaging each other in ways they find as positive and useful.

The solution-focused therapist will most likely work with the member(s) who wants to come in. Sometimes this is both parties, while other times it might only be one member of the couple. Usually, if only one member of the couple wants to come in, it is—in heterosexual relationships—the woman (Berg, 1988). This may be because the partner does not want to talk to a therapist or believes that what the partner views as problematic is not problematic for them. In the Johnson family, Natalie is most likely more motivated to attend therapy to make the relationship work; however, David has expressed his agreement to attend therapy and try to make things better. Given this, the therapist would work with both Natalie and David.

Although couples therapy can be done with only one member, this chapter will focus on having both members present. Because there are two people who are "the client," each with his or her own viewpoint, the therapist must develop **interactional bridges** (Hoyt & Berg, 2000). These interactional bridges bring together the visions of each member of the couple; displaying how the desired changes and possible solutions they have overlap.

Stages of Therapy

Solution-focused therapists may conduct an assessment in the first session; however, it is not an assessment about pathology, but rather one to find out how the clients view their situation and what solutions they have already engaged in that have been useful. Berg (1988, p. 33) provided several questions to keep in mind when conducting an assessment with a couple:

1. Whose problem is it? Who is most upset by the problem?
2. What is the presenting problem? How does the client explain the problem?
3. When does the problem not occur? What works?
4. What has been attempted that does not work?
5. What is the sign of initial change? What are the signs that therapy has succeeded and may be terminated?
6. Does the couple have positive regard for each other?

In exploring the couple's positive regard for each other, the therapist can assess each member's motivation to work toward mutual goals. Some questions that aid in this area include "Why haven't you left the relationship" or "In what ways does your partner show you that s/he loves you" (Berg, 1988). The answers to these questions help to determine the therapist's goal directedness. For instance, if the clients are together because of religious beliefs rather than love, the goal may be for decreasing conflict rather than moving toward greater emotional intimacy. In work with the Johnsons, their responses to why they haven't divorced would most likely be, "Because I still love him" or "We could have a good marriage together." They might answer how their partner shows love by saying, "There are times that he will switch the TV to a show he knows I want to watch—even without me asking" or "She wants me to stop smoking because she wants me to live a long life." This would lead the therapist to join in a goal of increased emotional connection.

Many couples come to therapy because they are dissatisfied with their partner and may spend time during sessions complaining about their partner or even more seriously, engaging in verbal conflict during the session. When this occurs, solution-focused therapists should redirect the couple as fighting does not enhance solution-building (Connie, 2013; Pinchot & Dolan, 2003). The therapist can ask questions to the couple about what their desires are for the relationship, which will have a greater chance of shifting the couple from problem talk to solution talk.

When SFBT was in its infancy, the therapists at the Brief Family Therapy Center developed a format for first sessions (de Shazer et al., 1986). This included an introduction to the process of therapy, statement of the complaint, exploration of exceptions, development of goals, examining potential solutions, a consultation break, and then delivery of a message from the team. SFBT was built on the process of live consultation where a team of therapists watched the session from behind a one-way mirror and during the consultation break discussed what had occurred during the session and developed some type of message or intervention to be given to end the session. Many solution-focused therapists, working alone or with a team, have continued to take a consultation break. One of the reasons is that it allows the therapist time to process and think about what occurred in the session while also heightening the expectancy of the client to receive the end of session message, task, or experiment.

Types of Questions

SFBT is an approach predicated on language (de Shazer & Berg, 1992). As such, the techniques used in the approach are primarily based in questions. These questions may be asked in any order, as they are usually quite intertwined—a question in one category leading into a question in another category. However, the therapist needs to decide which question to use, when, based on the context of the therapeutic relationship. Berg (1994) explained this dynamic, "Thus, *which* questions the worker decides to ask, and *how, when, whom* to ask, has significant impact on the client-worker relationship" (p. 84, italics in original). This section describes some of the most frequent and significant solution-focused questions.

Pretreatment Change Questions

Early in SFBT's history, the developers realized that between the time the client(s) made the appointment and the first session, there was usually something that was different—and better—for clients. This led to them asking the **pretreatment change question** (Weiner-Davis, de Shazer, & Gingerich, 1987). This question goes something like: "Often, people realize that between making the appointment and the session, things have been different for them. What have you noticed that is better."

   If the clients state things have gotten worse, the therapist can move forward in talking about what they want different in coming to therapy. If the clients explain that nothing has changed, the therapist can ask what they did during this time to ensure that things did not get worse (de Shazer et al., 2007). However, if the clients report any type of change the therapist can use this as the beginning of the solution-building process.

   When working with couples like the Johnsons, this question has added power. Since people are limited by their own perspectives, having two or more people discuss a situation allows the possibility of news of difference entering the session. For instance, Natalie may state that nothing is different from when she made the appointment. However, David may exclaim that they actually sat together for an hour and watched television together without having any type of conflict. This news of difference may spark observations in Natalie that she did not have in her awareness.

Exception Questions

The solution-focused therapist believes that problems do not always happen. There are times when the problem is not present at all or is there but to a lesser degree.

These instances are known as **exceptions** (de Shazer et al., 1986). Exceptions relate to the third rule of solution-focused therapy: once you know what works, do more of it. Exceptions are instances that have worked and been useful for clients. Berg (1994) explained, "The worker [therapist] and the client need to examine *who* did *what*, *when*, *where*, and *how* so that the problem did not happen, in other words, how the patterns around the problem were changed" (p. 91, italics in original).

Exceptions provide the clues toward solutions. Usually, clients are so focused on the problem that they lose sight that there were exceptions; and further what they did to help the exceptions occur. The more the therapist focuses on these times, the more clients can see that they have already engaged in useful behavior. Therapy can then focus on enhancing these past times into the present. Given that couples will undoubtedly have experiences of good times and bad times (to various degrees) in their relationship, the therapist has the opportunity to focus on the "up" times of the couple. Berg (1998) described the import of this: "If the couple had successful problem-solving experiences in an earlier part of their relationship, it would be helpful to have them recall those skills for use in solving current problems" (p. 37). These successful problem-solving experiences can be utilized as the couple's exceptions.

Exceptions can be distinguished as being deliberate or random (Berg, 1994). **Deliberate exceptions** happen when the client is able to clearly articulate what happened around the nonproblem event. For the Johnsons, David might be able to explain how he wanted to have a romantic evening with Natalie and he made reservations at a fancy restaurant and surprised her to dinner in which they enjoyed each other's company. Natalie may describe how she saw David come home tired from work one day and she went over and gave him a hug.

Random exceptions occur when people are not able to explain their success or think that it happened because of someone else's actions. When clients have random exceptions, the therapist might have them predict whether they will have the exception, and if they do, the therapist can ask how they were able to make that exception happen this time.

Coping Question

There are times, fortunately not too often, when clients have difficulty noticing and articulating exceptions. For them, life is too overwhelming at the moment to be able to focus on their own strengths and resources. At these times, solution-focused therapists might utilize **coping questions** (Berg, 1994). These questions highlight what clients have been doing to ensure that their situation has not gotten worse. The therapist might ask, "How is it that things aren't worse in the marriage." Natalie and David may then discuss that they tried not to call each other names, or even when they were very mad at each other did not lay a hand physically against the other person. The therapist would follow this up by asking how they were able to decide to do this. Their explanation would then become deliberate exceptions that can be used as a foundation for further change.

Scaling Questions

Clients sometimes express themselves in vague or abstract terms, such as saying that they are "not happy" or "are fearful." **Scaling questions** allow the therapist to begin to concretize a client's meaning (Berg & de Shazer, 1993). While one person's score on a scale may not necessarily translate exactly to another person's scale, the use of numerizing concepts allows therapist and client to assess movement in that concept. For instance, the Johnsons may be asked, "On a scale of 1 to 10 where 10 is the most, how motivated are you to make this marriage work." The answer to this question provides two benefits. First, it produces information into the conversation. Natalie may not have realized where David considers themselves/the relationship and this might engender a more productive conversation. Further, the number given becomes a baseline upon which to measure progress. If Natalie answers 6, the therapist might ask, "What would be happening in your life when you are at a 7." Her answer would become a possible solution for the couple.

Berg and de Shazer (1993) explained that scaling questions focus on three areas; the client's view of self, view of others, and perceptions of others' view of him. By exploring not only the client's scaling on the concept, but other people's as well, solution-focused therapists can utilize circular scaling questions to introduce news of difference into the conversation (Reiter & Shilts, 1998). For instance, the therapist might ask, "On a scale of 1 to 10, where are you Natalie in being committed to the marriage." This question focuses on the client's view of self. Another scaling question might be, "On a scale of 1 to 10, how committed do you think David is to the marriage," which asks one person about their view of others. Or the therapist could ask, "David, where on that scale do you think Natalie would rate you," which explores the perceptions of others on the person.

Miracle Question

The **miracle question** has become the hallmark of solution-focused therapy; however, it was not one of the original tools in the approach. It came into existence by happenstance when Insoo Kim Berg was working with a client who stated that a miracle was needed for things to get better. Insoo then explored what the miracle would look like for the client, which led to a solution-building process.

The miracle question gets clients to envision a future in which the problem they are dealing with is no longer present. The miracle question goes something like:

> Suppose tonight when you go home and go to sleep, during the night, a miracle happens. And the miracle is that all of the concerns that you are

dealing with are gone. When you wake up in the morning, what will be the first sign for you that something is different?

This question helps shift client's focus from their problem-saturated past that they have focused on to the probable exclusion of exceptions to a future where they are exploring what it is they want to have happen in their lives. In essence, the miracle question is a way of exploring client goals (de Shazer et al., 2007).

When asking the miracle question to couples or families, solution-focused therapists help the members to develop a miracle that each agrees with and desires (Pinchot & Dolan, 2003). This is an important point since both members need to believe the miracle picture is what they want to work toward. However, the question needs to be asked within a strong therapeutic relationship and connected to exceptions (Nau & Shilts, 2000). This is where the therapist, once getting the miracle picture, can explore when various aspects have already occurred in the clients' lives.

Just asking the miracle question is not sufficient for it to be useful. The therapist must know what to do after the miracle occurs (Shilts & Gordon, 1996). This is through a collaborative process of developing a detailed explanation of the miracle picture, since the larger number of signs that the person is moving toward the miracle, the more possibility they will see or create those pieces. As such, one of the most important solution-focused questions is "What else" as this question helps to explore further exceptions and expand the miracle picture.

Relational Questions

Since one of the reasons that people maintain complaints is that they get stuck in viewing a situation through their own narrow lens, helping clients see from multiple positions can be important. Sometimes people have difficulty explicating their viewpoint but can do so by taking the perspective of someone else—specifically the other person's view of what would be different in the client (de Shazer et al., 2007). One way to do this is to ask **relationship questions** (Pinchot & Dolan, 2003).

Relationship questions ask one person to answer the therapist's question from another person's perspective. This allows the client to shift from their own viewpoint to another person's viewpoint (in this case their relational partner), which provides the possibility for a binocular experience where two different viewpoints come together to produce a new perception and meaning (de Shazer & Berg, 1992). The Johnson's therapist might ask, "Natalie, what do you think David would see different in you that would let him know the miracle happened?" or "David, what do you think Natalie has seen in you that gives her the motivation to continue to work on the relationship?"

Another important aspect of holding a relational focus is to maintain neutrality (De Jong & Berg, 2013). A significant part of the solution-focused interview is to develop a binocular perspective—that is, the combination of the client's perspective with the therapist's perspective leads to a new way of understanding for the client; one that is more useful for them (de Shazer, 1982, 1991). If the therapist sided with one member of the couple, there would be a lack of new information—difference—into the conversation.

Compliments

Clients have engaged in some behaviors and mindsets that are not useful for them and continue to do so which leads them to come to therapy. However, they have also utilized some of their strengths and resources to ensure their problems do not get worse or actually get better. Solution-focused therapists highlight these times, providing what are known as **compliments** (de Shazer, 1988b; de Shazer et al., 1986). By letting the client know that they have been saying, thinking or doing things that are useful and good for them, the therapist joins with the client and infuses hope and expectancy for further change.

Complimenting can be classified into direct compliments, indirect compliments, and self-complimenting (Berg & DeJong, 2005). **Direct compliments** are given by the therapist to the client and specify clearly what the client(s) is doing that is useful and helpful. In the case of the Johnsons, the therapist might provide a direct compliment them by saying, "I am impressed that even during some difficult times you both have tried to get along, such as last week when you watched television together."

Indirect compliments happen when the therapist asks the client to describe what others in their relational field might see in them as strengths or resources. The Johnson's therapist might ask, "What would each of your parents say are the foundational components of your relationship."

Lastly, **self-complimenting** is when the therapist asks the client questions to elicit from them their own recognition of what they are doing that is useful. For instance, the therapist might ask, "Natalie and David, what have you each done this week that you think helped the relationship?"

Tasks and Homework Assignments

SFBT therapists utilize questions within sessions for some type of meaning change in the clients' perceptions and then usually attempt to get clients to do something different outside of the session. This notion of getting them to do something different is important as clients are coming into therapy doing more of the same—more of what has not been working for them. One way to accomplish a positive change is to infuse some type of randomness into clients' lives (de Shazer

& Molnar, 1984a). This may be in the form of exploring some aspect of their lives they haven't thought of before.

Formula Tasks

When originally developing the approach, de Shazer (1985) constructed skeleton keys; interventions that fit many different locks (client situations). These skeleton keys came to be known as "**formula tasks**." What all of the formula tasks have in common is that they attempt to get clients to initiate new behaviors—whatever they may be—in the hope that this new behavior will circumvent the previous problematic patterns and engage in productive patterns. In this way, therapists do not have to individualize the task to the specific client/couple; but rather, the tasks are generic enough to be useful regardless of the presenting problem. All formula tasks promote the notion of difference and expectancy for clients (Reiter, 2007). Some of the most famous formula tasks include the structured fight task, do something different task, and the first session formula task (de Shazer & Molnar, 1984b).

The Structured Fight Task

Many couples come to therapy in conflict rather than in stagnation; engaging in conflict through a nonproductive manner. To help these couples, de Shazer (1977, 1985) developed the **structured fight task**. This intervention appreciates the frustration that both members of the couple are experiencing, in which their arguments occur over and over. The ritual of the task occurs in four steps: 1) the couple tosses a coin to see who goes first; 2) the winner gets to complain for 10 minutes; 3) the second person complains for 10 minutes; and 4) the couple engages each other in 10 minutes of silence. If they think they need another round, then they toss the coin again and repeat the steps.

This formula task attempts to introduce a new pattern into the couple's repertoire. Normally, they may most likely try to defend themselves while the other person is yelling at them or perhaps one walks away once the other begins to argue. By engaging in this new way of having conflict, a change may happen where randomness and difference occur. As seen in the Johnson's previous arguments, they try to talk over one another and tend not to really listen to the other. The structured fight task may give them an opportunity to perhaps hear what their partner is trying to tell them or to not defend themselves in the moment.

Do Something Different Task

Given that clients have problems because they maintain their patterned viewing and acting toward problems rather than exceptions, one of the tasks for therapists is to get clients to do something different. This is in line with the second rule of

SFBT; if something does not work, don't do it again—do something different. De Shazer (1985) developed the **do something different task** to aid clients in getting out of the ruts of their problems.

The do something different task is given to clients when one person is complaining about the behavior of another person, has tried various attempts to change that behavior and those attempts have failed. This is the experience of most members of couples. The task may be presented something like:

> During this next week, when the problem happens, instead of doing what you normally do, you should do something different. It doesn't matter what that difference is, just as long as you are doing something you didn't do before.

The purpose of the task is to get the clients to shift their problem-maintaining pattern. Whatever the clients do will be random and perhaps sufficient for them not to language what occurs as being a problem. This new behavior may then become an exception, something to be built upon as a solution. If given to the Johnsons, when David begins to smoke in the house, instead of yelling at him to smoke outside (or not smoke at all), Natalie may instead stand right in front of him and begin to breath in the smoke. This may be different enough for him to appreciate her concerns. Or when Natalie gets upset with David, he might hold her hands while she is upset.

First Session Formula Task

Perhaps the most iconic formula task developed by SFBT is the **first session formula task**. This task is given at the end of the first session to help clients shift their perceptions from what has not been working in their lives to the unseen of what has been useful (Molnar & de Shazer, 1987). The task helps clients move from a focus on the past to the present and the future (de Shazer, 1985). The wording may go something like:

> Between now and next time we meet pay attention to all of things that are happening in [your life, your marriage, your relationship, your family] that you want to continue to happen.

The first session formula task changes the expectations of members of a couple who have most likely been paying attention to what their partner has been doing in the relationship that they do not like, so they can inform the therapist of these disturbances so the therapist could change their partner.

Since the therapist expects that there will be several events that occur in the client's life that are productive and useful, the client then begins to expect these to happen. Just this switch from expecting problems to expecting positive interactions can change the problematic patterns that have been occurring between the members of the couple.

Additional Solution-Focused Interventions

Ziegler and Hiller (2007) utilize a few additional tools in their solution-focused work with couples. These include normalizing, mutualizing, and the "good story" orientation. Many times couples come into therapy thinking that the problems they are experiencing are unique. **Normalizing** reframes their problems as common, which helps them realize that others have experienced the same thing and have overcome these problems. This is similar to the group therapy healing factor of universalization. A second beneficial outcome of normalizing is that it frames conflict and disagreements as part of human relationships. The Johnsons' therapist might say, "These types of arguments are normal for many couples, especially when they focus so much on them instead of what it is you are wanting in the marriage."

Mutualization is a process of creating bridges between people's experiences. Ziegler and Hiller (2007) explained this tool: "Mutualizing reframes the problem definition in a way that promotes a shift away from adversarial positions and puts both partners on the same side so that they can work together against a common problem or external force that is now seen as making trouble for them both, sometimes in different but related ways" (pp. 93–94). Because the SFBT therapist attempts to stay neutral and not take sides vis-à-vis one partner or the other, mutualization allows the therapist to adopt a collaborative relationship with both partners in a joint endeavor to overcome their problems and achieve their goals. The Johnsons' therapist could utilize mutualization as a way to shift David and Natalie from being combatants against each other to teammates working toward a win in their marriage. The therapist might say, "It is interesting that David is asking Natalie to not harp on him and Natalie is asking David for emotional fidelity. Really, you are both saying to the other, 'I want love and respect in this marriage.' Respecting each other seems what you are both wanting in the relationship."

The **"good story" orientation** is way of being that Ziegler and Hiller (2007) utilize to help build a bridge from clients' "bad story" narratives (problem talk) to their "good story" narratives (solution talk). This technique is in the realm of exceptions where the therapist hears how the talk down the path of problems is related to the path of solutions. For instance, the Johnsons' therapist might say, "You have been talking about how the relationship has been going in the wrong direction and every day a little more like you don't want it. And you can see that if you stop going in that direction, you go in a direction you want—such as you had during the beginning of your marriage."

While many of the techniques in SFBT are through the use of questions, many times first directed to one party of the couple and then to the other member, therapists can also utilize the couple's interactions with one another. As such, one way to engage a couple via solution-focused principles is through the use of enactments (Seedall, 2009). Enactments are most recognized via structural family therapy (Minuchin, 1974), yet are just tools to get two or more family members to interact with one another. They may be used just as points of observation. However, the therapist might also use them as ways that members of a couple can begin to be different with one another. This can occur through the solution-building process, where the therapist highlights exceptions seen during the transaction. Seedall explained, "Through enactments, clients are able to magnify not only self- but other-understanding, including partner experiences and perceptions of exceptions, thereby increasing awareness, motivation, and change expectancy" (p. 103). In working with the Johnsons, the therapist might say, "Can the two of you talk about how you envision the marriage to be when things are more-or-less as you want them to be." After the couple talks about it, even if it did devolve into arguing, the therapist can focus on those points of strengths between the couple; perhaps by saying, "I was very impressed just now. Even though part of the conversation did not go as you wanted it, I saw times where each of you was able to truly listen to the other person and show respect to their position." Thus, these solution-focused enactments can be used to help highlight exceptions, encourage the clients to do more of what worked, and be used as opportunities to provide compliments.

Goals in Therapy

Given that therapists take client complaints at face value, SFBT is predicated on the therapist and client having very clear goals. De Shazer (1988c) explained the general goal of therapy: "No matter how complicated the problem (or the description of the problem), and no matter its duration, a small and simple change often leads to unpredictably large changes" (p. 56). This happens by helping the couple to move toward their preferred future (Friedman & Lipchik, 1999).

While these are the generic aspects of goals for any client with any issue, when working with couples, therapists attempt to highlight those aspects of their relationship to which they've lost connection. Connie (2013) explained this process: "An important goal of SFT with couples is to awaken dormant successes so that they can play a role in the current relationship" (p. 7).

One way to start to construct goals is to ask the client questions regarding beginning indicators of where the client wants to be rather than the end product (Berg, 1988). This provides clients a way of looking at minimal differences in their lives that can be built upon in the future, but can be seen quickly. This focus on very short-term goals, as well as having long-term goals, helps to promote hope and expectancy of further change (Reiter, 2010). To help clients move forward rather than stay in their current patterns, solution-focused therapists help clients to construct useful goals. De Shazer (1990) provided six qualities of well-formed goals: 1) small; 2) salient to the client; 3) concrete/behavioral; 4) realistic; 5) involving the client's hard work; and 6) the start of something.

Goals need to be small because clients are already coming to therapy extremely frustrated, as they do not usually come to therapy at the first sign of distress. If the goal was large, such as a happy marriage, the time to attain that goal may be too long and the couple might drop out of therapy. The goal should be salient to the client as people are much more likely to be motivated to work toward a goal when it is one that they care about and want. Usually, in couples, both members desire the relationship to be better. Goals should also be concrete and behavioral so that both therapist and client know when it happens. Realistic goals are important as therapists do not want to help clients try to attain something that is not going to occur. Since SFBT therapists attempt to help people develop a customer-type relationship, they help construct goals that are inclusive of the client's hard work—it is the client that is doing something different rather than someone else. However, as we have discussed, a change in the client's behavior usually leads to a change in their partner. Lastly, the goal needs to be the start of something rather than the absence of something. People need to have something to work toward rather than away from. For instance, the Johnsons would not develop a goal of not fighting, as they would never know if they have achieved that goal. However, if their goal was to communicate in ways that were satisfactory for both of them, they would see more positive responses from each other. The therapist might help initiate a solution-focused goal conversation with the Johnsons about spending two hours together (small; concrete; realistic; the start of something) where they engaged in an activity they both enjoy (salient; inclusive of the client doing something).

Termination

When clients come back for the second session, the first question the solution-focused therapist asks is "What's better" (de Shazer, 1994) or "What has been happening that you want to continue to happen" (de Shazer et al., 1986). The answers to these questions become part of the solution-building process. Sessions focus mainly on the exceptions that have occurred throughout the time between sessions. If the couple was given a homework assignment/experiment, the therapist reviews the results and what "worked" for them.

Since the therapist's goal is to get the clients on track, rather than having to walk with them all the way to the end goal, sessions begin to get spaced out as progress is seen (de Shazer et al., 1986). If the Johnsons were given the first session formula task at the end of the initial session and come back with various lists of what each did that they want to continue to have happen, the therapist would focus on how they were able to make these events happen (deliberate exceptions) and what they can do to maintain and increase these actions. Whereas the space between the first session and the second may have been one week, from the second to the third may be two weeks, then three weeks, a month, or more as further movement towards their goals occur.

Termination in SFBT occurs when clients have achieved their goals. When a client's goals are met, therapist and client know that solutions are being or have been developed (de Shazer, 1991). Therapists and clients pay attention to whether the client still has the complaint they came in with or that it has lessened to a degree the client is comfortable with. However, during the course of therapy, the therapist should regularly review the initial goals and revise them if need be (Berg, 1994). De Shazer explained: "Once the clients are confident that the goal has been achieved and that the changes involved are likely to continue, then both therapists and clients can know that they can stop meeting" (p. 131).

Therapy with the Johnsons will continue until Natalie and David express that they are on the path toward their goals. Even if they have not attained all of the goals that they set out, if it is clear that they are on track toward them, therapy can terminate. The therapist wants to ensure to note the actions clients have taken to move toward their goals as this reinforces their sense of competence and control over the situation (Berg, 1988). They will then be more likely, even when no longer in therapy, to continue these behaviors that are involved in the solution-building process.

Case Transcript

Natalie made the call to set up the first appointment. The therapist invited both Natalie and David to the session once Natalie told her both of them agreed to go to therapy to work on the marriage.

> *Therapist:* Natalie and David, it is nice to meet you both. Thank you for coming. I hope that we can make this meeting useful for you. I will do my best and I assume each of you will as well. Could you tell me a bit about you, for instance, your jobs.
>
> > *This is a standard opening that Steve de Shazer used for many of his sessions. This taps into a sense of expectancy, where the clients can expect the therapist to be present and active as well as know that the therapist believes in them. The therapist decides to start the session by finding out about each member of the couple, hopefully outside of the saturated problem talk. This is the beginning of the joining process in the hopes that a strong collaborative relationship will ensue.*
>
> *Natalie:* Well, I'm a realtor and lived here in the Dallas area most of my life.
> *Therapist:* What's it like to be in real estate?
> *Natalie:* Sometimes good, but sometimes a bit frustrating, given the economy.
> *Therapist:* And you, David?
> *David:* I'm a schoolteacher.
> *Therapist:* What grade?
> *David:* Right now, tenth grade.
> *Therapist:* Okay. Looking back three months from now, what would let you know that this session was a little bit helpful?

Here, instead of asking what brought the couple to make the appointment, which would lead to problem talk, the therapist asks a question to get toward client goals. This opening offers the couple an opportunity to begin the solution building process.

Natalie: Well, if this was helpful, then David wouldn't be talking to other women anymore.

Therapist: Okay. What would he be doing?

Natalie: Keeping his penis in his pants when he's on the computer.

David: Hey, Natalie, watch it.

Therapist: All right, let's come back to that. David, how would you know this session was beneficial for you two?

The therapist tries to redirect an interaction that seems to be going toward conflict.

David: That she lays off of me.

Therapist: What do you mean by that?

David: She nags me all the time.

Therapist: Okay. How would she be with you instead?

Here, the therapist shifts from the problem focus of the client of what he does not want to what he does want. This is an early attempt to begin a conversation that focuses on goals—utilizing the notion that goals should be the start of something rather than the absence of something.

David: She'd be nice and caring.

Therapist: All right. Let's say Natalie is acting in that way. What impact would that have on you?

The therapist is asking a relational question to help bring forward a more in-depth description of possible behaviors that could be utilized as part of the solution-building process.

David: I'm sure I'd be nice and caring back.

Therapist: You would be nice and caring back. Natalie, how does that sound to you?

Natalie: It would be nice, but he hasn't been nice or caring in a long time. At least to me.

Therapist: Okay. There is a lot of frustration and resentment built up on both sides here. I'm going to ask you a strange question—as we ask a lot of strange questions here. This one deals with numbers. On a scale of 1 to 10 where 1 is you at your lowest and 10 is when you are at your highest, how motivated are each of you to make this marriage work?

The therapist does several things in this exchange. First, the therapist provides an empathic response to join with the clients around where they are currently at—with frustration and upset at their partner. The therapist mutualizes the feeling so that the couple has the possibility of joining together to move past the same experiences they are having. Second, the therapist introduces the first scaling question to assess how motivated each person is to enhance the marriage. This will help the therapist determine what type of client-type relationship there is with David and Natalie.

Natalie: I'm probably at a 6. I want it to work, but I don't quite trust him.

Therapist: All right. You're at a 6. And David?

David: I'm at a 6 also.

Therapist: You're at a 6? Natalie, did you know that?

Natalie: No. I thought he'd be lower.

Therapist: You thought he'd be lower. What do you think David sees in the marriage that you don't know that he sees so his rating is higher than you thought?

The therapist asks a relationship question to try to evoke a different perspective from Natalie since it seemed that Natalie did not expect a high response from David. This may open the pathway of each member understanding what the other wants in the marriage. At this point in the session, the therapist has a good idea that while both David and Natalie may have complainant-type relationships, they are very close to being customer-type.

Natalie: I don't know.

Therapist: Can you ask him and have a conversation about that?

The therapist initiates a solution-focused enactment, so that the couple can engage each other in exploring the available resources in the relationship.

Natalie: David, do you really think you're at a 6?

David: Yes, why wouldn't I be?

Natalie: Because you were talking to another woman and talking about divorcing me and moving in with her.

David: I told you, I wasn't really serious. Look, I married you. You are the only woman I ever asked to marry me. The only woman I ever did marry. I want to try. I think we've both given up this last year. But we don't have to.

Natalie: If I truly believed that you were going to try, I think it would really help things out.

Therapist: That was very nice to watch. The two of you really listened to one another and engaged each other in a very nice manner. Is that how you want your interactions to go?

Here, the therapist follows up the enactment by focusing on the strengths of the couple's interactions through a direct compliment.

Natalie: Yes, it would be nice if we could talk humanely to one another.
Therapist: David, is that type of interaction what you would like?

The therapist makes sure to get both party's viewpoints on the situation so as not to take sides in the relationship. This is part of the interactional bridges that are being built between the two.

David: Yeah, like we used to have.
Therapist: Can you tell me about how your communication used to be?

The therapist hears an opening into an exception to the problem and tries to expand it to see how readily able those behaviors can be for the couple so that they can repeat them. This is going toward the third rule of SFBT; once you know what works, do more of it.

David: We used to have fun together.
Therapist: Natalie, is that right? You two had fun together?
Natalie: Yeah.
Therapist: What did you used to do?
Natalie: We went out to eat, took long drives around the state, or watched sports.
Therapist: David, what else did you two do when you were communicating well?

The therapist utilizes the "what else" question to expand the assortment of exceptions, and possible solution-building experiences, for the couple.

David: We would watch shows on television, play scrabble, or have romantic dinners. But that hasn't happened in a long time.
Natalie: No, it hasn't. Why is that David?
David: Of course, it's my fault. Everything is my fault.
Therapist: Let's come back to that. Okay, I am going to ask you another strange question. This one requires a lot of imagination. From what I've seen, you both have a lot of that. Strange question is this; suppose tonight, you two go to sleep. And during the night a miracle happens and all of the concerns that you have been talking about today are gone. However, when you wake up in the morning you don't know that the miracle happened because you were sleeping. What would be the first sign for you that something is different? That a miracle has happened?

The therapist asks the miracle question to help further elucidate possible goals with the couple.

David: She wouldn't be so nasty to me.

Therapist: All right. How would she be with you?

David: Nice. Loving.

Therapist: And how would you know that she was nice and loving?

David: She'd actually smile at me. Maybe make me breakfast.

Therapist: And suppose she did. What would you do in response?

David: I would smile back.

Therapist: Natalie, how would that be?

Natalie: That would be nice. We haven't had that in a long while.

Therapist: What would your friends notice different about you that would let them know something is different about you two?

> *Here, the therapist asks a relational question to expand the scope of the miracle so that new possible miracle pieces can be explored.*

Natalie: They'd probably see that, first, we're out together with each other and second, that we're actually touching each other. Maybe holding hands.

Therapist: They would see you touching more. David, what else would they notice?

David: That we were laughing with one another.

Therapist: When is the last time that your friends saw this in you?

> *The therapist begins to connect the miracle picture of the future to the exceptions of the past. By realizing that they have already experienced pieces of their miracle, the couple can discover greater levels of hope and motivation to make the marriage work.*

Natalie: I don't know. Maybe a year-and-a-half ago. I do remember going to Bridget's wedding and we danced together and had a good time.

Therapist: David's a good dancer?

Natalie: In his silly way, yes.

Therapist: What else will you notice after the miracle happened?

Natalie: We would probably have date night again.

Therapist: So, if you were to take one night in a week and both decide on a place for a date, that would be a miracle?

> *Here, the therapist helps to engage in a conversation around goals. The goal of a date night is small, measurable, realistic, attainable, salient to the couple, and the start of something.*

David and Natalie: Yes!

Therapist: David and Natalie. We've talked about a lot here and I would like to take a few minutes to collect my thoughts and think things through. Then when I come back you can tell me about any ideas you had and I will let you know what I thought about.

The therapist takes a consultation break to collect thoughts as well as to bring forth a sense of expectation of what will be said once the session reconvenes.

Therapist: During the break I was thinking about how impressed I am by the both of you. While there were significant difficulties in your marriage and a hesitancy that you each had about really pushing forward, you found a way to get through it. Further, even during those times you each did things to show the other person that you still cared, even though at times it might not have been recognized.

The therapist begins the post-break statement by complimenting the couple as a further way to join them and reinforce actions that they have already taken that have been useful for them.

Therapist: I have one last strange thing to say, since I've said a bunch of strange things today! I am going to ask you each to do something this week that may be different for you. Between now and the next time we meet I would like you to pay attention to all of those things, the very small things and the very large things and everything in between that you want your partner to continue to do or to do more of. Keep track of these things but don't talk about them. We'll start the next session going over each of your lists. It was very nice meeting both of you and I look forward to next week hearing what you wrote on your lists.

The therapist decided to give the First Session Formula Task since both David and Natalie seemed to be on the borderline between complainant-type and customer-type relationships. By paying attention to what is happening that they want to continue to happen, each partner may see how he or she is involved in the interaction and what they can do to change things.

References

Berg, I. K. (1988). Couple therapy with one person or two. In E. W. Nunnally, C. S. Chilman, & F. M Cox (Eds.), *Troubled relationships* (pp. 30–54). Newbury Park, CA: SAGE Publications.

Berg, I. K. (1994). *Family based services: A solution-focused approach.* New York, NY: W. W. Norton & Company.

Berg, I. K., & de Shazer, S. (1993). Making numbers talk: Language in therapy. In S. Friedman (Ed.), *The new language of change* (pp. 5–24). New York, NY: The Guilford Press.

Berg, I., K., & DeJong, P. (2005). Engagement through complimenting. In T. Nelson (Ed.), *Education and training in Solution-Focused Brief Therapy* (pp. 51–56). New York, NY: The Haworth Press.

Berg, I. K., & Miller, S. (1992). *Working with the problem drinker.* New York, NY: W.W. Norton.

Connie, E. (2013). *Solution building in couples therapy.* New York, NY: Springer Publishing Company.

Davoodi, Z., Etemadi, O., Bahrami, F., Jafari, A. S. A., & Hosnije, A. H. S. (2012). The effect of the brief solution-focused approach (BSFA) on the tendency to divorce in divorce susceptible men and women. *Interdisciplinary Journal of Contemporary Research in Business, 4*(4), 865–879.

De Jong, P., & Berg, I. K. (2013). *Interviewing for solutions* (4th ed.). Pacific Grove, CA: Brooks/ Cole.

de Shazer, S. (1977). The optimist-pessimist technique. *Family Therapy, 4*(2), 93–100.

de Shazer, S. (1982). *Patterns of brief family therapy.* New York, NY: The Guilford Press.

de Shazer, S. (1984). The death of resistance. *Family Process, 23*(1), 11–17.

de Shazer, S. (1985). *Keys to solution in brief therapy.* New York, NY: W. W. Norton & Company.

de Shazer, S. (1988a). Utilization: The foundation of solutions. In J. K. Zeig & S. R. Lankton (Eds.), *Developing Ericksonian therapy* (pp. 112–124). New York, NY: Brunner/Mazel Publishers.

de Shazer, S. (1988b). *Clues: Investigating solutions in brief therapy.* New York, NY: W. W. Norton & Company.

de Shazer, S. (1988c). Once you have doubts, what have you got? A brief therapy approach to "difficult cases". In E. W. Nunnally, C. S. Chilman, & F. M. Cox (Eds.), *Mental illness, delinquency, addictions, and neglect* (pp. 56–68). Newbury Park, CA: SAGE Publications.

de Shazer, S. (1990). What is it about brief therapy that works? In J. K. Zeig & S. G. Gilligan (Eds.), *Brief therapy: Myths, methods, and metaphors* (pp. 90–99). New York, NY: Brunner/ Mazel Publishers.

de Shazer, S. (1991). *Putting different to work.* New York, NY: W. W. Norton & Company.

de Shazer, S. (1994). *Words were originally magic.* New York, NY: W. W. Norton & Company.

de Shazer, S., & Berg, I. (1985). A part is not apart: Working with one of the partners present. In A. Gurman (Ed.), *Casebook of marital therapy* (pp. 97–110). New York, NY: Guilford.

de Shazer, S., & Berg, I. K. (1992). Doing therapy: A post-structural re-vision. *Journal of Marital and Family Therapy, 18*(1), 71–81.

de Shazer, S., Berg, I. K., Lipchik, E., Nunnally, E., Molnar, A., Gingerich, W., & Weiner-Davis, M. (1986). Brief therapy: Focused solution development. *Family Process, 25,* 207–222.

de Shazer, S., Dolan, Y, Korman, H., Trepper, T., McCollum, E., & Berg, I. K. (2007). *More than miracles: The state of the art of Solution-Focused Brief Therapy.* New York, NY: Routledge.

de Shazer, S., & Molnar, A. (1984a). Changing teams/changing families. *Family Process, 23*(4), 481–486.

de Shazer, S., & Molnar, A. (1984b). Four useful interventions in brief family therapy. *Journal of Marital and Family Therapy, 10*(3), 297–304.

Friedman, S., & Lipchik, E. (1999). A time-effective, solution-focused approach to couple therapy. In J. M. Donovan (Ed.), *Short-term couple therapy* (pp. 325–359). New York, NY: The Guilford Press.

Hoyt, M. F., & Berg, I. K. (2000). Solution-focused couple therapy: Helping clients construct self-fulfilling realities. In M. F. Hoyt (Ed.), *Some stories are better than others* (pp. 143–166). New York, NY: Brunner/Mazel.

Lipchik, E., & Kubicki, A. D. (1996). Solution-focused domestic violence views: Bridges toward a new reality in couples therapy. In S. D. Miller, M. A. Hubble, & B. L. Duncan (Eds.), *Handbook of Solution-Focused Brief Therapy* (pp. 65–98). San Francisco, CA: Jossey-Bass Publishers.

Minuchin, S. (1974). *Families & family therapy.* Cambridge, MA: Harvard University Press.

Minuchin, S., & Fishman, H. C. (1981). *Family therapy techniques.* Cambridge, MA: Harvard University Press.

Molnar, A., & de Shazer, S. (1987). Solution-focused therapy: Toward the identification of therapeutic tasks. *Journal of Marital and Family Therapy, 13*(4), 349–358.

Murray, C. E., & Murray, Jr., T. L. (2004). Solution-focused premarital counseling: Helping couples build a vision for their marriage. *Journal of Marital and Family Therapy, 30*(3), 349–358.

Nau, D. S., & Shilts, L. (2000). When to use the miracle question: Clues from a qualitative study of four SFBT practitioners. *Journal of Systemic Therapies, 19*(1), 129–135.

Nelson, T. S., & Kelley, L. (2001). Solution-focused couples group. *Journal of System Therapies, 20*(4), 47–66.

O'Hanlon, W. H., & Hudson, P. O. (1994). Coauthoring a love story: Solution-oriented marital therapy. In M. F. Hoyt (Ed.), *Constructive therapies* (pp. 160–188). New York, NY: The Guilford Press.

O'Hanlon, S., & O'Hanlon, B. (1999). Love is a noun (except when it's a verb): A solution-oriented approach to intimacy. In J. Carlson & L. Sperry (Eds.), *The intimate couple* (pp. 247–262). New York, NY: Brunner/Mazel.

O'Hanlon, W. H., & Weiner-Davis, M. (1989). *In search of solutions.* New York, NY: W. W. Norton & Company.

Pinchot, T., & Dolan, Y. M. (2003). *Solution-Focused Brief Therapy.* New York, NY: The Haworth Clinical Practice Press.

Reiter, M. D. (2007). Utilizing expectation in solution-focused formula tasks. *Journal of Family Psychotherapy, 18*, 27–37.

Reiter, M. D. (2010). The use of hope and expectancy in solution-focused therapy. *Journal of Family Psychotherapy, 21*, 132–148.

Reiter, M. D., & Chenail, R. J. (2016). Defining the focus in Solution-Focused Brief Therapy. *International Journal of Solution-Focused Practices, 4*(1), 1–9.

Reiter, M. D., & Shilts, L. (1998). Using circular scaling questions to deconstruct depression: A case study. *Crisis Intervention and Time Limited Treatment, 4*, 227–237.

Seedall, R. B. (2009). Enhancing change process in Solution-Focused Brief Therapy by utilizing couple enactments. *The American Journal of Family Therapy, 37*(2), 99–113.

Shilts, L., & Gordon, A. B. (1996). What to do after the miracle occurs. *Journal of Family Psychotherapy, 7*(1), 15–22.

Stith, S. M., McCollum, E. E., & Rosen, K. H. (2011). *Couples therapy for domestic violence: Finding safe solutions.* Washington, DC: American Psychological Association.

Watzlawick, P., Weakland, J., & Fisch, R. (1974). *Change: Principles of problem formation and problem resolution.* New York, NY: W. W. Norton & Company.

Weakland, J., Fisch, R., Watzlawick, P., & Bodin, A. M. (1974). Brief therapy: Focused problem resolution. *Family Process, 13*, 141–168.

Weiner-Davis, M. (1993). *Divorce-busting: A step-by-step approach to making your marriage loving again.* New York, NY: Fireside.

Weiner-Davis, M., de Shazer, S., & Gingerich, W. (1987). Using pretreatment change to construct a therapeutic solution: An exploratory study. *Journal of Marital and Family Therapy, 13*(4), 359–363.

Ziegler, P., & Hiller, T. (2007). Solution-focused therapy with couples. In T. S. Nelson & F. N. Thomas (Eds.), *Handbook of Solution-Focused Brief Therapy: Clinical applications* (pp. 91–115). New York: The Haworth Press.

6

NARRATIVE COUPLES THERAPY

marcela polanco,[1] *Tirzah Shelton, and Catalina Perdomo*

Much like narrative therapists depart from the assumption that life is a social phenomenon, historically and culturally negotiated (White, 1995), so is narrative therapy and its practices. Practices informed by a narrative therapy framework are the outcome of therapists' engagements with particular modes of thought and life, which are, in turn, particular to the cultures in which they practice.

Before continuing with a brief historical revision of narrative therapy and our distillation of White and Epston's practice, illustrated in the work with Natalie and David, for purposes of inclusiveness, of respect, and of challenging homo- and heteronormativity (which disqualify and downgrade sexual diversity), we also want to clarify that the work we are discussing here will be focused on opposite-sex couples given that it was the way in which we situated Natalie and David. Other forms of relationships such as polyamorous or same-sex couples, for example, would require very different sets of considerations on cultural and social analysis to situate our practice.

History: Narrative Therapy's Adventures through Otherworlds of Life

Shortly after Michael White's sudden death in 2008, many publications of the history of the development of the work began to surface to honor his incredible legacy. This legacy greatly influenced narrative and family therapy and continues to do so. This historical documentation is easily accessible (Beels, 2001; Denborough, 2009; White, 2009; Epston, 2011) so we are emphasizing here only brief aspects of this history.

Featuring first as a *therapy of literary merit* (White, 1989) in the Dulwich Center Publications, which started as an underground, downunder press, narrative therapy emerged as a ground-breaking political approach to psychotherapy in the early 1980s (Beels, 2001). It was born out of the "brotherhood of ideas" (Epston, 2011, p. xxii) between David Epston and the late Michael White. They invented their own framework of practice at the fringes of mainstream psychotherapy out of the activist political undertone of social work and the ethics of respectful collaborations of anthropology. As family therapy, their practice did not look for a mental structure of experience as a guide and interest. They were interested in looking at experience not from a psychological but from a political perspective, which takes into consideration the influence of patterns of social structures in culture, kinship, and language (Chamberlain, 1990); as explained by the person seeking consultation, not the therapist, since people hold ultimate authority on the meaning of their accounts (Beels, 2001). Epston and White brought into the practice of psychotherapy concerns of broader social issues (Denborough, 2009).

A New Zealander born in Canada, David Epston's unquenchable thirst for ideas found its way first in anthropology studies at the University of Auckland, followed by social work at Warwick University in the UK. As Beels (2001) recounts, during a year-long training at the Family Institute at Cardiff, Wales, where Epston studied with his wife Ann, he discovered family therapy, particularly hypnosis, and found great interest in the work of therapists in the US. His work became widely known in child psychiatry and hospital settings working with life-threatening conditions such as childhood diabetes, asthma, and anorexia. Since 1987 he has been the co-director of The Family Therapy Center in Auckland, New Zealand.

Michael White, an Australian, had convictions in social, political, and ethical concerns when working with people (Epston, 2011). White found a home at first in social work when beginning his career in the department of psychiatry at a children's hospital in his home town of Adelaide. White believed that when working with children it was important to involve the participation of their families, in spite of hospitals' persistent refusal of his initiative. This led to his interest in family therapy. In 1979, he co-founded and became founding editor of the *Australian and New Zealand Journal of Family Therapy* with a group of colleagues having no formal training in the field, yet actively contributing scholarly work with families (Denborough, 2009). In collaboration with others, especially his wife, Cheryl White, he founded Dulwich Centre Publications in Adelaide, which is now well established as an international development and training center in narrative therapy and community work.

Epston and White met in 1981 during the Second Australian Family Therapy Conference in Melbourne. However different their styles were, they appreciated these differences, and they shared a common interest and commitment to the political wing of family therapy. As Beels (2001) wrote, when taking a closer look at their particular time and place, their culture tells more about their contributions than anything else. They were educated in the 1960s in a world of social activism and the profession's engagement in political action. New Zealand and Australia, in comparison with the US, had more of an emphasis on community organizing and less on psychotherapy. Their work in their respective countries—mostly in psychiatric contexts with young people and their families—was influenced by this activism, resulting in their disquiet with the alienation and rituals of degradation (Garfinkel, 1984) of families by psychiatry and psychology. Gently, yet radically, Epston and White set themselves out to invent their own practice to stretch rather than confirm ideas (Denborough, 2009) in their own terms. These are the terms of their convictions, giving it their own names even if they had to make them up for themselves. They coined vocabularies (i.e. externalization, unpacking identity conclusions, saying hullo again, etc.) to better capture in full the intentionalities of their work, while relishing the offerings of the potentiality of language in order to originate practices that refused to become merged into yet another set and definitive model of practice with faithful followers who would compromise, consequently, their cultural integrity, creativity, and freedom of experiment in doing so. Although in some cultures, as in the US, narrative therapy has become a "model" of practice, Epston and White (1992) meant to keep the creativity of the practice alive by keeping from conceptualizing it as such:

> So far, at least, our work seems to have defied any consistent classification…
>
> We have been steadfast in our refusal to name our work in any consistent manner. We do not identify with any particular "school" of family therapy, and are strongly opposed to the idea of our contributions being named as a school [or model]. We believe that such a naming *would only subtract from our freedom to further explore various ideas and practices, and that it would make it difficult for others to recognize their own unique contributions to development of this work, which we regard to be an "open book".* We are drawing attention to the fact that one of the aspects associated with this work that is of central importance to us is the spirit of adventure. Most of the "discoveries" that have played a significant part in the development of our practices have been made after the fact (in response to unique outcomes in our work with families) with theoretical considerations assisting us to explore and to extend the limits of this practice.
>
> *(p. xi, emphasis added)*

Influenced by anthropology, Epston and White sought to facilitate in their conversations the development of rich stories embedded in their social, cultural, and relational contexts on the preferred paths of the person's life and relationships through the means of questions. For this reason, it is common that narrative therapy conversations are regarded in terms of interviews, emphasizing inquiry as practice. In a narrative therapy interview, the therapist is an ethnographer:

> … being a guest, camping out in the other persons' world, receiving what the person has to tell you as a gift that is very precious to you… as the

ultimate authority on the meaning of his or her [hir][2] culture and experience... . Tell me this story, let us see what we can make of it together.

(Beels, 2001, p. 163)

Through the life of the practice, narrative therapy has ventured out of the downunder to travel to the upover worlds. This happened through their first book in 1990, *Narrative means to therapeutic ends*, as well as with White's teachings with Karl Tomm in Canada and the US, followed by David Epston. Almost 20 years after, in 2007, White's *Maps of narrative practices* significantly influenced the contemporary development of the life of the practice. This publication featured White's ideas of the last years of his work prior to his death. He had adopted the analogy of **maps**, among many other alternatives, as a supporting structure of lines of inquiry for therapists to scaffold their interviews with diverse couples, their families and communities' territories of life from what it is known, habitual, and familiar to them in their stories, to what it is possible for them to restory, hence to know, imagine, and invent. These maps are particularly focused on facilitating the development of rich or thick personal, social, historical, and relational stories about people's lived experiences that go against the grain of problematic stories. Commonly, the stories that unfold through these lines of inquiry result in the problematization of the problem (D. Epston, personal communication, May 2, 2011). White's inquiries seek to shed light on the unique outcomes or extraordinary results of people's lived experiences in their social and cultural contexts. He had particular interest in **subordinate experiences**. These are experiences that, while important for the person, become neglected or subjugated by the influence of social and cultural **dominant discourses**, which steer people away from their preferred aspirations, dreams, values, etc. Tension with dominant discourses result in the continued life of the problem and its effects in people's lives.

As a framework that is more interested in cultural and social analysis in relation to a person, their partners, families, and communities, rather than specializing on a theory of the mind, or of relationships, narrative therapy is a practice that makes itself available to work with a wide range of relational structures. It has been adapted to work with diverse couples. Jill Freedman and Gene Combs's (2002) collection of papers of their work with couples published by Dulwich Centre Publications has been very influential.

Stories and Their Imaginative and Literary Merit

Epston and White's political and ethical convictions are at the center of the practice along with their explorations of the analogy of text or story, hence its narrative therapy name. Drawing significantly from Jerome Bruner's (1986) analysis of literary texts, they arrived at the analogy of "**story**" as a theoretical framework to understand how a person organizes and gives meaning to experience. Epston and White (1992) translated the relationship between literary texts and readers into the interaction between people and the stories through which they live their lives. They adopted story as an interpretive, fluid framework (Goffman, 1961) of lived experience (Turner, 1986) by which people know of life in an ongoing manner (White & Epston, 1990).

Stories, woven like threads in a tapestry, provide context for Natalie and David to provide meaning to their experiences by connecting sequences of events through common themes, from their past toward an imagined future, in or out of the marriage. The stories about their lives and relationship are composed by their particular arrangements of a series of tellings that provide them with an organized chronological index of their history, according to a plot to arrive at a coherent account of themselves, their relationships, and the worlds around them (White & Epston, 1990). The arrangement of the recent events in their lives such as the internet affair, smoking, drinking, possible divorce, and conflict between them have taken Natalie and David to make up the most prominent plot of their stories, and hence their lives.

Stories, according to Bruner (1986), possess a structure comprising a **land-scape of action** of Natalie and David's actions (i.e. David's communication with Devyn through the internet) and a **landscape of consciousness**; the latter was re-named later by White (2007) as the **landscape of identity**. The landscape of identity provides the story with Natalie and David's intentions and purposes of their lives that shape their fluid identities (i.e. David's intentions in communicating with Devyn and in his marriage to Natalie in relation to his beliefs, aspirations, and dreams about his life).

For Bruner, the composition of stories, being stories about the problem or those that go against the life of the problem, however, is not based on information that has already been considered as such and has been filed in the person's consciousness for faithful recall. Natalie and David's multiple stories are not **secondary narratives** about former information stored by them. Instead, they are considered **primary narratives** that establish what they are counting as information. Natalie and David's primary stories *are* their realities instead of being stories that are concealing their real realities for the therapist to discover through introspection, insight, etc. As White (1995) wrote, "In so many ways, words are the world" (p. 30). In therapy, Natalie and David are not offering stories that were previously constructed. It is in the therapeutic interview, or any other communicative encounter, where their stories begin to be constructed. It is in their performance or storytelling about their coupling life, where Natalie and David's lives happen, not before or after. Life happens in the storying of their lives, not besides it. Every retelling of their story is a new telling. When they story their lives and relationship they are reconfiguring the worlds in which they live at the level of action and identity—or intentionality and purpose; and, consequently, the worlds in which they live become reconfigured by the tellings about their lives and relationships. In the performance or authoring of their stories, Natalie and David re-live, re-create, re-tell; hence, make up their experiences all over again (Bruner, 1986).

For White and Epston (1990) each partner is an author or participant in his/her/hir worlds and participates in the authoring and re-authoring of their partner's worlds and their lives and relationships in them. In every conversation between Natalie and David, and with a narrative therapist, they are re-authoring their lives by drawing from a rootstock of knowledges out of their everyday lived interactions within their respective cultures; they "… engage in performances of meaning under the guidance of the story" (Epston & White, 1992, p. 14). The co-storying about their marriage contributes to a transformative experience that takes place as the "reorigination" of their lived experiences by "… entering into stories with their experience and their imagination, and the process of taking these stories over and making them their own" (Epston & White, 1992, p. 14).

The development of such stories in a narrative therapy interview takes place through inquiries that seek to respect their authorship and open up new narrative spaces for Natalie and David to retell possible alternative perspectives, in order to reauthor the effects of the problem and re-engage with what is important to them, their dreams, aspirations, beliefs, etc. For White and Epston (1990), narrative therapy promotes couples' personal agency in the fashioning of their own lives. By **agency** White meant,

> a sense of being able to regulate one's own life, to intervene in one's life to affect its course according to one's intentions, and to do this in ways that are shaped by one's knowledge of life and skills of living.
>
> *(White, 2007, p. 264)*

Through the tellings and retellings of their stories, therapists privilege the couple's lived experience "… to stretch their minds, to exercise their imagination, and to employ their meaning making resources" (White & Epston, 1990, p. 62). For White (2007), "effective therapy is about engaging people in the re-authoring of the compelling plights of their lives in ways that arouse curiosity about human possibility and in ways that invoke the play of imagination" (pp. 75–76).

The emphasis on the narrative analogy guides narrative therapists' keen interests on the material with which the couple's stories are made up, in a manner of speaking, and that is their language embedded within their social, political, relational, and historical contexts (White, 2007). As White and Epston (1990) commented: "When engaging in language, we are not engaging in a neutral activity" (p. 27). Natalie and David's vocabularies (i.e. catfishing, divorce, alcoholic, smoker, cheating, etc.) are influenced by a stock of cultural discourses that shape their accounts for the meanings that they have conferred to their intentions, beliefs, aspirations, hopes, dreams, etc., about their relationship.

The focus on language is certainly not particular to narrative therapists. Practices informed by social-constructionist, postmodern, poststructural, and systemic perspectives share the same interest. What is particular to narrative practices instead is the unique ways in which language is situated in narrative therapy interviews.

It can engage compelling life predicaments and invoke the play of imagination to invite the couple to relive out the drama of their stories, fostering a dramatic, transformative engagement (White, 2007). This uniqueness stems from Bruner's (1986) emphasis on the literary merits of stories.

It is not sufficient for Natalie and David to tell a new story about themselves to make new claims about their lives, however. The literariness of stories, according to Bruner (1986), requires accounts of events in their real world, in a way that they render that world newly strange, rescued from its obviousness or habituated knowledges that, in therapy, are often saturated by the actions of the problem in their coupling life. The habituated stories about the problem are then turned newly estranged through the literary means of the therapist's inquiries. Literariness requires stories to be performed for an audience and in context. The audience authenticates the story. **Authentication**, according to Myerhoff (1978, 1992), means to bring the story to life, or declare its existence in their particular contexts, which happens in the interaction between the author, Natalie and/or David, while storytelling their lives; and, the audience, Natalie and/or David, while witnessing the storytelling of the other; and the interaction between the couple and the therapist. Hence, authentication means that their stories are relational and contextual in nature. The interrelation between an author and an audience is what constitutes stories as such, **stories of literary merit**. A one-sided, cognitive, and simplistic process of monologuing or catharsis robs stories of literariness.

The engagement of the imagination Epston and White emphasized in their work is critical to the formation of stories of literary merit, being these rich, evocative, and sustainable stories that are transformative. Narrative therapists seek to arouse the couple's **imaginative labor** (Freeman, 2010) to invite them to name experiences that may not have had a name yet, or speak of them in ways that have never been spoken of to counteract the languaging of the effects of their problems in their lives and relationships, and rescue them out of obviousness. The following excerpt describes ways in which the therapist engages the imaginative labor of Natalie and David in their descriptions about the problem and its effects:

> *Therapist:* So, the problem was weighing on you, Natalie, and the hope of possibilities has lifted it off your shoulders. And for you, David, knowing that Natalie wants to work on doing something about it and to reengage in the partnership has unblocked the light at the end of the tunnel you were not able to see before, finding yourself in the darkness instead? Did I get this right?

The most radical way in which Epston and White invoke the literariness of stories in narrative therapy interviews is by adopting a particular aesthetic treatment of language. This treatment shapes the grammatical arrangements of the therapist's inquiries. This is done to provide a context in the therapeutic conversations to rescue alternative, **subjugated stories** out of the obviousness of the context of the problem that could transform couples' lives and relationships. The subjugated stories of interest are those that speak to the couple's fluid identities shaped by values, beliefs, dreams, aspirations, etc. that are important to them, within their particular cultures of origin. This particular aesthetic treatment of language in narrative therapy is widely known as externalization (Epston, 1998) and we will discuss it when considering problem resolution.

Problem Formation: The Problem Internalized

Often, the ways in which couples organize their stories "contribute to the 'survival' of, as well as the 'career' of, the problem" (White & Epston, 1990, p. 3), which result in its internalization, becoming part of their identity in the couple's view (Epston, 1998; Epston & Maisel, 2009; Maisel, Epston, & Borden, 2004; Russell & Carey, 2004; White & Epston, 1990). Hence, Epston and White's work focuses particularly on "the requirements of the problem for its survival and on the effect of those requirements on the lives and relationship of persons" (White & Epston, 1990, p. 3). This is to invite the couple to offer a statement of their position (White, 2007) in relation to the problem as they respond to its requirements and effects in their lives and relationship.

For Epston and White the requirements for the survival of problems, therefore problems themselves, belong to social, political, relational, historical, discursive contexts and not to the person's mental structure; hence, their famous statement that has become the signature of their practice: the problem is the problem not the person. From a poststructuralist perspective, White (2000, 2004) took from the work of Michel Foucault (1984, 1988, 1997) on the history of the fabrication of the human subject and cultural habits of thought within systems of power in modern times. White did so to better understand how the requirements of problems are put in place so that it results in its internalization, hence objectification of the person. Foucault (1961/1965, 1963/1973, 1980) traced some of the developments during the seventeenth century in Europe that led to the objectification of the person or the internalization of problems as the person. Some of these developments were embedded in the growth of the status and prestige of the professions and their endeavors. They are, as White (2004) summarized from Foucault's work: a) dividing practices between the general population and the deviant (homeless, poor, mad, ill), for example, Natalie and David going to therapy under the assumption that there is something wrong with themselves, their partner, or marriage, setting themselves apart from other normal people and couples in their eyes; b) subjectification of people's bodies for classification or diagnosis as internalized disorders—David being considered as a possible cheater, smoker, and alcoholic, and Natalie and David being classified as overweight and their marriage currently asexual, may set the conditions for one or both to fit into some sort of a psychiatric dysfunction; and c) mechanisms of social control by which normalizing standards about life and development are set for people to judge themselves or measure themselves up against others—for example, Natalie and David comparing each other and their marriage against those of heterosexual peers who, in their eyes, they judge as performing normality in terms of their social life, sexuality, fidelity, parenting, etc. Hence, they feel that they are not up to par with other couples who seem to fulfill the expectations represented in the media, or religious views about coupling and sexuality.

The social and cultural standards of normality about coupling are of interest for narrative therapists' cultural analysis of couple's stories. These standards are embedded within contemporary systems of power that are regulated by **cultural discourses**, which are highly influenced and shaped by social institutions such as media, research, religion, professional knowledge, etc. These discourses influence the way in which the couple arranges their stories or the meaning that they attribute to their lives and relationship. They set expectations of being and relating as normality to be performed by couples, directing them on how to be in the world and in relationships to avoid the social implications of doing otherwise. Social expectations of coupling result in the subjugation of any other expressions of relating that would be counter-cultural or social. Discourses that go against social strands of heterosexuality or monogamy, for example, are subjugated as deviants from dominant truths of normality about coupling, and are sanctioned by social isolation, a sense of failure or professional psychiatric diagnosis, among others. For example, in David's situation, the normal expectations from his cultural Christian upbringing (according to his account) were strongly focused on ideas of normality in relation to monogamy and fidelity. He was required to be engaged faithfully in his marriage, as per the requirements of Christianity; hence engaging in an internet affair with a woman other than his wife kept him from fulfilling such expectation. Possibilities of an open marriage or polyamory would not be sanctioned by his Christian beliefs.

Social expectations of normality in relation to coupling, given their cultural contexts, not the therapist's, may leave little room for Natalie and David to draw from their preferred and fluid identities since they have been buried under the prospect of possible social sanctions such as divorce, shame, blame, guilt, inadequacy, isolation, etc.

According to Foucault's (1961/1965, 1963/1973) work on the understanding of how modern systems of power operate, the formation of social expectations that ultimately shape people's lives and relationships is of utmost importance in the participation of people in replicating and maintaining them. Unlike traditional systems of power where there is clearly an identifiable central authority that regulates people's performances to assure that standards and rules remain and are followed (e.g. law, the military system, etc.), in modern systems of power, people serve as mutual regulators and accomplices of the performance of social standards, disciplining one another when considering that the other is not engaging in socially acceptable and normal practices of living. For example, Natalie and David's critical comments to one another in terms of their weight further replicates social expectation of normality within their cultures about how their bodies ought to be shaped to be desirable for the other and accepted within their communities. What the couple deems acceptable is based on highly influential social institutions that, in a manner of speaking, produce cultural expectations of normality. Some examples of these influential institutions are the media, religion, education, etc. It is in the intimacy of their relationship where and when couples participate in the further replication of those social expectations of normality. When the expectations are not met accordingly, the person engages in conclusions of their identity as a failure, being inadequate, deviant, etc.

Foucault's studies mean that the couple can be active participants or consumers of the creation, sustenance, and/or change of such dominant discourses. If they are influential in the life of dominant discourses in the social realm, then they are equally influential in the life and career of the problem in the intimacy of their lives and relationships. For White and Epston (1990), stories of problems and subjugated stories are "history-making" instead of "history-taken" (p. 41). In narrative therapy interviews, therapists facilitate ways in which such dominant discourses are made visible for couples to deliberate about their effects, their responses, and consequently their options for action in relation to what brought them to therapy.

Theory of Problem Resolution: Externalizing Treatment of Language

Reliving, reconstructing, therefore retelling stories that reverse the internalization of social constructs as personal identities that result in the objectification of the couple, takes place through externalizing narrative therapy interviews (White & Epston, 1990). These interviews situate the problem outside the couple's bodies, consciousness, psychology, and relationship, placing it where it belongs: in its social, cultural, and historical contexts. **Externalization** means to de-psychologize or post-psychologize the problem (Mcleod, 2004). By drawing from the rootstock of the couple's skills and knowledges that speak to their fluid identities, meaning to what they give most value to in life, it is possible to story aspects of the couple's lives that contradict the life, career, and requirements of the problem. In Natalie and David's narrative therapy interview, the therapist is interested in inquiring about what they give most value to in their lives and relationships that contradict the values and life of the problem and its effects in terms of infidelity, alcohol, smoking, and divorce. In the next excerpt, the therapist adopted an externalizing treatment to language of a unique outcome in the conversation, "the hope," rather than a problem. This contributed to the couple's discernment of what is important for them in their marriage:

> *Therapist:* … for you David, how is it for you to know that *this hope* takes Natalie to want to do something about the marriage and that it makes a difference for her?

David: Well, it makes me feel that we can finally talk so that we can start thinking about the changes we need to make.

Therapist: And how is this for both of you that you can finally talk, and work
together to do something about the marriage and address mistakes?

David: It is very important for me. It feels that I am back to working with a
partner in the marriage.

Natalie: Yes, it feels that we are in partnership again.

Therapist: How come it is important for both to have a sense of partnership in
your marriage?

In the interview, the therapist would be interested in setting up a context, through
the means of questions that externalize the problem, to reveal the socio-historical
context of their problem given their cultural heritage. The way in which externalization features in narrative therapy interviews is through a play of language
or a particular treatment of language that conveys this theoretical stance. In an
interview with Lesley Allen, White (1995) commented:

> I think that the main point about externalizing conversation is that it intro-
> duces a different way of speaking about, and a different way of thinking
> about, that which is problematic—and, of course, a different way of acting
> in relation to that which is problematic. There are ways of speaking, thinking
> and acting that are at odds with the ways of speaking, thinking and acting
> that are associated with the internalizing discourses. In promoting these
> externalizing conversations, we are engaged in an activity that is not entirely
> a pro-cultural activity.
>
> *(p. 41)*

White (2005) proposed that objectifying the problem, personifying it or situating it as an idea or a person's sense, making of it an external entity, challenges the
taken-for-grantedness of some cultural ways of speaking about couples' lives and
relationships in internalizing terms.

The literary perspective of stories, previously discussed, holds a critical role in
externalizing interviews for the therapist to adopt what could be considered an
uncommon and playful use of language in their inquiries when interviewing the
couple. By speaking about the problem in externalizing uncommon and playful
ways, the language of the problem becomes unfamiliar, consequently creating an
opportunity for the couple to reengage with words that better describe what
matters to them. For example, in the uncommon playful use of language often
adopted in Epston and White's work, it is possible for encopresis to speak, to be
sneaky and to run people's lives (White, 1984); for dead people to say hullo again
in their state of biological finality to bring with them their teachings (White,
1998); and for dogs to police terrifying fears in the middle of young people's

nights (Epston, 2004). Epston and White's language treatment includes a particular literary approach to stories for this to be possible.

Epston and White's treatment of language is rather subtle yet revolutionary and transgressive with radical implications; it is "playful, lightheaded and joyful" (White, 2007, p. 24). It gently inserts a gap between the couple and the problem. It also introduces a treatment of language that characterizes the problem in ways that reveal its tricks and treats when recruiting the couple into its truthful, universal, and normalizing ways. The aesthetics of their treatment of language as externalization makes explicit the construction of a relationship between the person and the problem that was only potentially or virtually implicit at first within the couple's accounts (Carey, Walther, & Russell, 2009; White, 2000). This is demonstrated in the following dialogue with the couple:

> *Therapist:* So, now that you are experiencing that the weight of the problem was lifted off your shoulders by the hope, Natalie, maybe no longer feeling its pressure on your back, legs, and knees. And you can see the light at the end of the tunnel, no longer being in the dark, David; what does feeling lighter in your body, no longer feeling the pressure of the weight of the problem doing to you, Natalie? And what does seeing the light at the end of the tunnel allow you to do in that tunnel, David? Perhaps I am thinking about these developments considering the idea of giving your marriage a last chance in partnership.
>
> *David:* I can see a future with Natalie and I don't feel alone. I feel that I have a partner back. The light is pointing at a future with Natalie and she is waiting for me at the end of the tunnel so that we can move forward with the marriage.
>
> *Natalie:* Yes, I feel that I can do something about our marriage and work together with David. I feel that David sees me now after having ignored me for so long. I think he hasn't seen me in a long time. Also I like that he wants to walk towards me to get out of that tunnel he has been in lately, so that we can meet and be together. I feel lighter.

The aesthetic treatment to language in narrative interviews via externalization requires what White called **double listening** (White, 2003) or what we have considered a *bilingual ear* to listen to the language of the identity of the problem and the language of the preferred fluid identity of the formerly subjugated couple, to open up a relationship out of a seemingly single, internalized, or monolingual account. Other narrative therapy authors have called this particular externalizing language treatment: *a novel form of speech* (Pare & Lysack, 2004), *a linguistic shift* (Freedman & Combs, 1996), and a *new manner of speaking* (Maisel et al., 2004).

An uncommon, externalizing treatment of language in narrative interviews inserts a gap through a counter-cultural way of speaking about the problem that tends to erase context and relationships, removing the experience from what

White (2005) considered to be the politics of local relationships. This makes it possible for Natalie and David to be no longer stuck in truths or single expectations about how their identities and relationship should be, and the consequently negative conclusions about one another while attempting to achieve it unsuccessfully. These are restricting truths that lock their marriage into deterministic intrinsic qualities about each other's failures (e.g. cheater, alcoholic, overweight, smoker, asexual, etc.), resulting in their considerations of divorce. Thereby, externalization exposes the politics of the experience of the couple's problems (White, 2007). It includes a critical intentionality that is often missed:

> ... it is never a matter of whether or not we bring politics into the therapy room, but whether or not we are prepared to acknowledge the existence of these politics, and the degree to which we are prepared to be complicit in the reproduction of these politics.
>
> *(White, 2011, p. 49)*

By opening a space between the couple and the problem, situating the problem into its corresponding discursive, cultural, and socio-historical contexts, externalization opens opportunities for the couple's initiatives to be expressed. The couple has the opportunity to explore other coupling options that may contribute to arriving at conclusions about their identities that are more in tune with what they hold important and valuable in their lives and relationship (White, 2007). Externalizing conversations set up a context in the interview for other purposes and values than the ones of the identity of the problem, to become more richly known, for the history of the purposes and values of the couple to be discussed, and for the couple to engage in practical options for action that are in harmony with these purposes and values. This is made available by offering the opportunity for the couple to scrutinize the problem, rather than the problem scrutinizing the couple, and to evaluate its effects. The gaze is re-focused onto the life and career of the problem and the cultural and historical practices of normality and objectification from systems of power that are likely implicated in it. Couples can retell ideas of their preferred identities in tandem with possibilities that are now available to take action in response to the effects of the problem in their lives. White (2007) considered this as one of the primary tasks of narrative therapy work; to assist people to derive alternative meanings in order to create the conditions for couples to reinterpret their lives. He explained further:

> If we can play some part in assisting... people to break their lives from those very negative personal stories that have such a profound effect on shaping the expression of their experience, and if we can help them to step into some other more positive account of who they might be as a person, then it will become possible for them to actively engage in the reinterpretation of the [problem]... that they were subject to. And this reinterpretation will

change the shape of the expression of people's experiences... and therefore shape of their lives.

(White, 1995, pp. 83–84)

For White and Epston, externalizing interviews challenge psychological notions of the self that seem contained within the boundaries of the person's skull and skin. Instead, they call attention to the social, cultural, relational, and historical constitution of fluid identities of the person as a moral agent—a person with a sense of commitment or ethical obligation toward life and relationships according to aspirations that are held valuable and important to them in carrying out in their lives.[3] A narrative therapist draws from what the couple give importance to and want to manage well in their lives, holding a moral obligation to do so. By couples holding on to what they deem important as a moral responsibility, they are shaping their lives and relationships in their everyday lives as a consequence; led by their aspirations, beliefs, dreams, hopes, for their lives and relationships that shape their fluid identities.

Therapy Process: Transformative and Sustainable Story Development

The development of stories in narrative therapy interviews is of critical importance in the therapy process, considering who the couple is and what they do are influenced by the stories that they tell about their worldviews, relationships, lives, and identities. By adopting an externalizing treatment to language, the therapist sets up a context in the interview to create points of entrance into the development of the couple's stories that will capture more positive conclusions of identity in relation to what they aspire to in life and hold as valuable and important.

The development of couple's stories is assisted in many different ways, particularly by the therapist's questions. The therapist seeks to ask questions to facilitate the development of the couple's stories that become transformative for them, meaning that the stories make a difference in how the couple decides to address the problems of their lives and thereby sustaining them through the effects of the problem. This process may vary across different narrative practices in many different cultures. Here, we are focusing on White's (2007) therapeutic process informed by the metaphor of maps. White looked at maps as a metaphor of his work as a guide to engage in an exploratory journey of neglected aspects of the territories of the couple's life under the influence of the problem. He acknowledged, however, that the use of maps is not at all necessary in the therapy process given that it is a metaphor that may not fit for some narrative therapists, in which case the development or translation of the maps metaphor into other exploratory metaphors would be required.

The metaphor of maps refers to guides of multiple paths that interviews can take, influenced by the therapist inquiries that contribute to the development of the couple's transformative and sustainable stories which were unknown and unpredictable at the beginning of the exploration. White proposed a series of maps of lines of inquiry. One of these maps in particular seeks to assist therapists to navigate through externalizing conversations: **Statement of Position Map I** (White, 2007). This map includes four lines of inquiry: 1) the name of, or the ways to, characterize the problem by Natalie and David: "Natalie and David, how would you describe the problem that ultimately brought you here today so that you could bring me up to speed?" "If you were to give this name a proper name to better capture the life it has had in your lives, what name would that be?"; 2) the effects the couple identify the problem has had on their lives and marriage: "Would you mind telling me a bit about the ways in which the problem [its name] has effected your lives and marriage?" "How it has been for you to live with this problem?"; 3) their statement of the position they are taking in relation to the effects that the problem is having on them and their relationship, meaning their evaluation of the effects: "Although I could speculate how it has been for both of you to experience these effects in your lives and relationship as a result of living with the problem, I am very interested in hearing from you about how it has been. Has it been positive, negative, neither or something else?" This level of inquiry draws from an assumption that couples are not passive recipients of suffering, no matter how paralyzing it may feel (Denborough, 2008; White, 2003, 2011). Hence, the effects of the problem call necessarily for a position or response, whatever this may be, in protecting that which the problem affected and the couple judged as important and valuable enough for them to act upon. 4) The justification that the couple offers to support why they judged the former valuable and important. It consists of an inquiry about the couple's foundations of their former statement in relation to what they hold most important in their lives, which they were able to discern through the effects of the problem in their lives: "Would you mind speaking about how you make sense of how you have judged the effects of the problem in your lives? What does this say about what is important to you?"

Interviews do not necessarily follow these levels of inquiries in a certain order and timeframe. They may take different directions that are unpredictable as they depend on the contributions of each conversational partner; and each contribution depends on the unique direction each interview takes. This is illustrated in the disorderly ways in which these lines of inquiry take place in the transcript below. Having said that, often the last level of inquiry of the **Statement of Position Map II** leads to the adoption of White's re-authoring map. This is to assist the couple in the rich storytelling within a historical and relational context on that which the couple gives importance in their life both from a remote history toward a remote future, zigzagging between a landscape of action and identity, as discussed above: "You have shared with me what is important to both of you in your relationship and lives, which have been affected by the actions of the problem [name] in your life. Can you tell me a story of when was it when you first became aware that this value was important to you in your life and who do you remember lent a hand in this development?"

For White (2007), by substituting an internalized version of the problem for an externalized version, people start coming together to address the effects of the problem in community. Recruiting the couple's allies, or significant relationships in their lives that are supportive of initiatives that counteract the life of the problems in Natalie and David's lives, is of significant importance.

Other implications of externalization include rendering opportunities to take responsibility (White, 2011) for the effects of the problem as well as for the person to be influential in the problem. It invites the couple's personal agency in the fashioning of their own lives, being able to draw from the skills of living to intervene in the effects of the problem, according to their preferred intentions and aspirations. Unlike some misinterpretations of externalizing conversations to free the person from responsibility, responsibility is rather taken up not as a word but as a concept (White, 2011), in terms of accountability, or answerability (Emerson, 1983; Morson & Emerson, 1990).

White (2011) clarified, however, that it is not externalization in itself that makes this possible but the effects of externalizing conversations by inviting the couple's actions into a relationship with their consequences so they reflect upon them in order to extract from them new learnings about their coupling lives.

> *Therapist:* … I recall that at the beginning of the conversation you exchanged some ideas among yourselves about cheating, messing around, attributing blame, and making mistakes. So, how do you think what we spoke about today will be of use, or not, in addressing those concerns? I am thinking about how the hope, love, wanting to give the marriage a chance in partnership, not giving up, wanting to do something, and feeling visible to the other may help you address these concerns?
>
> *David:* Well, I know that I hurt Natalie and that was not my intention, as hard as it may be to believe. I made a stupid mistake and want to fix it. I don't want to lose Natalie. All these things that we have been talking about I hope help us to be able to sit down and talk. I owe Natalie an apology for what I did. I grew up in a Christian household and what I did goes against my values. I lost sight of things.
>
> *Therapist:* Did you get lost in the darkness of the tunnel and lose your Christian values in it?
>
> *David:* Yes, definitely!
>
> *Therapist:* But I understand that now you can see the light and see Natalie under the spotlight as a partner who you have always loved. So what does this mean in terms of undoing the hurt that you said you caused Natalie, and that Natalie and the hope themselves have reminded you about since you acted against your Christian values?
>
> *David:* I have to work toward getting Natalie's forgiveness.

Externalizing conversations highlight that there are always aspects of lived experiences not fully captured by a narrative (Bruner, 1986), which become potential material for the unfolding of the performance of alternative, subjugated, or counter-narratives (Freedman & Combs, 1996; Morgan, 2000; White & Epston, 1990). This potential material is known in the narrative therapy literature as **unique outcomes**. White and Epston (1990) borrowed this term from Goffman, who wrote about the ways in which experiences are structured. Goffman (1961) considered that in "… any social strand [or dominant story] of any person's course of life… unique outcomes are neglected in favor of such changes over time as are basic and common to members of a social category although occurring independently to each of them" (p. 137).

In practice, narrative therapists pay close attention to the gaps in people's stories that free up space for the rich story development of what White (2007) called **subordinate storylines** of people's lives, or also, alternative or **counter stories**. Unique outcomes are often overlooked under the effects of the dominance of the narrative of the story, turning significant events in the couple's lives silent. They contrast existing deficit-focused conclusions that are associated with the dominant storylines that have been limiting the couple's lives (White, 2007). They help guide the therapist in supporting people to derive new conclusions about their lives and relationships. While the conversation can heavily lean on the description of the problems that affect couples' lives, the therapist maintains a keen ear for openings for unique outcomes that serve as avenues to explore other coupling territories:

> *Therapist:* So, thus far I have heard Natalie use the word cheating, which David described instead as "messing around." Also, David, you mentioned the idea of attributing blame. But, as Natalie said when she called to set up an appointment, you are both in agreement that you want to give your marriage one last chance. Is a last chance something you are interested in talking about today in spite of the ideas you have shared so far about blame, messing around, or cheating?

White's Statement of Position Map I serves as a scaffold for the therapist to guide conversations for the development of rich stories of literary merit. They include the same four levels of inquiry of the Statement of Position Map II but focus on the unique outcome rather than the problem. They include the name of the unique outcome, its effects, the couple's statement of their evaluation of the effects, and the justification of their evaluation.

Narrative Therapist as Decentered but Influential Co-Researching Position

When engaging narrative therapeutic interviews to unveil the negative effects of the problem in a couple's life and relationship, drawing from the couple as moral agents, White (2005, 2011) situated the role of the therapist in a decentered but influential position. In essence, therapists are foreigners in the territories of the couple's domestic lives and relationship, hence, they need to be educated about them. Narrative therapists are like inquisitive foreigners. As foreigners, therapists are decentered from the authorship of the couple's territories of life and relationships. Therefore, they need to work behind or alongside the couple so as to not specify for them how their lives should be, but rather be caught up in the couple's views (White, 1995). White (2011) considered that a **decentered therapist** privileges the larger world of life over the local world of therapy. He found imperative:

> … the development of therapeutic practices that decenter the voice of the therapist. Practices that decenter the voice of the therapist have the effect of bringing to the center of the therapeutic endeavor some of the 'knowledges' of life and skills of living of the people who consult therapists. These are often knoweldges and skills that are not very visible at the outset of therapeutic consultations.
>
> *(White, 2011, p. 3)*

The curiosity of the decentered therapist is not naïve but clearly intentional and shapes the ways in which they listen to the couple's stories (Hibel & Polanco, 2010). It carries a political consciousness that plays out in the externalizing treatment of language to support the development of rich stories of literary merit. This intentionality makes narrative therapists influential in the ways in which the territory of the couple is explored and shaped along with them. For narrative therapists, "personal and community ethics […] emphasize our responsibility for the consequences of what we say and do in the name of therapeutic practice" (White, 2011, p. 40). White (2000) considered this notion:

> We're certainly playing a part that is directive in terms of what gets taken up, from these conversations, for further explorations… But that is not to say that we are directing things in the sense that we are authoring the actual accounts of people's lives that are expressed in these conversations.
>
> *(p. 98)*

This sort of decentered but influential co-exploration has also been articulated by Epston (1999) as one of "**co-research**." The co-explorations or co-researches, unfolding through the influential and responsible posture of a decentered but influential therapist, allow for respect towards the particular storytellings of the couples' statements of their positions about their problem, hence, their values, dreams, aspirations, beliefs, or fluid identities. The therapist holds no expert knowledge on how couples should perform in their relationship. In narrative therapy interviews, the therapist takes this posture to consult with the couple throughout the process on their preferred paths of exploration in the conversation, in accordance with what they hope for or is of interest to them:

> *Therapist:* … if you don't mind me, I would like to interrupt briefly to consult with both of you on something at this point. Since at the time of calling to set an appointment, Natalie, you said that you wanted to give your relationship one last chance and that David was on board with that perspective. I wanted to consult with both of you if you get the sense that the exchange of ideas up until this point feels promising to continue in the direction you had hoped in coming here? Is this how you envisioned exploring the option of giving your marriage one last chance? It may be too soon to tell, so you can continue if you wish to see what it brings to both of you; unless you have tried something similar with no results. Knowing this will help me know what to do. I would be glad to step back for a moment so that you can continue and see where this takes you.

An influential but decentered co-researching position facilitates the development of a relationship between the therapist and couple as one of solidarity, in which the therapist is an interested ethnographer. In White's (1993) terms:

> And what of solidarity? I am thinking of a solidarity that is constructed by a therapist who refuses to draw a sharp distinction between their lives and the lives of others, who refuses to marginalize those persons who seek help, by therapists who are constantly confronting the fact that if faced with the circumstances such that provide the context of troubles of others, they just might not be doing nearly as well themselves.
>
> *(p. 132)*

In solidarity, a narrative therapist assumes a position of humility, holding on to their understandings about cultural systems of power while surrendering all pretenses of knowledge, understanding, and clarity of the worldviews of couples and how they name, discern, experience, respond, and hence story these systems in their lives.

Discontinuing the Interviews

Narrative therapy interviews unfold in unpredictable ways. Since the outset, interviews are unpredictable in terms of where they are going to take the couple and the therapist in their exploratory journey of inquiries and storytellings and when they are going to arrive at unimaginable destinations. This is due to the nature of the development of a story. The continuation or discontinuation of the process then is a decision that is made along the way and it highly depends on the couple. Through the course of each interview and when the interview comes to an end, the therapist checks in with the couple about how the process is going for them in relation to what they had hoped for when deciding to come to therapy. For Natalie and David, the therapist checks in with both on how things are developing in relation to their intention to come to therapy to give their marriage one last chance. The therapist consults with them about how they judge the development of the process and if they consider that scheduling a further appointment makes sense to them or if they think they can continue with giving their marriage a chance out of the context of the therapy.

It is not uncommon that couples rely on the therapist for such a determination instead of deciding for themselves, thinking that the therapist "knows best." In those circumstances, among other options, the therapist provides a summary of what he or she has learned from the couple's skills and knowledge in addressing the problem, emphasizing how this has developed through each one of the interviews, or the interview if it is only one session. In doing so, the therapist serves as a reflecting surface for the couple so that they can witness themselves through the reflection of the therapist, engaging with what they have achieved through the process. On the basis of that information, they could proceed to determine if they have an interest in scheduling another appointment or not. Different couples judge when to end therapy using different criteria. It is possible that the couple continues enduring the effects of the problem in their lives upon termination, but feel that through the interviews their skills and knowledge to address the problem have been made more tangible and accessible to them. Hence, therapy is no longer needed and they can continue with the work themselves and with the support of significant relationships in their lives.

Natalie and David

Natalie and David came in for a first session. Over the phone when Natalie called to set up the appointment, the therapist learned that they were coming to therapy to give the relationship one last chance before they contacted divorce lawyers. Natalie clarified that this was a shared decision and that her partner, David, was very well aware of this and would not mind the therapist sharing her description with him. For a narrative therapist it is important to determine the authorship of perspectives shared and those who have had access to them.

> *Therapist:* It is good to meet you both. Before we start, I want to bring you up to speed quickly on a few things about how I work. Through our conversations I will be asking many, many questions. They come from a place of having no single clue about your lives. Some questions will be for us to figure things out together and others for me to better learn about your circumstances. Some questions may sound a bit strange to you, so if that is the case let me know so that I can lend you a hand with the question if you find

interest in addressing it. If you have any questions for me at any time, please feel free to ask. Any questions?

Natalie: No, that is helpful thank you.

David: I am good.

Therapist: So, before we start I want to bring you up to speed about what I know about you from when you, Natalie, called to set up an appointment. I know that you are here to give the relationship one last chance before you go ahead and contact divorce lawyers. And I know that David shares this perspective. So, where do you think it would be a good place for us to start to make the best use of our time together today?

> *The therapist provides a context in preparation for the possible uncommon external-izing treatment of language that is countercultural to the ways in which the problem may have been spoken about by the couple. The therapist also highlights the process of the interview by means of asking questions. Transparency on what the therapist knows about the couple—either by the account of the partner who called to set up an appointment or by a referral source—plays out here as well with purposes of involving everybody's input in the process openly.*

Natalie: Well, I really don't know where would be a good place to start but to say that I think that we are here because I want to keep our marriage together.

David: Jesus, Natalie, you told me this morning that you had changed your mind and now you were ready for a divorce and we were coming to therapy to finish things off smoothly. This is bullshit!

Natalie: Well, if we don't work things out, yes, I am ready for a divorce. I can't do this anymore. Since you're the reason we're here anyway, why don't you go first then?

David: Do you see what I am talking about? (*looking at the therapist*)

Therapist: I am unsure that I see what you are pointing out, David? Could you give me a hand so that I can better understand what you would like me to see?

David: This! This crap about throwing the blame on me.

Natalie: You are the one to blame! You cheated on me, not the other way around.

David: I wouldn't call it cheating.

Natalie: What would you call it then? What would you call having sex online with another woman as a married man?

David: I told you I was just messing around. It was nothing serious.

Therapist: (*Interrupts*) Excuse me, if I come across as a bit rude here but if you don't mind me, I would like to interrupt briefly to consult with both of you on something at this point. At the time of calling to set an appointment, Natalie, you said that you wanted to give your relationship one last chance and that David was on board with that perspective. I wanted to consult with both of you if you get the sense that the exchange of ideas up until this point feels promising to continue in the direction you had hoped in coming here? Is this how you envisioned exploring the option of giving your marriage one last chance? It may be too soon to tell, so you can continue if you wish to see what it brings to both of you; unless you have tried something similar with no results. Knowing this will help me know what to do. I would be glad to step back for a moment so that you can continue and see where this takes you.

David: No, no, no. We need you here. We have gone around this many times and end up nowhere.

Therapist: How about for you, Natalie?

Natalie: He doesn't want to come clean and I want to know the truth. How can we move forward if he keeps lying?

Therapist: Then would you like to continue this conversation with David so that you can get to the truth of things?

Natalie: No, obviously I have not gotten to him. We need to do something different which is the reason why we are here.

> *The therapist consults with the couple (Epston & White, 1990) about the direction of the interview. It would be easy for the therapist to assume that this point of the conversation is not working for the couple but instead leaves it to the couple to make that judgment for themselves so decisions can be made on how to proceed according to what they hope for the meeting. Also, the therapist is sustaining the couple's hopes for a last chance at the forefront, as a possible opening for a unique outcome in the interview.*

Therapist: Great. Well, since you want to do something different, maybe by inviting me into this conversation is one way in which you have started to do something different, and, so, I would like to ask you some questions to see where this will take us. What do you think?

Natalie: Yes, of course.

David: Go ahead.

Therapist: So, thus far I have heard Natalie use the word cheating, which David described instead as "messing around." Also, David, you mentioned the idea of attributing blame. But, as Natalie said when she called to set up an appointment, you both are in agreement that you want to give your marriage one last chance. Is a last chance something you are interested in talking about today in spite of the ideas you have shared so far about blame, messing around, or cheating?

> *The therapist acknowledges the account the couple has offered about the problem while highlighting the unique outcome of giving the marriage a chance, consulting the couple on the direction they prefer to take in the conversation.*

Natalie: Yes, yes, of course.

David: Well, I am fed up with it. I don't know that it is possible for the marriage to have a last chance at this point.

Therapist: Well, David, since you don't know that this is possible or not at this time, do you want to know? Are you interested in us talking about it to see if that helps you know if it is an option or not at this time before calling a divorce lawyer?

David: Well, we are here so we might as well.

Therapist: Well, great, in that case, I am certainly interested and intrigued to learn more about the developments that led both of you to consider this as a possible option for your marriage at this time. Would you mind catching me up about what you mean by giving your marriage one last chance, even if at this point you no longer know if it is still a possibility (*looking at David*)?

The therapist is engaging in the characterization of the unique outcome, drawing from White's (2007) Statement of Position Map II. Giving the marriage one last chance is located by the therapist as a unique result of their experiences in their marriage that seem to go against the grain of the problem of cheating, messing around, and attributing blame.

Natalie: Well, let me tell you what happened so that you understand better. Six months ago, I found out that David was having an internet affair. I found his messages to a woman named Devyn, including conversations about divorcing me, so he could be with her. He denied it until I made him open his email. He thought I was so stupid I was never going to find out but I caught him. I was heartbroken, of course.

David: I am just not going to say anything at this point because I don't know how to make her understand that I was just saying that to keep Devyn interested and didn't have any intention to divorce.

Therapist: I see. So am I right in thinking that these are the events that led your marriage to be at a place that only one last chance is left for it?

Natalie: Yes, of course. If we don't do anything I doubt I will continue in the marriage.

David: We have had problems long before I met that woman on the internet so all of that together made me consider recently that divorce is an option.

Therapist: So, would you mind speaking about what would be involved in the process of giving a last chance to your marriage for each one of you?

The therapist is interested in the meaning of the unique outcome as well as what this meaning means in terms of actions by each one, following Bruner's understanding of the two landscapes included in a story, one of meaning and another of action.

Natalie: I am not sure about David, but I am not ready to give up completely, so it involves not giving up.

David: Well, we continue talking about things needing to change, but we don't do anything about it, but I know things do need to change.

Therapist: So, not giving up completely on the marriage and a call for needing to do something to change is what giving a chance to the marriage means in terms of what you would do?

Natalie: Yes, not giving up and doing something about it.

David: We just don't know how.

Therapists: I see. So, I understand so far that you decided to come to therapy based on the knowledge of other options than calling the divorce lawyer. This is the knowledge of you not giving up completely on the marriage (*looking at Natalie*), and you knowing things need to change (*looking at David*), or something needs to be done about "it." Did I get you right?

David: Yes, if we don't do something about it, I don't think this marriage is going anywhere.

Natalie: Yes, you are correct.

Therapist: Good. So is that knowledge that you both have of not giving up and knowing you need to do something about it a recent idea?

> *The therapist is inquiring about the history of this development in the couple's life, hoping to enrich the development of the story about not giving up, aspiring to construct this story as one that is transformative and sustainable for the couple.*

David: Well, I honestly didn't know that Natalie did not want to give up on the marriage. When we talk, I always get something different. I get that she wants to leave me.

Therapist: So, how is it to hear that Natalie does not want to give up completely?

David: Well, it makes me feel hopeful. I feel that we will be able to do something, which I haven't heard in quite a while.

Therapists: Can you say a bit more about this hope, David? I am curious about it. Are you curious as well, Natalie? Are you interested in hearing about David's hope?

Natalie: Yes, yes of course. I also have not heard David talk about hope before.

Therapist: David, do you want to bring us up to speed about this hope? What does this hope look like for you?

> *The therapist is engaging an externalizing treatment of language to speak about hope in relation to David. David initially located hope as a personal quality as in "I am hopeful." The therapist inserted a gap, linguistically, between the hope that may look like something, and David.*

David: Well, this hope always reminds me that I made a mistake with Natalie, like she does, and that I have to do something about it. Natalie always wants to remind me about it and talks to me in a way that makes me consider that she is tired of this marriage and wants a divorce so there is no point in me trying to do something. I understand her. If she says that she is not ready to give up, however, this means to me that the marriage still means something to her and she is willing to work things out. This is the message of this hope for me. It looks like possibilities to fix things.

Natalie: Of course it means something to me, David. Things have been hard during the last six months. I cannot pretend that you did nothing.

David: Well, I understand that. I get the sense sometimes that you are giving up and are not giving options to do something about it. That makes sense. But if we are going to work, I can't do this alone.

Natalie: I know and I am not saying you have to.

Therapist: So, how is it for you to know of this hope that looks like possibilities and that is making David want to do something about his mistake, Natalie?

> *The therapist continues an externalizing treatment of language by giving the hope intention, leading David to wanting to engage in actions. The therapist in inquiring about the effects that the hope has for both.*

Natalie: Well, it makes me want to work with him about all the problems we have had in the marriage. This really makes a difference to me.

Therapist: And, for you David, how is it for you to know that this hope makes Natalie want to do something about the marriage and that it makes a difference for her?

David: Well, it makes me feel that we can finally talk so that we can start thinking about changes we need to make.

Therapist: And how is this for both of you that you can finally talk, and work together to do something about the marriage and address mistakes?

> *The therapist is inviting the couple to evaluate the effects of the hope in their marriage.*

David: It is very important for me. It feels that I am back to working with a partner in the marriage.

Natalie: Yes, it feels that we are in partnership again.

Therapist: How come it is important for both to have a sense of partnership in your marriage?

> *The therapist is inviting the couple to provide a justification to the value they have identified by evaluating the effects of the hope in their lives.*

Natalie: That is what defined our marriage before. Our friends and relatives always admired us by the way in which we got along as truly partners.

David: Yes, I miss that.

Therapist: So, is reconnecting to the partnership related to giving the marriage one last chance?

David: Definitely.

Natalie: Yes, yes, of course.

Therapist: So, I have learned from you that both have been able to hold on to this knowledge about your marriage as one that is not to be given up completely, even when heartbroken, as you said earlier Natalie, and that there is hope that looks like possibilities and leads David to want to fix mistakes and lead both to want to do something about it, which may involve reconnecting to a sense of partnership? So, how is it for you to speak about these ideas? How is this going for you?

> *The therapist could have also followed a line of inquiry at this point to include the contributions of friends and relatives to further learn about the sense of partnership from their vantage point.*

Natalie: Well, I feel a weight has lifted off my shoulders.

Therapist: And for you, David?

David: Yes, I see the light at the end of the tunnel.

Therapist: So, the problem was weighing on you, Natalie, and the hope of possibilities has lifted it off your shoulders. And for you, David, knowing that Natalie wants to work on doing something about it and to reengage in the partnership has unblocked the light at the end of the tunnel you were not able to see before finding yourself in the darkness instead? Did I get this right?

> *The therapist is playing off the couple's language, drawing out as much as possible the expressions they used to characterize their experiences in relation to the effects of the ideas discussed on the problem.*

(*Both agree*)

Therapist: So, now that you are experiencing that the weight of the problem was lifted off your shoulders by the hope, Natalie, maybe no longer feeling its pressure on your back, legs, and knees. And you can see the light at the end of the tunnel, no longer being in the dark, David; what does feeling lighter in your body, no longer feeling the pressure of the weight of the problem, doing to you, Natalie? And what does seeing the light at the end of the tunnel allow you to do in that tunnel, David? Perhaps I am thinking about these developments considering the idea of giving your marriage a last chance in partnership.

David: I can see a future with Natalie and I don't feel alone, I feel that I have a partner back. The light is pointing at a future with Natalie and she is waiting for me at the end of the tunnel so that we can move forward with the marriage.

Natalie: Yes, I feel that I can do something about our marriage and work together with David. I feel that David sees me now after having ignored me for so long. I think he hasn't seen me in a long time. Also I like that he wants to walk towards me to get out of that tunnel he has been in lately, so that we can meet and be together. I feel lighter. I wish I could shed the extra weight I have this way as well, sitting down talking to you and losing weight. Wouldn't that be great?

(laughs)

David: I would be coming here regularly instead of going to the gym.

Therapist: Ah! You would be surprised to know about the power of words, and their effects on people's lives, bodies, or relationships, starving the problem to death for people to be in good shape to move forward with their lives out of their tunnels, finding partners along the way *(laughs)*!! Let me check with you here to make sure that we are talking about things that you were hoping to discuss?

Natalie: Yes, this is going great.

David: Yes, I agree.

Therapist: Good. Well, David, earlier you said that you did not know that giving a last chance to the marriage was an option now. Do you know now if it is a possibility or not? I am curious if throughout the course of our conversation up until this point, you found some knowledge about it.

David: Yes, of course. I know it is possible. I want to work on the marriage and give it a chance. I know we love each other; otherwise we would not have been here after all that has happened within the last six months.

Therapist: So, are you connecting to the love that you have for one another, David?

David: Yes, it has always been there. I know I don't show it to Natalie.

Therapist: What is it like for you to have this connection with the love to Natalie and speak to it, making it visible during this conversation?

David: Well, loving Natalie is what at the end of the day keeps me in the marriage. I want her to know this. I want her to know that I do love her. I always have. I admire Natalie as a person.

Therapist: Natalie, I am curious to know how are you hearing David's words about love and admiration toward you?

Natalie: I had doubts that he still loved me.

Therapist: Would you mind speaking about what David's words are doing to your doubts?

Natalie: I want to believe.

Therapists: I see. So, I have learned through our conversation today that you came with the knowledge that you, Natalie, were not ready to give up completely, and David knew that something needed to be done differently. When learning about each other's knowledge, hope came to play in this conversation, lifting the weight of the problem off Natalie's shoulders for her to feel lighter and feel that she can move to do something about the marriage. For you, David, the hope brought light into a dark tunnel, seeing now that Natalie is standing under the spotlight at the end of this tunnel; which consequently made Natalie become visible to you again, David. David, you were able to connect to the love that has kept both of you together, in partnership, which, as you said, Natalie, the love has been something about which you have had doubts but now you want to believe in. Did I get the picture here?

Natalie: Wow, you have a good memory.

(laughs)

David: Yes, you got the picture.

Therapist: Well, my memory has been playing nicely today. It is not always the case! So, if my memory continues to play nicely, I recall that at the beginning of the conversation you exchanged some ideas between yourselves about cheating, messing around, attributing blame, and making mistakes. So, how do you think that what we spoke about today will be of use, or not, in addressing those concerns? I am thinking about how the hope, love, wanting to give the marriage a chance in partnership, not giving up, wanting to do something, and feeling visible to the other may help you address these concerns?

David: Well, I know that I hurt Natalie and that was not my intention, as hard as it may be to believe. I made a stupid mistake and want to fix it. I don't want to lose Natalie. All these things that we have been talking about I hope help us to be able to sit down and talk. I owe Natalie an apology for what I did. I grew up in a Christian household and what I did goes against my values. I lost sight of things.

Therapist: Did you get lost in the darkness of the tunnel and lose your Christian values in it?

David: Yes, definitely!

Therapist: But I understand that now you can see the light and see Natalie under the spotlight as a partner who you have always loved. So what does this mean in terms of undoing the hurt that you said you caused Natalie and that Natalie and the hope themselves have reminded you about since you acted against your Christian values?

David: I have to work toward getting Natalie's forgiveness.

Therapist: Natalie, does forgiveness fit with the hope of working together with David, feeling visible to him, while you give the marriage a last chance?

Natalie: Yes. I have been waiting for those words for the last six months.

Therapist: Ah! Was it worth the wait?

Natalie: Of course.

Therapist: Well, given that the time that we had available for our conversation today has come to an end, I want to consult with you about how it was for both of you to have this conversation?

Natalie: I feel that we finally talked and listened to one another. I don't want to give up and want to hear what David wants to say. I am willing to forgive and want to know what it is that I am forgiving David for.

David: Yes, I agree that today was helpful to talk. I don't want to lose sight again of my love for Natalie, my values, and my desire to continue in the marriage. Talking here helped me with this.

Therapist: Well, do you feel that you are at a good place to continue to talk on your own, in partnership, to explore ways to give your marriage a chance? Or do you want to continue this talk here among the three of us for a bit longer? What are your thoughts, and please know that I would be delighted to support either option, or additional ones you consider that make sense to you and your hopes at this time.

Natalie: I definitely want to come back to make sure that we continue on this track for a little bit before moving forward just the two of us.

David: Yes, I think that is a very good idea.

Therapist: That makes a lot of sense to me. I am very interested in hearing about how the knowledge that you hold now about yourselves and your partnership will have an impact in your everyday lives in the next few days. So, what timeframe do you have in mind for a next meeting?

David: If you have time next week, right (*looking at Natalie*)?

Natalie: That would be great.

In a following session the therapist would begin with the summary of the development of the previous conversation for purposes of continuity. The therapist would check with the couple where those developments took them in the days that followed. The therapist would check with Natalie and David if they are still interested in exploring options to remain connected with the hope and love, and David's desire to ask for forgiveness, consulting with them if any of those threads would be in their interest to continue to talk about that day, or if new developments transpired in between meetings that they considered more important to discuss. The therapist will continue consulting on an ongoing basis the impacts of the developments of the session in their everyday lives, and to consult with the couple on the most appropriate time to discontinue meeting.

Notes

1   The use of lower case is intentional and preferred.
2   Various non-standard pronouns have been developed with purposes to include people who do not subscribe to the gender binary he/she. For the purposes of this chapter, we choose the pronoun "hir" to include non-conforming binary gender positions of identity.
3   Foucault wrote about four elements of the constitution of an ethical self as a moral agent, which were influential on White's work, particularly on his work on conversations about failure. The ethical substance—the life events whose main relevance lies on the ethical judgment as whatever we take on as what we want to manage well in our lives; the mode of subjectification—moral obligations and efforts in managing

the ethical substances well; asceticism—self-forming activities as obliged techniques of practices for the formation of relationships; and telos—the mode or kind of being shaped by aspirations that the person has for his or her identity project of a life that is a work of art.

References

Beels, C. C. (2001). *A different story: The rise of the narrative in psychotherapy*. Phoenix, AZ: Zeig, Tucker & Theisen, Inc.

Bruner, E. M. (1986). Ethnography as narrative. In V. W. Turner & E. M. Bruner (Eds.), *The anthropology of experience* (pp. 139–155). Chicago, IL: University of Illinois Press.

Carey, M., Walther, S., & Russell, S. (2009). The absent but implicit: A map to support therapeutic enquiry. *Family Process, 48*(3), 319–331.

Chamberlain, S. (1990). The new ethnography: "Windmills and giants." *Dulwich Centre Newsletter, 2,* 39–46.

Denborough, D. (2008). *Collective practice: Responding to individuals, groups, and communities who have experienced trauma*. Adelaide, Australia: Dulwich Centre Publications.

Denborough, D. (2009). Some reflection on the legacies of Michael White: An Australian perspective. *Australian and New Zealand Journal of Family Therapy, 30,* 92–108.

Emerson, C. (1983). The outer word and inner speech: Bakhtin, Vygotsky, and the internalization of language. *Critical Inquiry, 10*(2), 245–264.

Epston, D. (1998). Internalising discourse versus externalising discourses. In D. Epston (Ed.), *"Catching up" with David Epston: A collection of narrative practice-based papers published between 1991–1996*. Adelaide, Australia: Dulwich Centre Publications.

Epston, D. (1999). Co-research: The making of an alternative knowledge. In Dulwich Centre Publications (Eds.), *Narrative therapy and community work: A conference collection*. Adelaide, Australia: Dulwich Centre Publications.

Epston, D. (2004). Sasha, Amber, Joel Fay, and Isha [Special Issue]. *Journal of Brief Therapy, 3*(2), 97–106.

Epston, D. (2011). Introduction. In D. Denborough (Ed.), *Narrative practice: Continuing the conversations* (pp. xxii–xxxviii). New York, NY: W. W. Norton & Company.

Epston, D., & Maisel, R. (2009). Anti-anorexia/bulimia: A polemics of life and death. In H. Malson & M. Burns (Eds.), *Critical feminist approaches to eating dis/orders* (pp. 209–220). New York, NY: Routledge & Kegan Paul.

Epston, D., & White, M. (1990). Consulting your consultants: The documentation of alternative knowledges. *Dulwich Centre Newsletter, 4,* 25–35.

Epston, D., & White, M. (1992). Consulting your consultants: The documentation of alternative knowledges. In D. Epston & M. White (Eds.), *Experience, contradiction, narrative and imagination: Selected papers of David Epston and Michael White, 1989–1991* (pp. 11–26). Adelaide, Australia: Dulwich Centre Publications.

Foucault, M. (1965). *Madness and civilization: A history of insanity in the age of reason* (R. Howard, Trans.). New York, NY: Random House. (Original work published 1961.)

Foucault, M. (1973). *The birth of the clinic: An archeology of medical perception*. London, UK: Tavistock. (Original work published 1963.)

Foucault, M. (1980). *Power/knowledge: Selected interviews and other writings*. New York, NY: Pantheon.

Foucault, M. (1984). *The history of sexuality* (R. Hurley, Trans.). New York, NY: Vintage Books. (Original work published 1976.)

Foucault, M. (1988). The technologies of the self. In L. H. Martin, H. Gutman, & P. H. Hutton (Eds.), *The technologies of the self: A seminar with Michel Foucault* (pp. 16–49). Amherst, MA: University of Massachusetts Press.

Foucault, M. (1997). *Ethics, subjectivity and truth: Essential works of Foucault 1954–1984* (R. Hurley and others. Trans.). New York, NY: The New Press.

Freedman, J., & Combs, G. (1996). *Narrative therapy: A social construction of preferred realities.* New York, NY: W. W. Norton & Company.

Freedman, J., & Combs, G. (2002). *Narrative therapy with couples… and a whole lot more: A collection of paper, essays and exercises.* Adelaide, Australia: Dulwich Centre Publications.

Freeman, M. (2010). *Hindsight: The promise and peril of looking backward.* New York, NY: Oxford University Press.

Garfinkel, H. (1984). *Studies in ethnomethodology.* London, UK: Polity Press.

Goffman, E. (1961). *Asylums: Essays in the social situation of mental patients and other inmates.* New York, NY: Harper.

Hibel, J., & polanco, m. (2010). Tuning the ear: Listening in narrative therapy. *Journal of Systemic Therapies, 29*(1), 59–70.

Maisel, R., Epston, D., & Borden, A. (2004). *Biting the hand that starves you: Inspiring resistance to anorexia/bulimia.* New York, NY: W. W. Norton & Company.

McLeod, J. (2004). Social construction, narrative and psychotherapy. In L. E. Angus & J. McLeod (Eds.), *The handbook of narrative and psychotherapy* (pp. 351–365). London, UK: SAGE Publications.

Morgan, A. (2000). *What is narrative therapy? An easy-to-read introduction.* Adelaide, Australia: Dulwich Centre Publications.

Morson, G. S., & Emerson, C. (1990). *Mikhail Bakhtin: Creation of a prosaics.* Stanford, CA: Stanford University Press.

Myerhoff, B. (1978). *Number our days.* New York, NY: Simon and Schuster.

Myerhoff, B. (1992). *Remembered lives: The work of ritual, storytelling, and growing older.* Ann Arbor, MI: The University of Michigan Press.

Pare, D., & Lysack, M. (2004). The willow and the oak: From monologue to dialogue in the scaffolding of therapeutic conversations. *Journal of Systemic Therapies, 23*(1), 6–20.

Russell, S., & Carey, M. (2004). *Narrative therapy: Responding to your questions.* Adelaide, Australia: Dulwich Centre Publications.

Turner, V. W. (1986). Dewey, Dilthey, and drama: An essay in the anthropology of experience. In V. Turner & E. Bruner (Eds.), *The anthropology of experience.* Chicago, IL: University of Illinois Press.

White, C. (2009, October). Where did it all begin? Reflecting on the collaborative work of Michael White and David Epston. *Context,* 57–58.

White, M. (1984). Pseudo-encopresis: From avalanche to victory, from vicious to virtuous cycles. *Family Systems Medicine, 2*(2), 150–160. doi:10.1037/h0091651

White, M. (1988). *Selected papers. Saying hullo again: The incorporation of the lost relationship in the resolution of grief.* Adelaide, Australia: Dulwich Centre Publications.

White, M. (1989). The process of questioning: A therapy of literary merit? In M. White (Ed.), *Selected papers* (pp. 37–46). Adelaide, Australia: Dulwich Centere Newsletter, Winter. (Reprinted from Dulwich Centre Newsletter, 1988, Winter, 8–14.)

White, M. (1993). Commentary: The histories of the present. In S. Gilligan & R. Price (Eds.), *Therapeutic conversations* (pp. 121–135). New York: NY: W. W. Norton & Company.

White, M. (1995). *Re-authoring lives: Interviews & essays.* Adelaide, Australia: Dulwich Centre Publications.

White, M. (1998). Saying hullo again: The incorporation of the lost relationship in the resolution of grief. In C. White & D. Denborough (Eds.), *Introducing narrative therapy: A collection of practice based writings* (pp. 17–29). Adelaide, Australia: Dulwich Centre Publications.

White, M. (2000). *Reflections of narrative practice: Essays and interviews.* Adelaide, Australia: Dulwich Centre Publications.

White, M. (2003). Narrative practice and community assignments. *The International Journal of Narrative Therapy and Community Work, 2,* 17–55.

White, M. (2004). *Narrative practice and exotic lives: Resurrecting diversity in everyday life.* Adelaide, Australia: Dulwich Centre Publications.

White, M. (2005). Workshop notes. Retrieved December 31, 2015 from www.dulwichcentre.com.au/michael-white-workshop-notes.pdf.

White, M. (2007). *Maps of narrative practice.* New York, NY: W. W. Norton & Company.

White, M. (2011). *Narrative practice: Continuing the conversations.* New York, NY: W. W. Norton & Company.

White, M., & Epston, D. (1990). *Narrative means to therapeutic ends.* New York, NY: W. W. Norton & Company.

White, M., & Epston, E. (1992). Introduction. In D. Epston & M. White (Eds.), *Experience, contradiction, narrative and imagination: Selected papers of David Epston and Michael White, 1989–1991* (pp. 7–9). Adelaide, Australia: Dulwich Centre Publications.

7

QUEER INTERSECTIONAL COUPLE THERAPY

Sheila Addison

> *Knowledge is not made for understanding; it is made for cutting.*

(Foucault, 1984, p. 88)

> *We all want an identity that makes life worth living.... I believe in the truth of you, and so do a lot of other people"*

(Bornstein, 2006, pp. 31–32)

The choice of a mixed-gender, presumably heterosexual couple as the model case for this book inevitably limited how authors constructed their chapters. Just like Foucault's "knowledge," this choice "cuts" – cuts some couples out of the conversation, cuts some clinicians out of the mainstream of couple therapy, cuts off opportunities for cross-pollination of ideas about relationships and change. This kind of cutting has real impact on the lives of lesbian, gay, bisexual, and transgender[1] people who have been so often cut out of conversations about marriages and families, but also on straight and cisgender[2] people, who miss the chance to learn from those different from themselves.

I brought this to the editors' attention when they sought me out as a potential author. They readily agreed it would be a mistake, in 2016, to publish a book on couples that overlooked the needs of sexual and gender minority clients in relationships. Fortunately, as a participant in the production of knowledge, I have been given this opportunity to include another view of couples and couple therapy, one that sees LGBTQ people as part of the body of knowledge all couple therapists should be familiar with. But in order to do so, I have had to make some changes to David and Natalie's story.

In my version of this case, David is a transgender man, or "assigned female at birth." He identifies as heterosexual—attracted to women—but when he was living as female prior to his transition, he identified as lesbian. Natalie identifies as lesbian, but also dates trans men. Thus, the couple identifies as **mixed-gender**, but also as **LGBTQ-identified**, or **queer**.[3] I decided that David's gender identity is known to his family, but not to Natalie's. I also decided that Devyn, David's chat partner, is a transgender woman, which adds another layer to the emotional affair.

David and Natalie's case as written also did not identify any family member's race, ethnicity, or cultural identity, with the exception of Jordyn, adopted from China. Research has suggested that LGBTQ couples are "often more dissimilar than opposite-sex [*sic*] couples" in terms of race, age/generation, level of education, socio-economic status, and other identity variables (Connolly, 2004, p. 7). Because the **intersectional approach** considers how different dimensions of identity influence one another, I opted to make David's family White (as would be typical of most families in Maine), and Natalie's family African American, creating an inter-racial relationship for the couple. I also opted to make Natalie's stepfather, Nicholas, White as well, adding a second inter-racial marriage to the mix. These changes will obviously impact the couple's story in ways I will explore in this chapter.

History of the Model

The field of couple therapy has suffered from tremendous homeostasis in terms of incorporating the needs of sexual and gender minorities. While Hartwell, Serovich, Grafsky, and Kerr (2012) identified only 2 percent of articles in couple and family therapy (CFT) journals between 1996 and 2010 related to gay, lesbian, and/or bisexual issues, this still represented more than a 200 percent increase from Clark and Serovich's landmark 1997 study that found only .06 percent of articles during a 20-year time span addressed sexual minorities. Blumer, Greene, Knowles, and Williams (2012) investigated CFT publications from 1997 to 2009 for transgender-related information, and found a dismal 0.0008 percent, or nine articles out of nearly 11,000.

Early writing often focused on the issue of gay men married to heterosexual women (Buxton, 2004). Authors were more concerned with whether the "heterosexual" marriage could or should be preserved, and with the pain and outrage of the straight spouse. But despite the challenges of systemic change, the mental health fields have produced increasing amounts of scholarship and clinical literature that represent more experiences. Today, there is ample support for a "gay-affirmative" or "LGB-affirmative" psychotherapy approach (Davies, 2000; Stone Carlson & McGeorge, 2015) that assumes sexual minority identities and same-gender relationships are valid and healthy. And a body of both professional and popular works has emerged that has created an increasingly nuanced picture of the needs of sexual minority clients in relationships, as well as particular challenges faced by same-gender couples.

A variety of common stressors have been identified in queer-specific couple literature, but Green and Mitchell (2015) cluster them into three themes or factors:

- LGB minority stress
- Relational ambiguity
- Obstacles to forming cohesive support systems

The first factor includes the effects of stereotypes, stigma, and devaluation (also termed homo-negativity or homophobia) from outside sources including the culture at large, families of origin, and one's community/ies. It also includes the internalized prejudices that queer people inevitably confront, and the way these attitudes interfere with a couple's ability to bond with one another and value the relationship. For example, the lack of visible long-term, satisfied same-gender couples in significant numbers gives rise to fatalistic and negative predictions about whether such relationships can last. At the same time, the very public debate over same-gender marriage, and the subsequent religious backlash, serves as a constant reminder that many people do not value LGB relationships and, in some cases, even wish them harm.

The second factor, **relational ambiguity**, involves the difficulties of clearly defining the boundaries of relationships that have, until recently, often been denied the recognition of marriage and its accompanying legal, financial, and social protections. Even with the 2015 *Obergefell* Supreme Court decision that cleared the way for marriage rights in all 50 US states, it can still be hard for couples to talk about what marriage means to them. Those who choose not to marry (e.g. because of personal objection to an institution some see as heterosexist, or the risks created by marrying a same-gender partner in one of the many states that does not prevent discrimination in employment and housing based on sexual orientation) still face the challenge of managing what may feel like an ambiguous commitment, easily severed by either party.

The third, obstacles to forming cohesive support systems, relates to the difficulties that LGB couples often face with integrating their various networks of friends, family, colleagues, etc. When sexual minority individuals encounter homo-negative attitudes from those close to them, it is often the case that they develop separate spheres of relationships—an LGB **"family of choice"** that offers the validation and support not available from one's family-of-origin. Varying degrees of openness or "outness" about one's identity at work, in school, at church, and so on can create a kind of balkanized social network, where only certain circles can know certain information. Multiplied by two in the case of a couple, the problem of managing information and boundaries can become overwhelming and contentious, while the couple's sense of support feels increasingly fragmented and uncertain.

However, clinicians should resist the impulse to assume that same-gender couples' troubles are always related to sexual orientation; they have most of the same conflicts that "heterosexual" couples do as well. As Green and Mitchell (2015) say, "We are not implying that one needs a whole new theory of therapy to work effectively with same-sex couples" (p. 490). Concepts from most couple therapy models (e.g. Bowen's differentiation, EFT's adult attachment, Gottman's Sound Relational House) can assist in explaining same-gender couple difficulties too. But therapists who work with same-gender couples must be familiar with these unique stressors, as their effects can sometimes be subtle, masquerading as "typical" couple arguments about chores or money.

It is also important for clinicians to recognize the significant strengths and resiliency that comes with the territory of being part of a same-gender couple. Gottman (2006) has concluded that "gay and lesbian couples are a lot more mature, more considerate in trying to improve a relationship, and have a greater awareness of equality in a relationship than straight couples" (cited in Rutter, 2015, p. 91). Lesbian couples consistently show a high level of equality in their division of labor and resources, and share the most emotional closeness compared to gay male or heterosexual couples (Green, 2012). Other research suggests that same-gender couples in general have more egalitarian relationships, handle conflict more effectively without resorting to aggression, and take a more collaborative, less invalidating stance with one another in disagreements. Rutter (2015) observes that the gay male couples he works with in sex therapy are "quite scrappy, willing to be creative and purposeful in maintaining the couple through difficult times" (p. 93).

Unfortunately, information on couples that include bisexual and transgender members has lagged behind that for lesbians and gay men. Bisexual clients are often mis-identified as either gay or straight, based on the gender of their partner. When in a same-gender relationship, bisexuals are often living with the dual stigma of **biphobia**[4] (Collins, 2004) as well as heterosexism/homophobia. And bisexuals, whether in same-gender or mixed-gender relationships, experience biphobia from their own partners, and from the couple's social networks. Bisexuals in mixed-gender relationships also often must cope with the stresses of being "in the closet," as their identity is frequently denied, even if they repeatedly come out (Bradford, 2015; Mulick & Wright, 2002).

Transgender people regularly experience cissexism and transphobia/trans-negativity,[5] often from their own partners if they come out and transition while in a relationship (Malpas, 2015). Cisgender partners often report a great deal of grief, rage, and feelings of betrayal as a partner transitions gender, in part because their own sexual identity is called into question if they remain partnered with their post-transition spouse. For example, if Jason, a heterosexual man, opts to stay married to Shannon as Shannon transitions from female to male, Jason will now be perceived as a gay man.

Trans people may postpone coming out and transition due to worries about their partner's reaction, or fears of a battle over child custody if the relationship does not survive (Lev, 2004). Couple work around transition may involve a mixture of individual and conjoint meetings, as each partner moves at their own pace through the complex feelings about the inevitable changes to the relationship, with the goal of developing a mutual plan for how to manage challenges in both the couple and parenting arenas (Malpas, 2015).

Although clinical understanding of partners of transgender people has improved, in the past a pre-existing marriage that the partners intended to continue was sometimes used as a reason to deny gender confirmation surgery by doctors afraid of lawsuits from the cisgender spouse (Lev, 2004). Heterosexual wives of transgender women have received the most clinical attention thus far, with considerably less research done regarding male partners of trans women, or any partners of trans men.

The couple literature is, at this time, still very thin when it comes to exploring problems other than transition that transgender people and their partners bring to therapy (e.g. Lev & Sennott, 2015; Malpas 2006). Gender minority people who do not fit into a clear binary gender (e.g. male or female, often described by terms like "**genderqueer**" or "**gender fluid**") have also been largely ignored by the literature on couple relationships.

Literature addressing the GLBT population, at large or in therapy, has been justly criticized for relying heavily on a White, middle-class frame of reference and focusing largely on sexual and gender identity as loci of oppression. The result is a conversation about the lives of sexual and gender minorities which excludes concerns related to race, class, and other dimensions of power and privilege which may be more or differently salient for queer people of color, disabled and poor queers, and others for whom sexuality and gender are not the primary ways they experience devaluation and marginalization.

Attempts to focus on "diversity" or increase multicultural competence have often, in practice, meant looking at race, gender, and class (or more recently, sexual orientation), each in its own "diversity ghetto," with little if any discussion of who might inhabit multiple categories. As critical social theories on individual dimensions of diversity have converged and influenced one another, multiple scholars have noted that examining the effects of a single dimension of privilege and oppression produces an analysis with only limited ability to generalize.

For example, White women and women of color often experience the effects of sexism in very different ways, and may prioritize gender differently in their concerns. A poor family with citizenship who belong to the dominant racial group has different options for coping with their poverty than a family of undocumented immigrants. Urban White middle-class gays and lesbians have been the typical client for much of the development of gay-affirmative therapy; it is likely that they experience heterosexism and homophobia, as well as their same-gender relationships, differently from those who are disadvantaged in terms of race, class, gender identity, and so on.

Several frameworks have been proposed for how to talk about the effects of valued and de-valued identities in a more complex fashion. Falicov (2014) developed the Multidimensional-Ecosystemic-Comparative Approach, or MECA model, using the metaphor of each family's "ecological niche." McDowell (2015) proposes a Critical Decolonizing Family Therapy that works toward transformation based on Gregory Bateson's Level III learning (contemplating the system that produces alternatives), cybernetics' third-order change (a transformation in how the world is viewed), and Soja's "third space" of resistance and social change, as well as ideas about critical consciousness and reclaiming indigineous knowledge from Friere and Laenui.

I personally prefer the term "**intersectionality**," originally proposed by Crenshaw (1989) as a means for talking about race and gender without a sole focus on either axis of oppression (Cho, Crenshaw, & McCall, 2013). Its name evokes the metaphor at the heart of its analysis: that identity can be thought of as running along multiple dimensions, all of which intersect to create each individual. See Figure 7.1 for an illustration of the intersectional model, which I adapted from a diagram originally by Diller, Houston, Morgan, and Ayim (1996).

In the diagram, any given person's life is shaped to some degree by all the dimensions of identity. How much each of their identities is valued by the existing power structure, called "**kyriarchy**"[6] by the feminist historian Schüssler Fiorenza (2001), informs their access to power; kyriarchy grants more power to those whom it values more.

More valued identities are shown above the line marked "kyriarchy," while devalued or oppressed identities are below it. Each identity spans a continuum

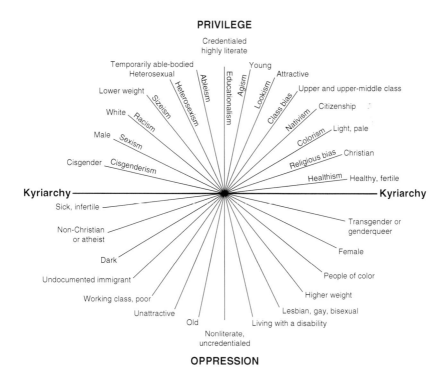

FIGURE 7.1 The intersectional model.

Adapted from Diller, Houston, Morgan, and Ayim (1996).

from most to least valued, rather than binary options of "privileged" or "marginalized."[7] So along the dimension of "healthism," while a robustly healthy and fertile person might be most valued, a person with a chronic but easily managed condition might also be above the line, yet in danger of slipping below it if their condition worsens and impacts their ability to work or reproduce.

However, the intersectional view would also consider the way other axes influence one's experience of healthism. For example, a more literate and formally educated person is likely to be treated better by health professionals, even if they are more sick, than a healthier person who cannot read and is unfamiliar with how to self-advocate in complex systems. A poorly educated person with a "Cadillac" health care plan from their middle-class union job may get more help recovering from an injury or illness than an adjunct professor with a PhD but no insurance who is among the "working poor."

Rather than oppressions being "cumulative" in a strictly additive way (more valued identities always equals a smoother path; each added oppression equals an added burden), their interaction for each individual is complex and sometimes idiosyncratic. For example, while some queer people of color identify with the experience of "double" or even "triple jeopardy"—oppression along the lines of race, sexual orientation, and for women of color, gender—others find that the bonds of collectivist cultures make it easier for parents and children to navigate a child's coming out process together, because in doing so, they can remain a family (Addison & Coolhart, 2015; Glass & Few-Demo, 2013). At the same time, difficulty in integrating multiple identities can result in identity fragmentation, in which some aspects of identity are suppressed or ignored in order to avoid conflict with identities that are most critical to one's sense of self (Singh & Harper, 2015).

Thus, an intersectional perspective on power acknowledges that context always matters. A White, well-educated, cisgender bisexual woman such as myself will, in all likelihood, be most in touch with the way my gender and sexual orientation are devalued by the system of kyriarchy which privileges straight men. But my experience of that devaluation will be different from a transgender bisexual Latina who dropped out of high school. When working with such a client, intersectionality reminds me that our differences and our similarities are both in play in the therapeutic relationship, and that while my valued identities (race, education, gender identity) may not be "visible" to me, they likely will be to my client. For couple therapists, the intersectional lens adds depth and richness to the list of well-established concerns for queer couples—both partners have perhaps experienced homophobia and coming out, but each did so with the different influence of their many intersecting identities (Addison & Coolhart, 2015).

Theory of Problem Formation

Like feminist and multicultural therapies, an intersectional approach to couple work is often more of a lens than a particular model for intervention. It can be used by therapists as an "overlay" on any model that accommodates directly addressing power and privilege. I personally rely most often on the work of Susan Johnson and other proponents of Emotionally Focused Therapy (see Chapter 3), based on attachment theory and in-session enactments. But I find some clients take more readily to the Sound Relationship House model of John and Julie Schwartz-Gottman with its blend of behavioral, psycho-educational, and affective work. I will also sometimes reach for scaling, exception, and miracle questions from Solution-Focused Brief Therapy (see Chapter 5); metaphors, re-frames, re-structuring techniques, and unbalancing techniques from Structural Family Therapy; differentiation work and relationship experiments from Bowen Therapy; and even the occasional paradox or restraining technique from Strategic Therapy. And as I tell my students, I always feel guided by the ghost of warm, nurturing Virginia Satir sitting on one shoulder, and provocative, double-talking Carl Whitaker on the other.

So I am usually thinking about attachment injuries, negative cycles, and the lack of a "safe harbor" when assessing couple problems (per EFT), and often I am also mentally noting neglected relational friendships, problems responding to bids for connection, gridlock around perpetual problems, the Four Horsemen of the Apocalypse in conflict, and a lack of effective repair (per the Gottmans). However, I am also thinking about how these problems are specifically difficult for this couple because of the effects of devaluation, oppression, and unequal access to power.

Contextual Stressors on the Couple

Natalie and David's case shows ample evidence of the three factors identified by Green and Mitchell (2015): LGB minority stress, relational ambiguity, and obstacles to forming cohesive support systems. It is likely that both partners, like most LGBTQ people, grew up in a household in which they were the only queer- or trans-identified person. Looking at their genogram and family story, there are no other members of their families identified as lesbian, gay, bisexual, or transgender, and no evidence of same-gender couple relationships (though we can't assume no one in the family has engaged in them in the past). The **heteronormative**[8] definition of "family" forces queer people into the category of "other" or "different," an experience which can be both enraging and exhausting, as well as a daily **microaggression**[9] (Hudak & Giammatei, 2014).

While Maine (David's home) prohibits discrimination on the basis of sexual orientation (but not gender identity), permits same-sex adoption, and allows transgender people to amend their birth certificate, these have all been developments within the past decade. The path to marriage equality prior to the 2015 *Obergefell* decision encountered setbacks such as a state referendum overturning a marriage equality law in 2009 before it could go into effect. A 2013 survey of school climate by the Gay, Lesbian, and Straight Education Network (GLSEN) found that the majority of LGBT students in Maine reported regularly hearing remarks that were homophobic, sexist, and negative toward someone's gender expression; most experienced verbal harassment, three in ten reported physical harassment and one in ten was physically assaulted. Only 12 percent of Maine schools reported having conduct policies that forbid bullying and harassment based on sexual identity and gender expression (GLSEN, 2013a). In all likelihood, school during David's youth was similar if not worse.

Natalie's years growing up in Texas likely were even more difficult. Texas laws in 2016 do not bar discrimination against sexual or gender minority people, and do not provide for transgender people to amend their birth certificates. Texas does not specifically prevent LGBTQ people from adopting, but does not allow a child adopted by a same-gender couple to receive a supplemental birth certificate to prove the parents' rights. Although *Obergefell* legalized same-gender marriage everywhere in the US, some Texas counties still refuse to issue marriage licenses to same-gender couples as of this writing. GLSEN's (2013b) school climate survey of Texas showed similar, high rates of negative remarks, verbal and physical harassment, and physical assault of GLBTQ students. Only 6 percent of schools explicitly prohibited such behavior.

Given that these surveys represent contemporary students' experience, both David and Natalie were likely exposed to high levels of heterosexism, homophobia, cissexism, and transphobia as they grew up and came out to themselves and others. Both likely experienced negative attitudes toward their sexual/gender identities from those around them, and have had to face everything from microaggressions to verbal abuse as they have come out.

Relational ambiguity may have been a particular problem for this couple. Same-gender marriage was not available in Texas until 2015, and although David has been living as male for some time, a number of Southern states have refused to allow transgender people to marry different-gender spouses without a corresponding birth certificate. Even if David and Natalie married in Maine, their marriage would not have been recognized by Texas until *Obergefell*, and any employer, organization, or official who questions its validity can still force the couple to have to defend their relationship, perhaps at the cost of a legal battle. The couple has likely lacked role models for queer married life, particularly ones that reflect their cross-cultural and trans-inclusive relationship. Some of Natalie's insecurity about David's online relationship with Devyn may be driven by the sense that she can never be sure whether their marriage is as "real" as a heterosexual one, and thus safe from outsiders.

Many relationships in the couple's families of origin have been impaired by heterosexism, homophobia, cissexism, and transphobia. David and Natalie's families, like most families, assumed their children were heterosexual and pictured them in a heterosexual relationship from the very beginning. Friends, teachers, and community members did likewise. The images of committed and married couples offered as role models were all heterosexual. What little information family members communicated about queer people was either confusingly mixed or clearly negative. There was no awareness in either family about the existence of gender minorities; images of people who somehow transgressed gender roles were limited to "humorous," usually degrading images of cross-dressing men. In such an environment, neither David nor Natalie could develop the kind of secure attachment relationships that children need from their caregivers. I'll look at David's side of the genogram first to explore these effects.

David's family assumed he was a heterosexual girl/woman, assumptions which were informed by heteronormativity and cissexism. David internalized this belief as well, though from a young age, like many gender-variant children, he felt different from the girls who were supposedly his peers. He was labeled a "tomboy" from an early age, but his lack of athletic ability and quiet nature made that label a poor fit as well. He recalls hiding in the bathroom on Valentine's Day multiple years in a row, afraid of receiving a valentine from a boy in his class, but unable to articulate why this idea was so distressing.

Heteronormativity also plays a role in the larger system of family relationships. David's mother, Sheila, is intensely involved with his older sister Susan, and Susan's adopted daughter Jordyn. Sheila's focus on this traditional "family of creation," with its heterosexual couple and child, aggravates David's sense of being devalued by his family. It likely has a similar effect on his sister Regina. Although she is heterosexual like Susan, she is an unmarried mother parenting alone, who has not always been able to care for her child herself, and thus she falls short of the image of the "normal, healthy family." The support network among all family members suffers because of the pressure to conform to a limited view of what a family can and should be.

David's family expresses homophobia/homo-negativity to varying degrees. Before coming out as transgender, David presented as female; thus, when he dated female partners in high school, he described himself as lesbian. Sheila told David she supported his "lifestyle choice"—language that carries stigma for most sexual minority people because it implies their orientation is a conscious decision—but his father and sisters both reacted negatively. Dana stayed later and later at work, while Susan and Regina rolled their eyes at their sibling's "play for attention" and asked him not to "make a big deal out of it" at school, or people would think their family was "weird." Now that he is fully transitioned to living as male and married to Natalie, however, his mother views him as a heterosexual man, which she finds easier to cope with.

The family's transphobia/trans-negativity has made their relationship with David even more complicated. Again, Sheila makes the most effort, using his male name and pronouns, but she still describes David as her "daughter," and talks about "David's gender thing" in ways that make David feel uncomfortable. David is reluctant to confront her about this and potentially lose the relationship with her. He sees her closeness to Susan as evidence of unacknowledged cissexism as well as heteronormativity.

Regina attributes her cut-off with David to their fight over her parenting, but David suspects she is uncomfortable with his transition as well. David resents the fact that at the time of their fight, he was presenting as female but androgynous, so although he was younger and smaller than Regina, the police labeled him a "troubled type" and assumed Regina was the victim: a cissexist view which led to only him being arrested and charged.

Susan refuses to use David's male name, and will only say "my sister has issues," although she came to David and Natalie's wedding and is pleasant to Natalie. Dana, rather than expressing interest in finally having the son he wanted so much, has made little effort to connect with David, and did not even come to the wedding.

Natalie's family is subject to the same systemic forces as David's. Natalie has identified as lesbian since middle school, though now she uses the term "queer" more often because of her relationship with David. Her brother Scott said he was comfortable with her same-gender relationships, but wanted her to stay "in the closet" in school as he was afraid she would be bullied. He was willing for her to be out to his partners, but not to his male friends, particularly his college fraternity brothers. Robyn, her half-sister, says she feels "fine" about Natalie's sexuality, but doesn't understand "why she's with a guy now." Her mother Laura has tried to reconcile her Baptist faith with her love for her daughter, but held out hope for many years that Natalie would "find the right man." Now that David and Natalie are together, Laura is relieved to think that she was correct, and wants Natalie to keep quiet about her dating history and queer identity.

Natalie's relationship with her father is a distant one, so she has not come out to him; heteronormativity allows him to assume she is heterosexual unless told otherwise. Laura's second husband, Nicholas, has tried, ineffectually, to communicate support to Natalie, but she sees his efforts as trying to make up for her father's absence, and resents them. Ironically, there may be some influence of heteronormativity here as well—the heterosexual nuclear family is idealized; therefore, there is only room for one "father figure" in the picture.

Natalie has chosen not to tell anyone in her family that David is a transgender man, telling David "they wouldn't understand something that far out of their experience." Privately, she worries that if her family knew David was originally identified as female, they would continue to see him as a woman. She wants to protect him from their anticipated transphobia/trans-negativity, but there is an element of self-protection here as well: despite her lesbian identity, her family sees her relationship as a heterosexual one and thus treats it as more "legitimate" than the relationships with women in her past. She benefits from the cissexist assumption that everyone is cisgender unless identified otherwise.

Natalie's feelings about David's online relationship with Devyn is also colored by cissexism and transphobia, specifically **transmisogyny**.[10] Although she is comfortable with trans men, she has less experience with trans women and is not sure she feels the same kinship with and attraction for them that she does for cis women. She has a hard time understanding David's interest in Devyn, and although she would never say it to him, she feels he should relate to her better than to Devyn since they were both assigned female at birth and grew up with similar bodies and gender roles. She feels guilty about this thought, since she knows David would be hurt by the comparison.

Although the influences of gender and sexuality are clear, an intersectional perspective suggests that other dimensions of privilege and oppression influence David and Natalie's life together, and shape how the queer-specific issues influence them as well. To understand this couple, then, we must look at them in a more nuanced context and consider other dimensions of identity.

Racism

In an era of increasing racial tensions that has spawned (at the time of this writing) greater public attention to police killings of Black people, the #BlackLivesMatter movement, and overt hostility toward immigrants and Muslims from Presidential candidates, the White privilege held by David and his family is an obvious consideration. This privilege has "smoothed the road" for them in imperceptible ways as members of the dominant racial group in an overwhelmingly White state.

David's family is deeply uncomfortable in conversations about race, as evidenced by their inability to discuss the cross-racial adoption of Jordyn from China. Sheila has acknowledged that she worries about how to relate to Natalie because of her own inexperience with Black people, but David's White privilege allows him to attribute her awkwardness to sexuality- and gender-related microaggressions, rather than the racial microaggressions that Natalie perceives as well. Natalie also is left wondering how much Dana, Susan, and Regina's antipathy toward the couple is based on race, but attributed to sexuality and gender because it is "safer" for White people to criticize sexual and gender minorities than to express racial hostility.

This disconnect in meaning-making has the potential to fuel conflict in the couple, as invoking race may be experienced as a threat to the security and harmony of the relationship. Discussing race with White people often gets derailed by White fragility, described by DiAngelo (2011) as "a state in which even a minimum amount of racial stress becomes intolerable" due to a lack of skills for dealing with cross-racial communication (p. 54). Even apparently simple invocations of race, such as identifying a racial microaggression, or acknowledging racial inequality, may result in "the outward display of emotions such as anger, fear, and guilt, and behaviors such as argumentation, silence, and leaving the stress-inducing situation" (p. 54). This is likely a factor in the way many cross-racial couples de-emphasize or dissociate from the topic of race and racialized experiences (Killian, 2003). It is common for such couples to deny that race is an issue in their relationship, and to minimize the impact of racial microaggressions or overt discrimination they experience, as a way of preserving harmony in the relationship

While the traditional narrative about race, gender, and sexuality has held that African Americans are less accepting of homosexuality than Whites, this conclusion has been increasingly questioned (Adamczyk, Boyd, & Hayes, 2016).

Religiosity appears to be a more reliable predictor of attitudes than race, and indeed in Natalie's family, her mother is the most religious member, and also the person who feels the most ambivalence about Natalie's queer identity. At the same time, her mother Laura manages to maintain a relationship with Natalie in spite of her misgivings, which may in part be due to the traditional Black community's focus on maintaining family ties at all costs—a value developed as a means of resisting the destruction of family ties during slavery when spouses and families could be ripped apart at the whim of a White owner.

Still, Natalie's conflicts with Laura and her brother Scott over her queer identity can also have racial undertones. Natalie perceives their desire for her to keep her identity hidden in certain circumstances (e.g. around her mother's church friends and Scott's fraternity brothers) as an example of "**respectability politics**." Higginbotham (1993) coined the term to describe the way devalued groups attempt to increase their status by adopting assimilated values and norms to prove their "worthiness" of acceptance, rather than challenging the kyriarchy's exclusionary tactics. For Natalie, her family's desire for her to pass as heterosexual is an affront to her values, and an effort to mimic the values of dominant White culture. Although her mother seems to like David, Natalie feels conflicted over her mother's cross-racial marriage that mimics her own, and privately feels shame that neither of them chose a Black male partner like her father Fred.

Race is also likely a factor in the tension between Natalie and her stepfather Nicholas. While a clinician might expect her to feel close to him because he accepts her lesbian/queer identity, she experienced his efforts to connect as reflecting a sense of entitlement to affection and respect driven by White privilege. She believes his dislike of Fred is based in racist attitudes toward working-class Black men, and feels protective toward Fred as a result, even while she resents her father's disengagement. Natalie also doubts that Nicolas understands how to cultivate a positive racial identity in her half-sister Robyn, and is torn about whether Robyn's acceptance of her sexual identity is representative of Robyn's assimilation into a largely White group of friends at her college in Oregon.

Sexism

David's family illustrates the multi-generational effects of sexism, beginning with his father Dana's preference for a son, to the point that he insisted on a third child that his wife Sheila didn't want. His expectations were thwarted, though, when David was assigned female at birth (AFAB). Although David (born Danae) wasn't particularly feminine, his lack of athletic interests still disappointed his father, who wanted an outgoing, competitive "jock" like he was, even if he had to settle for those qualities in a daughter. When David came out as male, rather than bringing his father closer, his "failures" provided an excuse for Dana to disengage even further.

David seems to have internalized his father's beliefs about gender roles in the family. His fight with his sister Regina, before she got sober, was more about her failures to live up to his expectations of a mother than any concern for her or for her daughter Anna. He also seems to have very stereotypical expectations of Natalie—wanting her to lose weight, wanting her to provide him with sex—and some of his frustrations may be masking feelings of insecurity. Natalie's income as an established realtor likely far exceeds his as a public school teacher, a situation most men find difficult to tolerate in their marriages, and which raises the risk of a divorce (Bertrand, Kamenica, & Pan, 2015).

But David has experienced the disadvantages of life as a man under kyriarchy as well. When he and Regina fought, he was the one arrested and sentenced to probation, although Regina is older and taller than him and both were intoxicated. The police chose to arrest him, however, on the assumption that he must have been the aggressor toward his sister. His transgender status put him at tremendous risk of violence while he was jailed awaiting trial; lacking a policy for how to house trans prisoners safely, the county kept him in the medical unit until Sheila convinced Dana to pay for bail.

Natalie has an uneasy relationship with her gender role, complicated by her race and sexual identity. Black women, who are much more likely to have worked outside the home than White women over the past century, have historically been left out of traditional narratives about motherhood and femininity while being expected to be "strong" and hold together their families in the absence of Black men. Natalie loves her mother Laura deeply, and respects her sacrifices for her children in Fred's absence, but she does not want to be pigeonholed as a "traditional" Black woman herself. Coming out as lesbian/queer represented two steps away from that gendered role, but her relationship with David can at times feel to her like "a step backward" into a heterosexist norm, especially since her family does not know David is trans.

Her work as a real estate agent exposes her to risk on a regular basis, as she accompanies clients to empty houses and meets with clients in their homes. She has heard stories of agents who were harassed, robbed, or narrowly escaped sexual assault, and feels doubly vulnerable because as a Black woman, she is wary of involving police in her life even if she were a crime victim. She is encouraged by her brokerage to flirt with clients to encourage them to list properties with her, although she has doubts about whether this helps her prospects in the way it might for a White woman. She also wonders whether she is any good at flirting with straight men, and feels awkward when she tries.

Weight Stigma

Both David and Natalie experience weight stigma in their lives, as internalized self-loathing, negativity from others, and ironically, from one another as well. Both have gained weight as adults and particularly since their marriage. For Natalie, gaining weight undermines her sense of herself as an attractive woman, even though Laura tells her, "Black women look good with a little padding." She feels angry at herself for being unable to reject White norms of beauty, and angry at the dominant culture for its rejection of Black women.

David's weight gave Dana an excuse for rejecting his child, even after David came out as male. Although David was more comfortable with his weight before transitioning, in part because it kept him somewhat "gender-less" and insulated from the expectations for cisgender girls, it has been particularly troubling for him as an adult. David feels that his body fat works against his desire to be accepted as male, and undermines his sense of masculinity by giving him a more androgynous or feminine shape. Testosterone has shifted where his body fat deposits, but he has been unable to get the flat chest or slim rear end that characterizes many men's bodies.

The clients' internalized weight stigma is made worse by their criticism of one another's bodies. David feels betrayed by Natalie's weight gain since the marriage, which he blames for his reduced interest in sex, while Natalie couches her complaints in terms of concern for David's health. Neither is comfortable in their own skin—a situation potentially complicated by David's experiences as a trans man, and Natalie's experiences as a Black woman—and their discomfort gets externalized as contemptuous criticism. Stigma against higher-weight people has significantly increased in recent decades, along with public health campaigns against the "obesity epidemic" and projections about a nation of obese children (Greenhalgh, 2015; Seacat, Dougal, & Roy, 2014). Criticizing one another's bodies is bound to result in deeply hurt feelings and a lack of trust in the relationship.

Migration/Geography

Although migration and geography are not depicted on the intersectional graphic in Figure 7.1, they are a part of this couple's context as well. David and Natalie grew up in very different regions of the United States, and navigated a long-distance relationship before deciding to settle in Natalie's home state of Texas. This immediately set up a disparity between them: they were on Natalie's "home turf," surrounded by her family and friends, while David had to start from scratch to make professional and personal connections, job hunting and creating a community of friends for himself.

For a straight couple, that would often clearly tip the balance of power toward Natalie. But as a queer woman in a secretly queer relationship, she may have more to lose in terms of her relationships and community status if one or both of them are outed, because she still lives and works within a network that largely believes she is heterosexual. At the same time, as a transgender man, David is very poorly protected in Texas; although neither state includes gender identity in its hate crimes law, the Maine Human Rights Act prohibits transgender discrimination in housing, employment, public accommodations, and credit, assurances he lacks in Texas.

The social, systemic, and intra-psychic processes of heterosexism, homophobia, cissexism, transphobia, and biphobia complicate the lives of the queer couples I work with by adding stress, shame, and opportunities for couple conflict, while diminishing their internal and external resources (Meyer, 2003). Intersecting oppressions in other areas raise the stakes even further. Singh and Harper (2015) argue that systemic devaluation harms intimacy by adding to couples' stress levels, leading to arguing, sexual problems, and difficulties managing "outness." Green, Rubio, Bergman, and Katzuny (2015) found that social stressors even impacted gay fathers' parenting; they found an association between experiencing specifically anti-gay microaggressions and either permissive or authoritarian parenting styles, less positive co-parenting, and more couple aggression.

Queer communities are not immune to the influence of kyriarchy, and often carry significant biases in terms of cisgenderism, sexism/misogyny, biphobia, racism, classism, and so on. My belief is that all families are immersed in kyriarchy, and thus, all families contain the seeds of these ills; like the old Palmolive commercial, we're "soaking in it." David and Natalie's families are not unique in the fact that they have internalized these values, just in how they are expressed.

These multiple, intersectional stressors act as ongoing catalysts for friction in the couple. While even a relatively healthy couple might find their resources taxed by these contextual issues, when the couple also has difficulties due to relational dysfunctions (e.g. attachment injuries, poor differentiation, etc.), the scene is set for problems to erupt into regular conflicts. Thus, in order to help David and Natalie address the inciting incident of the online relationship with Devyn, I would argue that the therapist must be sensitive to and prepared to address these underlying dynamics as well.

Theory of Problem Resolution

Just as queer intersectional couple therapists are free to use their preferred model of therapy to assess problems, they can use these same models to direct treatment, so long as the resolution process is: 1) informed by the intersectional issues present in the case, 2) a good cultural "fit" for the couple, and 3) cognizant of the influence of the therapist's own intersectional identities and biases. Personally, I typically use Emotionally Focused Therapy and attachment theory as "home base," but sometimes switch to a Gottman Sound Relationship House lens to prompt my thinking or engage a particular couple more readily.

Minority Stress Coping Tools

Green and Mitchell (2015) suggest that clinicians working with LGB couples can use a variety of techniques to help the couple cope more effectively and reduce the negative consequences to their relationship, relying on the feminist concepts of "**resistance**"[11] and "**subversion**."[12] They encourage:

- talking overtly about the negative beliefs and attitudes toward LGB people that create minority stress
- critically examining internal and external heterosexism and homophobia (and, presumably biphobia)
- talking frankly together about the dangers as well as the benefits of being "out" in order to negotiate couple differences in this area
- exploring options for increasing the couple's time in affirming environments and decreasing their time in homo-negative situations
- developing a joint plan for coping with discrimination and microaggressions that fits with each partner's coping style
- finding opportunities to work for social change

However, these strategies may not work for all couples, especially when considering intersectional factors. In their study of young gay men, Madsen and Green (2012) found that some of the young men's coping strategies for dealing with anti-gay discrimination were more indirect and subversive than overtly resistant. Some of their strategies included hiding or moderating their reactions, discounting the source as unworthy or ignorant, distracting from feelings with other absorbing activities, and focusing on the hope that the future will get better. Some of these strategies, born out of the relatively little power that adolescents have over many aspects of their lives, may suggest adaptive means of coping for multiply-marginalized couples as well.

Glass and Few-Demo (2013), in their study of Black lesbian couples, found that many chose to selectively hide or de-emphasize the couple aspect of their relationship in certain situations in order to maintain close ties with Black family and community members who disapproved of same-sex pairings. By downplaying the sexual aspect of their relationship, these couples could still be welcomed to family events as friends; in turn, by coming to events together, the couple might weather any overt homophobia more effectively, and still have access to the family support system. Given that many of these couples talked about their lack of access to a supportive GLB community, maintaining their family ties while cultivating a shared "homeplace" as a safe space to be themselves is an ingenious and adaptive response to multiple oppressions.

Cultural Humility

When it comes to understanding the contextual and intersectional elements of a case, I start from a position of **cultural humility**. The concept of cultural humility was originally developed for physician training (Tervalon & Murray-Garcia, 1998) as an alternative to the idea of "cultural competence." The authors suggest that competence implies "a detached mastery of a theoretically finite body of knowledge" (p. 117) and may impart a false sense of security in clinicians who then resort to stereotyping, ignoring clinical evidence, and devaluing the perspective of others with "relevant cultural insight" (p. 119). While the competency model emphasizes the acquisition of cross-cultural knowledge, the humility model, since expanded to mental health (e.g. Hook, Davis, Owen, Worthington, & Utsey, 2013; Ortega & Coulborn Faller, 2011), assumes that "one's own knowledge is limited as to what truly is another's culture" and therefore humility requires "accepting one's limitations" (Reynoso & Friend, 2015, p. 190).

This model emphasizes a commitment to life-long self-evaluation and critique in which clinicians develop "an interpersonal stance that is other-oriented rather than self-focused, characterized by respect for others and a lack of superiority" (Hook et al., 2013, p. 2). Hypotheses, rather than conclusions, are emphasized, and clinicians are expected to cultivate awareness of the tendency to center their own beliefs and values, then work to "put these aside and learn from clients" (Reynoso & Friend, 2015, p. 190). This stance provides a kind of "brake" on the tendency to get carried away with one's own clinical brilliance, and the frustrations that can arise when clients do not share our appreciation for our own perceptiveness about their culture. It echoes the "not-knowing stance" encouraged by Anderson and Goolishian in their Collaborative Language Systems approach (Anderson, 1997), as well as other postmodernists, but specifically punctures the false sense of mastery so often created by "multicultural" educational approaches.

Broaching Difference

Despite the emphasis on multicultural competence in the past several decades, many majority-culture clinicians are still ambivalent or avoidant about directly addressing issues of culture and identity, particularly race (Knox, Burkard, Johnson, Suzuki, & Ponterotto, 2003), leading to ruptures in the therapeutic relationship. For example, although the majority of African American clients report experiencing racial microaggressions in therapy, less than a quarter actually discussed the issue with their therapist, to the detriment of the therapeutic alliance (Owen, Tao, Imel, Wampold, & Rodolfa, 2014). "Race-avoidant" therapists have been found to derail client concerns, resulting in interactions where clients seem to be "deterred from discussing [racialized] aspects of the experiences that they initially thought were relevant" (Thompson & Jenal, 1994, p. 490).

Hardy and Laszloffy (2002) assert that multicultural therapists must at times act as a "broker of permission," "using power to help clients… find the safety and comfort necessary to risk saying things that they have been unable to say" (pp. 580–581). They believe that this is particularly the case in terms of "politically sensitive, volatile topics" like marginalized and oppressed identities (and, I would add, privileged ones as well). Although such a direct approach may make some therapists uncomfortable, there is ample evidence that it is both necessary and beneficial for effective clinical work.

Day-Vines et al. (2007) explore the benefit of directly addressing race via a direct style they term "**broaching**." The authors summarize a wealth of clinical evidence that suggests minority clients are poorly served by the mental health field, beginning with the high rate of premature termination of services (50% of minority clients, versus 30% of white clients) as well as the ongoing suspicion many minorities have regarding "talk therapy" and medicine in general. Noting that "counselors who demonstrate cultural responsiveness are consistently perceived by clients of color as being more credible and competent" (p. 403), the authors argue that directly broaching cultural issues combats the denial, repression, and silence about difference that contributes to intergenerational legacies of shame and superficial cross-cultural relationships.

Although the broaching model was developed specifically to prompt more direct engagement with racial issues in therapy, I would argue that this technique is equally applicable to other dimensions of diversity in the intersectional approach. Thompson and Jenal's work on race (1994) suggests that power dynamics within the counseling dyad can promote or inhibit culture-specific discussions, leaving clients feeling frustrated and unheard; similarly, LGB clients often want to know whether their therapist is also a sexual minority like themselves (Petford, 2005; Riggs, 2015). Although sexual and/or gender identity are important to broach when working with GLBTQ clients, other dimensions of privilege and oppression should be considered as well, as they intersect with and impact clients' experiences of queerness.

Day-Vines and Holcomb-McCoy (2013) explore four domains of broaching behavior: intra-individual issues, intra-cultural issues, inter-cultural issues, and inter-counseling issues and dynamics. The first domain, **intra-individual issues**, involves inviting clients to consider their intersecting identities and suggests they may be relevant to the clinical conversation; for example, "What has it been like for you to come to terms with your identity as an Arab gay man?" The second domain, **intra-cultural issues**, evokes conflicts that may arise within a client's community, such as the question, "Some older lesbians are uncomfortable with the term 'queer.' Does that ever come up for you with your friends and peers?" The third domain, **inter-cultural issues**, opens space for discussion of conflicts between the client's identities and the dominant culture, or other cultural groups. Here, the sociopolitical context of oppression may be invoked by questions or statements such as, "It seems like you're feeling quite happy about being out as a woman these days, and the problem now is really more coping with the stress of other people's microaggressions—is that right?"

With couples, the intra-cultural and inter-cultural domains may also be opportunities to explore how each partner experiences their similarities or difference. For example, noting that one partner identifies as lesbian and the other as bisexual can lead into the question, "When does this difference in identity come up for the two of you as a couple?" (See Day-Vines and Holcomb-McCoy for further ideas on broaching statements, and Cardemil and Battle [2003] for other examples of how to specifically discuss race and ethnicity.)

Therapist's Identities

The fourth domain of broaching, **inter-counseling issues and dynamics**, may be the most challenging for some clinicians, as it directly addresses the therapist's own identities and how they interact with those of clients. Efforts to broach in this domain may create a great deal of anxiety for clinicians fearful of seeming insensitive or encountering strong negative reactions from clients as the power dynamics of kyriarchy are evoked in the room. Often, broaching attempts take the form of requests for permission or validation from the client, for example, "How do you feel about the fact that I'm a heterosexual therapist? Is that OK with you?" In a 2008 interview, Hardy suggests that "[a] permission-granting maneuver requires some subtlety. I don't agree with the strategy where white therapists ask clients of color, 'How do you feel about being in therapy with me?'" (Wyatt, 2008). He argues that because he has the more powerful role as the therapist, "It's my job, the way I see it, to put my views out there about it and not require an answer" rather than putting the client on the spot without revealing anything about his own beliefs or attitudes.

However, even a more sophisticated broaching maneuver, such as "I know that as a straight person, I can't be an expert on your experience as a queer couple, so I hope you'll let me know if I assume too much" focuses conversation on a relatively safe aspect of difference, while asking the client to keep the therapist culturally honest. Watts-Jones (2010) encourages clinicians to consider their "location of self," linking this exploration of personal identity to family systems approaches such as Almeida's Cultural Consciousness model, Narrative Therapy, feminist family therapy, and other models, as well as exploration of the self of the therapist. She suggests a need to "leav[e] the comfort zone," asking:

> How does a White therapist say to clients of color that s/he fears unknowingly saying something racist, or that s/he is anxious about Black families getting too angry if they talk about racism? How does a Black therapist say to a White client, I wonder if you will be able to take me seriously given the history of racism in this country?
>
> *(p. 409)*

Watts-Jones encourages therapists to lean into the discomfort of broaching, even along dimensions where they feel less fluid and confident, arguing that "the question about oppression is not if but how," and therefore "we as therapists need to be curious about how oppression shows up in every family, and not simply those who present with discrete trauma, or those who come in identifying the second shift as a source of conflict" (p. 411).

Day-Vines, Bryan, and Griffin (2013) found that a distinct group of clinicians, which they label "avoidant," consider cultural topics to be inappropriately complex for counseling, promote a lack of personal responsibility in clients, and distract from "legitimate counseling issues" (p. 218). Another group, labeled "continuing/incongruent," is characterized by awkward efforts to avoid giving offense, a fear of losing the client, and a feeling of being tongue-tied or incoherent when it comes to talking about race and ethnicity. These clinicians may by particularly challenged by a case conceptualization that puts cultural identity and broaching at the center of clinical work. However, as Watts-Jones (2010) writes, "Making identities transparent is an invitation to clients to participate with the therapist in being mindful of how our mix of experiences may at times create tension, misunderstanding, or frustration and to *talk about it* [emphasis added]. It extends the collaboration" (p. 413).

Broaching involves giving selective attention to the contextual factors that may be impacting clients' experience. This makes it possible to include these factors in conversations about clients' experiences of their couple relationship, and look more closely at how power and privilege contribute to the current problem. The therapist has an obligation, thanks to the power differential, to make sure that discomfort with difference does not lead to screening out clients' clues to the salience of cultural factors. For example, when a couple is discussing whether to go out to a club with friends, and one partner, who uses a cane and leg brace, says "I just don't feel comfortable there," the observant therapist will broach the topic of disability, asking something like "when you say you're not comfortable, could you say more about what you mean? Is there something about accessibility that makes it difficult for you to enjoy going there? Is that something your partner knows about, do you think?" "In intersectional couple therapy," Addison and Coolhart (2015) write, "there will inevitably be cultural similarities and differences within the couple, and in their family and community contexts, but also with the therapist; we recommend that clinicians look for chances to bring them into the conversation" (p. 451).

First Session

The more I do and teach therapy, the more I realize that clinical work for me is an interlocking sequence of assessments and interventions. Gathering information allows me to hypothesize where there might be an opportunity for change. Attempting an intervention yields more information—about the clients, about me, about our work together—that is part of another assessment. In the flow of a good session or course of therapy, assessments turn into interventions and interventions turn into assessments, moment by moment, week by week.

However, developing a clear picture of where we are starting from makes it easier to begin therapy with purpose. While my assessment is certainly shaped by my particular family systems orientation, the broad-spectrum approach I take would generally work well for most approaches. However, other therapists might wish to use the intersectional lens with a more present- or future-focused method, and their first-session goals might look different. The challenge, I believe, is that if we omit a systematic history-taking, it can be difficult to gather enough information to build an intersectional hypothesis, as clients may not spontaneously present enough context to help us fill in the blanks. (This touches on a larger conversation in the family therapy world about whether more ahistorical approaches do a disservice to contextual issues of power and privilege, among other dynamics.)

First, I want to take a broad history of the couple, including a simple version of Bowen's genogram for each client's family-of-origin (FOO), and touching on contextual factors such as (but not limited to) race, ethnicity, religion, class, gender dynamics, and attitudes toward sexual/gender minorities—depending on the clients' presentations. For queer couples, I particularly want to understand something about how each partner has experienced heterosexism, homophobia, cisgenderism, and transphobia from their FOO, both growing up and now in adulthood. I also want to know how each FOO has reacted to the clients' coming out processes, and the fact of the queer relationship. I am also interested in a brief version of each partner's coming out experiences, which is one way I assess internalized heterosexism, homophobia, cisgenderism, and transphobia.

I gather a short history of the relationship from its beginning to the present, looking for opportunities to identify power and control issues, cross-cultural issues, and via my EFT lens, partners' attachment styles, with a beginning idea about how their negative cycle might look. I ask briefly about substance use, the quality of their sexual relationship, and any history of violence, explicit or sub-clinical; these are topics I will delve into more deeply in future sessions as needed. I am interested in the history of the problem that brought them to therapy, and the decision to come into therapy itself. If the couple seems deeply ambivalent, I may try to assess the degree of commitment to the relationship and the therapy process, versus hopelessness and thoughts of exiting the relationship. I also want to find out the couple's strengths, particularly what has kept them together through such difficult times.

As I get a sense of what each partner wants from therapy, I look for a way to re-frame their conflicts in terms of mutually acceptable goals. "You both want to feel secure and close in this relationship," "You want to be able to manage difficult times and feel like you're on the same team," or "Each of you wants to find a way to repair this hurt between you and find a way to move forward together" are types of re-frames that fit many couples. I frequently lean heavily on attachment themes—reaching out, connecting, having a safe harbor, etc.—and I find that ending the first session on this note, along with having taken a history that makes each partner feel I am beginning to understand them, usually instills some hope in the couple and leaves them willing to commit to giving therapy a try.

Throughout the first session, I look for opportunities to identify or ask about intersectional factors, creating multiple chances for broaching the similarities and differences in the room. "Do you talk much about your different religious backgrounds?" I might ask, knowing that the answer will give me clues about the couple's dynamics as well as the salience of religion and their comfort with directness and difference. I always broach race with clients of color, given the code of silence around race that prevails in the US, particularly when a White person like myself is in the room. I usually broach gender, even with other women, since it would be unwise to assume, based on our surface similarity, that our experience of femaleness is something we experience the same way. With mixed-gender couples, I find it helpful to acknowledge that gender could lead to the feeling of "two against one" or a competition between women if we don't address those dynamics as they arise. I also always broach gender identity when I work with trans and gender-queer clients, who can be exquisitely sensitive to my cisgender privilege and very fearful of talking about it, even though I advertise as a trans-competent therapist.

In general, if there is a dynamic where my identity is more valued by kyriarchy than my client's, I feel a duty to take a one-down stance by pro-actively broaching the topic, making myself and my values visible to the client. Like Watts-Jones (2010), I am probably least comfortable doing this around class, but cultural humility is a life-long process. By doing so, I am acknowledging that difference may influence our relationship, giving permission to the client to comment on their experience of difference in the room, and making it clear that it is OK to discuss the effects of outside cultural forces on our lives and relationships, in or out of the therapy room.

Therapy and Termination

To echo Green and Mitchell (2015), I see no need to adopt a uniquely different approach to the actual therapy process with my LGBTQ clients. I typically use the three-stage, nine-step Emotionally Focused Therapy model, beginning with assessing and de-escalating their negative cycle; helping them change from their frozen and reactive positions (often pursue–withdraw or a variation) to more accessible and vulnerable positions so they can experience safety and bonding; and helping them to integrate their new way of connecting so they can continue the process themselves. Sometimes a couple's style seems more suited to working on the bids for connection, effective conflict and repair, and accepting influence from the Gottman's model, so I use that language predominantly instead. Throughout the process, my stance is warm, curious, and active, as I help couples unfold vulnerable feelings and then talk directly with one another in enactments.

However, my sessions will also regularly return to intersectional issues of power and privilege, devaluation, and places where partners feel unseen or wounded by each other and the world. Together we will unfold tender places where old hurts have festered, and practice noticing when there is a fresh moment of "ouch" in the room because one partner doesn't "get it." We will also build the strength to sit with the uncomfortable knowledge of our own privileges in relationship to one another. As clients are more able to articulate how kyriarchy pits them against one another or even against themselves, the "safe harbor" of the couple relationship can provide an opportunity for bonding in new ways per EFT, and the increasing amount of "cognitive room" each partner devotes to the other can provide a stable foundation for the relational friendship per Gottman.

In the case "transcript" below, I will demonstrate how this looks in a beginning session as I am gathering the information I need for a beginning intersectional understanding of the couple, and planting seeds of challenges to the existing stuckness that we will come back to in future sessions.

Case Transcript

David found me when searching for couple therapists with trans-affirmative experience. Natalie called to feel me out, and told me that David was willing to come if she thought I was a good fit. She summarized their relationship, including telling me that they are an interracial couple and that David is trans, but that her family does not know this. She described finding his emails with Devyn, and the conflict that followed when she confronted David about them, then decided to make an appointment.

Both partners seemed nervous, tense, and sad, avoiding eye contact, sitting on opposite ends of the couch. I summarized what I'd learned from Natalie, watching David closely to see if any of his reactions suggested my summary was biased.

> *Therapist:* So if I understand right, you two have been feeling out of sync for a while now, like things weren't going so well between you? Like you've been missing some of the closeness you had when you were first married, and it's been feeling pretty lonely?
>
> *I'm using language that is either neutral—"out of sync," "weren't going so well"—to avoid the implication of blame, or that invokes attachment longings — "closeness," "lonely"—to set a positive frame for the session.*
>
> *David:* That's right.
>
> *Therapist:* And then a couple of weeks ago, there were these messages…
>
> *I'm very neutral, as I don't want to provoke a conflict before I've even had the chance to join with them both. I'm watching Natalie to see if my neutral framing upsets her.*
>
> *David:* Yeah, she went into my computer because we were using hers to play music, and I guess she found some stuff that she took way too seriously. I mean, I know it looks bad, I get that, but she would not listen when I told

her it wasn't serious, and she got really pissed, started telling me I was going
to leave her, calling names, it just got really crazy. And I know things haven't
been so good with us, but I'm not the one who's talked about divorce every
time we have a little fight over something, that's her. But now it seems like
this thing is blown all out of proportion and we don't know how to get over
it on our own.

Therapist: So how long have you felt like things "weren't so good?"

I'm echoing his language purposefully—to start with a framing that he accepts.

David: I guess a while now. We haven't been having sex for eight or nine
months…

Natalie: Seven months. We had sex on your birthday weekend.

David: OK, seven months I guess, but for a while it just seemed like everything
was really busy and stressful, what with Natalie's job trying to move a lot of
properties, and the school year starting for me which is a really stressful time.
The fall was just really busy and it seemed like we were always stressed out
and tired.

Therapist: So that's how you made sense of not having sex—a problem of time
and stress? The two of you just couldn't make time for each other?

David: I guess. I mean Natalie has never had as high a sex drive as me.

Natalie: It's the T.[13]

David: I always had more of a sex drive.

Natalie: But when you increased your dose, you got more focused on
wanting sex.

David: The doctor said my levels needed adjustment last year because of my
weight.

Natalie: But you just let them adjust your dose, and it's made you so unpleasant
to live with, you're irritable, you're always crabby about how we don't have
sex often enough, you get on me about my weight but then you won't take
care of yourself.

Therapist: So, Natalie, your sense is that it goes back longer than that.

*I'm moving to gently block this conflict from escalating right now, but I want to join
with Natalie as well as David so I move to her.*

Natalie: Absolutely. It's been three years of marriage, and it seems like after
that first year he really changed; he pulled away and just wasn't excited to be
together any more.

Therapist: You felt like he wasn't there for you in the same way.

Natalie: Yes, it's like he just closed me out.

Therapist: David, do you know what Natalie is talking about here? When she
says she felt like something changed a couple of years ago?

*I want to keep both of them engaged in the conversation and focused on collaborating
with me in giving history rather than attacking one another.*

David: I guess, although I don't see it like that. She blames me but she's not
telling the whole story, it's not like I just randomly changed personalities or
something.

Therapist: What's missing? Was there something that happened?

David: Look, so we met on OK Cupid, right? But I was living in Maine,
and she was living here, near her family. When we were getting serious, we
started talking about where we were gonna live. We talked about Maine, and
I thought she'd really like it for a change of pace, though she might not like
the winters you know? But she said the real estate market isn't so big in some
of these little villages and she was worried about making a living. And most
places need teachers, so we said, OK, not Maine.

Therapist: That made sense to you, felt OK? [*he nods*] Was your family still there?

I'm probing a bit to see if David resents leaving his family to move out of state.

David: I wasn't worried about the family thing. I just wasn't necessarily
thinking Texas.

*I take note of his casual dismissal of family, and bookmark it for later. I'm also keep-
ing an eye on Natalie to see if she seems to object to his story at any point.*

Therapist: Did you talk about somewhere else?

David: We did, a little, we talked about Boston or New Haven, but Natalie,
I don't know, she just has this whole family that she's really close to, and so
she was just really strong about wanting to stay near them. She knew the
market here, so I guess it made sense to me really. But it was a big change.

Therapist: I bet. Maine to Texas, that's really different [*he nods*]. Natalie, how is
he doing so far? Is he telling it fairly, you think?

I'm attending to the alliance. I don't want Natalie to feel silenced and then erupt.

Natalie: I mean, I guess so, you know, we did talk about a lot of things, but yeah,
family is important to me, and I was really just seeing my career here start to take
off, which takes a lot of time in real estate, you have to do a lot of networking.

Therapist: I bet.

Natalie: So, there were good reasons, I didn't just say "I want it my way,"
you know.

*I sense that she's feeling a little defensive, so I decide to broach the subject of race,
which wasn't mentioned in their re-telling of their discussion but which can be a*

very salient factor in where one lives—many American cities are still heavily segregated in practice, if not in policy, and the Northeastern US is overwhelmingly White dominated.

Therapist: Sure, I hear that. You two tried to work out your options together, figure things out as a team? [*they both nod*]

I'm framing this in an optimistic way, hoping that each will identify with the implication that they tried to be collaborative, even if they feel their partner wasn't so much.

Therapist: So I wonder, what was that conversation like for you as an interracial couple? Was that something you talked about much? [*they look at each other and frown, shaking their heads*] I'm just thinking, Maine, that's a pretty White place if I understand right? Boston, New Haven—not so diverse, am I wrong?

I'm broaching an inter-cultural issue here, and what might also be termed an intra-couple issue: how their differing racial identities interact with White-centric culture, and with one another's identities. I'm trying to stay curious and humble though.

David: Yeah, yeah you could say that [*he laughs a little*]. It's pretty White.
Therapist: Was any of that part of the conversation about Maine or wherever, how it might be for Natalie to live somewhere like that?
David: [*looks at Natalie*] I guess it crossed my mind, but we didn't talk about it really, because it was pretty clear from the get-go that it just wasn't going to work for her career.

I look at Natalie here to invite her to add her thoughts. I'm also looking to see how comfortable she is with my initiating this line of conversation.

Natalie: Well, I mean, I thought about it you know.
Therapist: Did you visit David in Maine while you were dating?
Natalie: A couple of times.
David: Mostly I went to see her, because I had summer break but she had to work, and then the holidays are so important to her family, so I did a lot of the travel. She bought some of the tickets though, you know, teacher's salary [*we laugh together*].

I sense that this is an uncomfortable topic. I want to assess how much they have actually talked about race, and make it clear that I'm prepared to talk frankly with them about it.

Therapist: Natalie, I know that I'm coming from a White perspective here, and I don't want to assume anything, but I wonder, how were those visits for you?

Here, I am broaching the inter-counseling dimension of my own racial identity.

Natalie: Oh, they were nice, very nice visits. It's really nice up there, really peaceful.
Therapist: Nice?
Natalie: It's peaceful, it's really quiet, you know everybody thinks Texas is just a bunch of tumbleweeds but we're right near Houston, so, you know, there's actually a lot of traffic and city lights and things, and Maine just wasn't like that, it was really tranquil.
Therapist: Yeah, I bet [*we smile a little awkwardly*].

I can tell this is uncomfortable, so I broach the inter-counseling dimension again.

Therapist: I feel like maybe I made it awkward when I asked so directly about race. I know that a lot of times it's not so easy to talk about, especially with someone like me—I'm White, you just met me, you know, there's no history between us yet.

I'm saying this mostly to Natalie, but I'm also observing David. He looks cautious, but also a little relieved, like he's interested in this conversation, but glad he's not the one asking questions. I deliberately used self-deprecating humor to ease into this broaching statement; this is congruent with both my personal style in therapy, and also with my commitment to cultural humility.

Natalie: [*with a laugh*] Well, that's true [*a pause*]. You don't want to complain when you're a guest of someone else, right? So when I think about those trips, I choose to focus on what I liked, and it really was nice to be there together, just the two of us. David lived at the end of this really long road, with all these trees, and we could go take a walk together and it would just feel like we were the only two people for miles around.
Therapist: Right, so it really was a special time together.

I'm validating her strength-based re-frame of her visits, but I'm gathering this also covers for more complicated feelings. She's switched to talking in second person, a clue that this topic is anxiety-provoking. I'd expect that, talking about race with a new client.

Natalie: Right, exactly, really special. My mom taught me to focus on the positives, so that's what I think about.

Her echoing of my language suggests to me that we're joined enough for me to see if we can talk more directly about the racial difference, perhaps other identities as well.

Therapist: So you really treasure those memories. And… can I ask? What's the other part, that's maybe harder to talk about?

I'm using tentative language deliberately, hedging my request to soften it.

Natalie: Well, I guess… you know, when you travel, you know you're going to run across all certain types of people, and you just have to be prepared for that, because it's not going to be like where you came from everywhere you go.

Therapist: Say more about that.

Natalie: Well, so, like in Houston, at the airport you know, you go to the ticket counter and there's people who think a certain way, and then the screeners, the people in the Starbucks, and so on. And then you get somewhere else, and you get off the plane, and you stop in the bathroom, or to get a coffee, and suddenly there's all these people who look like "uh, what's she doing here?" They're not mean about it or anything, they're not snapping your picture or something, but you can tell, it's different for them.

Therapist: Seeing a Black woman travelling there.

She's been talking in "code" and I decide to be direct, but gentle.

Natalie: Yeah, exactly, it's like "um, did you get on the wrong plane?" [*we all laugh a little*]. You know. Suddenly people are looking like they maybe have somewhere else they need to be when I ask if they can use skim milk for my latte, you know?

Therapist: It's uncomfortable.

Actually it sounds like it might be enraging, but I'm deliberately choosing more mild language since we're early in the session and the therapy relationship. Also, I don't want to scare off David, who right now is listening.

Natalie: Exactly. It's not like it's the end of the world, but it's a long trip, I'm tired, so I kind of put it out of my mind and just focus on "you get to see your guy in just a little bit."

This is an adaptive coping strategy, analogous to Madsen and Green's (2012) findings regarding their young gay interviewees' strategies for coping with anti-gay experiences. However, I'm curious whether David has made "cognitive room" (per Gottman) for this part of Natalie's experience, or whether White privilege has kept him from noticing it.

Therapist: You try to let it go, but it can be exhausting.

I want to push a little deeper into the vulnerable, exhausted part and heighten that.

Natalie: Yeah, it really can.

Therapist: You show up at the end of a long, hard day, and now there's this extra "tax" you have to pay, for Traveling While Black, you have to put up with a bunch of White people having feelings about you being there.

Natalie: Exactly. The first time I visited, I took a cab downtown so I could meet David after work, and the cab driver was all trying to chat me up like "hey, I can tell you're not from around here," and then he says some shit like "where do they make fine chocolate girls like you? Maybe I can show you around town later? You need a guy like me to come with you" and I just thought oh my God, pull over because either I am going to stab this guy or jump out of this cab.

Therapist: Wow. Yeah. Wow. That's, like, so many different ways of injuring you, all wrapped up in one. Race, gender…

Natalie: Exactly. And you know, one thing I really hate, as a queer woman, is some straight guy hitting on me, but then he has to go and add in some racial comment, like oh, he can tell I'm not from around here because I'm Black.

Natalie has broached the topic of sexual identity herself—not entirely surprising as I advertise as LGBT-friendly, but still not something every client will do right up front. I hope that my broaching race has started to set the expectation that we can talk about identity and how it affects their lives in our sessions.

Therapist: It's like he's invalidating everything about you, all at once. Treating you like you're less than human. He's hitting you in all these vulnerable spots. Telling you, "I have all this power to hurt you, and what are you going to do about it?"

Framing homophobia, racism, sexism, etc. as an abuse of power is one way of resisting and subverting the dominant assumption that they are "just words" that have no real meaning unless the de-valued person allows themselves to be hurt by them.

Natalie: Exactly. Just like that [*she's nodding, and I can see her eyes tearing up*].

Therapist: I can see how painful that is, even thinking back on it now.

I hold her gaze for a bit. This exchange gives me some confidence that she feels understood, and this conversation about race is feeling safe enough to continue with.

Therapist: David, as you're listening to this, I'm wondering what's happening for you? Have you heard about this before, this exhausting part for Natalie?

I'm wrapping David into the conversation—he's been a silent participant long enough. I also want to assess whether her vulnerability evokes any softer feelings in him, per EFT, while still gathering more contextual information.

David: I don't know, I guess, I mean I know Maine is really White. That's certainly true. But it's not… I've never seen somebody be outright rude to her or anything.

Therapist: You haven't seen that go on, that you're aware of.

I'm validating him, but with a careful choice of words to make it clear: this is his perception. I don't want to attack his view, but I also don't want to invalidate Natalie. This is a common response from someone with more privilege; when a person describes an experience of devaluation like a microaggression, the more privileged partner denies their experience because "I've never seen it."

David: Right, I haven't seen it, but I guess… I dunno, she never really said anything to me about it, so I didn't know that was happening.

Therapist: You didn't realize she was being hurt like this.

Natalie didn't say "hurt," I didn't echo "hurt" to her, but I want to see if this evokes some tender feelings in David. I'd also like to bring him into the conversation about race, which is one that White people often avoid.

David: I guess I didn't think about it that way. She never said anything to me and so I didn't think there was a problem.

Therapist: What's that like, to realize that she didn't tell you about this experience, that Natalie was hurting and exhausted and you didn't know about it?

I'm asking him to attune to his present moment experience of recognizing his wife's pain. This is an EFT-style intervention, but it's also an assessment of his general ability to tolerate negative emotional states in himself and his partner. If they're going to repair the trust violation of the emails, it will be important for him to be able to tolerate hearing about her pain and access some of his softer feelings at the same time.

David: It kind of sucks, you know, to think about that. That she wouldn't say anything.

Therapist: It feels bad, to think that she'd be hurting, and not say anything to you.

David: Yeah.

Therapist: To think that you didn't recognize this might be going on for her, like there's this distance between the two of you that you didn't even know about.

I'm using some heightening techniques per EFT.

David: Yeah. I mean, I get that being a White guy, I don't always see some things. I just thought, you know, I asked her "does it bug you to be here?" and she said it was fine, so I thought that was the truth.

David has now broached race himself. I suspect he's unaware of how much taboo there is for many Black people against complaining to White people about racialized experiences, even friends and intimates.

Therapist: So when you hear your wife say that just in visiting you, she'd have these hurtful experiences, and yet she didn't tell you; you even asked her about it but you didn't know that was going on for her until she talked about it today, and you can see that little tear come up in the corner of her eye, what's happening for you inside?

We've been talking about thoughts; now I want to hear about feelings.

David: Well it's bad, you know, I feel bad.
Therapist: That feels bad? [*he nods*]. I almost wonder if maybe it feels a little guilty?

I'm using empathic conjecture from EFT to get to a less generic word than "bad."

David: Yeah, I guess so, I mean… OK, so I know I'm a White guy, trust me, living with her and her family around, I'm really aware these days that I'm a White dude, you know, my kids at school, half of them are Black and half of them are Latino, and I teach Chemistry you know, so one day one of them goes "Hey, our Chemistry teacher is Mr. White!" like on *Breaking Bad*, you know? So now that's what they call me sometimes, "Yo, Mr. White, we gonna cook some blue ice today?" stuff like that…

This is White Fragility—David can join in a conversation about race to some degree, but when he has to face how race has limited his knowledge of the world and his partner, he gets defensive and copes by distracting with humor. It's useful information—in part, it tells me I over-reached with the conjecture "guilty"—but I want to get us back on track.

Therapist: So there's something really hard about knowing that Whiteness can get in the way of your relationship with Natalie. It can get in between the two of you, and the closeness you'd like to have with your wife.

I go back to attachment language to evoke "closeness."

David: Yeah, exactly. It's like, I even know what she's talking about, you know, with the airport thing, because I get it myself but in a different way.

I'm looking at Natalie, who looks interested.

Therapist: Tell me about that.

David: Well, up in Maine, everybody grows up learning that you just mind your own business. I mean my oldest sister Susan was a real typical "girly girl" type, just like my mom, but my middle sister Regina, she was never into all that. She was real practical, she liked to ride horses, so she worked at the stables, and you don't wear dresses to muck out stables, you know [*we all laugh a little*]. I guess growing up somewhere else she would have been called a tomboy; she was tough and strong. But nobody said anything to her about it, because that's not how you do it in Maine.

I have a sense of what David is driving at with this story about gender presentation; I prompt him very gently to include himself in the story.

Therapist: Sure, OK. And so how did that Maine attitude work for you?

David: Well, it's complicated. My dad wanted a boy, and Mom said she was done after two but he really bugged her about it, so they got pregnant again. When I was born, you know, here was another girl [*he looks unhappy*].

Therapist: So they assumed.

I take advantage of a little pause from David to gently affirm that for him, the gender he was assigned at birth did not turn out to be a good fit for him.

Natalie: Exactly.

I take this as a sign that she is feeling compassion toward David as he talks about gender in his family—a complicated and awkward subject for many transgender people.

David: Right. So on the one hand, I was kind of more like Regina. I was really good with practical stuff, like taking apart this old alarm clock to figure out how it worked, I got into technical theater and would do the sets for the school plays, so I was always wearing flannel and covered in sawdust, kept my hair real short, and it wasn't too big a deal.

Therapist: That Maine attitude kind of worked out where you were concerned, "do your own thing."

David: Yeah, except Dad wanted an athlete to be in varsity baseball like he was in college until he threw out his shoulder pitching, but I'm just no good with anything with a ball. That's not a trans-guy joke, by the way [*we all laugh*].

I'm encouraged by his appropriate use of humor—perhaps he's self-soothing some anxiety about telling his story, but it's an effective coping tool and a mechanism for managing relationship conflict that gay and lesbian couples are often quite good at, per Gottman. But he has now directly broached gender identity, which tells me that we're establishing a therapy culture where we talk about these identity issues.

David: So, most people didn't really pay a lot of attention to me; when I started to quietly transition, which was mostly in college, when I would come home on breaks, nobody said much. I could tell some people were wondering "what is going on there?" but mostly people don't say anything. And by the time I started the T and had my top surgery[14] and then came back for my first teaching job, that was like an hour from where I grew up, so people didn't know me, and it was pretty much not an issue.

Therapist: So you're saying, you could sort of fly under the radar to some degree as a younger person, with this "mind your own business" culture around you, and then once you transitioned, it seems like people in Maine generally don't read[15] you as trans.

We're broaching the inter-cultural domain again, talking about David's experience with the dominant culture in his home region. I want to be curious and not make assumptions; even though I feel generally pretty aware of issues for transgender people, I'm not part of that community, so David is the expert here.

David: Right, I mean half the time I don't think Mainers even pay enough attention to the rest of the world to know that there is such a thing as a trans person. I can go into just about any barbershop or bathroom or whatever and not get a second look.

Therapist: So it felt pretty safe for you in Maine?

David: Well, on the one hand, when you're trans, you can never really afford to just assume "oh, I'm probably safe." You never know how someone is going to react.

Therapist: True. That sounds like a hard way to live.

David: Sure. But I guess I had it easy, compared to guys I know who live other places.

I have been keeping in mind that this topic started as a parallel to Natalie's experience as a Black queer woman in Maine. I can guess what the connection is in David's mind, but I want him to articulate it, and bring Natalie back into the conversation.

Therapist: It can be really different in different areas of the country.

David: Yeah, exactly. You know, in Texas, they are not kidding around about the whole homophobia, transphobia kind of thing, especially in the suburbs and the sticks. In Houston, they elected a lesbian mayor, they have a big Gay

Pride parade, but if you don't fit that really buff, cowboy, masculine kind of image, as a guy, even a straight guy, someday you're going to have somebody say something to you. Half the time you don't know if somebody is going to try to convert you or kick your ass.

> *I'm a little worried we're losing Natalie, and she has lived her whole life as a queer Black woman in Texas, so I want her to weigh in, although her experience may be different due to gender, race, gender identity, etc.*

Therapist: Natalie, what do you think about David's description here?
Natalie: Well, sometimes I think he's a little dramatic about it, you know, I mean people have all these assumptions about the South.

> *She's feeling a bit defensive of her home, I think, and may also be upset that David is looking to compare his experience in Texas with hers in Maine.*

David: You said yourself that it can be a hard place for people like us.
Natalie: That's true.

> *It's a good sign that she can accept his influence here and concede some of his viewpoint, so I stay out of the way.*

Natalie: I know it's different in some ways for David. It's not like when you're a queer Black woman, you get the red carpet treatment, but. . . . When you're a Black woman, you're no threat to a White man, unless you're coming for his job or his tax money.
David: Or his girlfriend [*we laugh together*].
Natalie: They never see that coming, though [*we laugh again*].

> *Again, this feels like an appropriate use of humor to soothe themselves as a couple and keep conflict from escalating. They're playful, even in a difficult conversation.*

Therapist: So you're saying, it's possible that for David, Texas might really be a pretty unfriendly place, even though since he's also a straight White guy, supposedly he's "at the top of the pile" so to speak.

> *I am making an intersectional observation here: while David and Natalie share some things about their general experience of "queerness," the specific day-to-day experiences can play out very differently for them because of the way their various identities intersect.*

Natalie: Right, right. He gets off easy in the world, is how I was brought up to see it, you know. But I know it's complicated.

David: It is complicated.

Therapist: Sounds like it.

Natalie: I think I thought, oh, well, Houston, it's so diverse, and David's pretty confident, he's smart and he's a great teacher, he'll do pretty well wherever he lands.

> *My interpretation here is that Natalie was focusing on David's racial and gender privilege, without considering the disadvantages of being transgender, not traditionally masculine, etc. as well as the differences in culture between locations.*

Therapist: Yeah, Natalie, I hear you—you saw David as this guy with a lot of strengths, right? [*she nods*]. And so, David, it seems like although on the one hand, you could see all the points Natalie made about why Texas was the right choice, there's been a cost for you that maybe hasn't been talked about so much.

David: Yeah. I mean, the way she talks about people looking at her in the Starbucks in Portland? I feel like I get that, not because of my race obviously, but when I go order a coffee, what do they do?

Therapist: They ask for your name.

> *I would have let him answer this question himself, as it's probably rhetorical, but I want to demonstrate that I'm following him, and I have a sense of how vulnerable this common situation can be for a transgender person. However, I'm wary of accepting his view, that his experience around gender is equivalent to Natalie's around race.*

David: Exactly. And every time, I'm wondering if the barista is going to do a double take, or when they call out "David?" and I show up, if someone's going to give me a funny look. Because it happens—not a lot, but it happens. It never happened in Maine, but it happens here. Forget about using the bathrooms sometimes.

Therapist: That feels really unsafe for you.

David: Right. Maybe they don't say anything, but all it takes is one person saying to someone else "I think that's a WOMAN!" and then who knows what happens. I'm waiting for the day that some kid brings it up at school.

Therapist: It's dangerous.

> *Again, I'm heightening the vulnerable emotion.*

David: It sure is [*Natalie is watching him with concern on her face*].

Therapist: And even if it doesn't go there, you still have those little looks to tell you, you're not one of us, you're not a person, you're "other."

David: Yeah.

Therapist: And so when you say, "I think I get what Natalie feels like in Maine," what you're saying is, "I have my own experience of being made to feel less than human, too."

David: Right. I get it, you know. The same thing happens to me.

> *I take this chance to broach the inter-counseling dimension again, this time around my racial similarity with David.*

Therapist: I hear you, David. I want to be careful here, because, one White person to another, I think maybe when we say "I get it, I've been there" about our experiences, it doesn't feel so good to Black people? [*Natalie is nodding*] But I think it's clear that you as a trans man really know what it can feel like to have that moment of feeling dehumanized, and I think you're trying to say that, that's not something you want Natalie to feel either. It hurts you, to know that she felt that kind of hurt, both because that hits close to home, and because you care about her. Is that right?

> *I'm hedging and being sure to validate him, while framing his point in terms of the relational message: He hurts, knowing that Natalie hurts.*

David: Yeah. That... you've hit it on the head [*there are tears in his voice*].

Therapist: And that's not something you've talked with her much about—how, basically, you two faced the choice of, not only "where are we going to live?" but also "who is going to get hurt by this decision and how?" Even if you didn't realize at the time that was part of what was at stake, there was this question "what will the decision cost each of us?" And that never really got talked about.

David: Exactly.

Natalie: It's true. I think we were just kind of rushed you know, it was so hard having that long-distance relationship, and it was going so well, but we couldn't keep flying back and forth all the time, and we just wanted an answer, like "well what next?"

Therapist: And you made the best decision available to you at the time, the best you two knew how, but that doesn't mean there was no fallout.

> *I'm referencing the relationship to emphasize their bond and their shared history as a couple. I assume neither one wanted the other person to wind up feeling resentful.*

Therapist: And so I'm guessing, David, that a while ago when you said Natalie wasn't telling the whole story, at least some of what you feel like was left out was this, the story of how you two got started as a married couple, and what that's meant for you personally.

David: Right. I mean, yes, we had a great first year here. It was really different from anywhere I've ever lived, and being with Natalie was so great. But
that was the honeymoon, and honeymoons don't last forever. And Natalie's
family means so much to her, her career means so much, this place means
so much…. It's just hard to not feel the same way about it, to know that she
doesn't really get how this feels for me.

Therapist: I hear that.

*I decide to take a risk here, and offer a conjecture about the affair. I am feeling pretty
joined with the couple, and I don't want either of them to leave this first session with
the feeling that I'm minimizing or colluding with the affair because I don't take it
seriously. I also think that there is a link here, and I want to test out my idea. I'm
going to hedge a lot, though, and be ready to step in to "catch the bullet" per EFT
if things escalate.*

Therapist: You know, David, hearing you say that, I'm wondering…. I don't
want to set off a powder keg here, but I know you two came because of these
emails and things you shared with another woman…. Did Devyn seem like
she would be able to "get it?"

David: That's… yes. I would have to say, yes, that's a lot of it.

*I can see Natalie's face cloud over, but David is present and attuned enough to see it
too, I think because he is feeling heard and seen by me thus far.*

David: I know that's not an excuse, and I know that doesn't justify some of the
things I said and did, but that was definitely a factor.

*Now, I feel like the couple is ready to address the emotional affair more directly. David
seems open to acknowledging at least some responsibility for hurting Natalie, and she
seems able to let me take over the job of challenging him for the time being. It will be
more effective for me to challenge him for now, because he feels understood and less
worried about being attacked as "the problem."*

*At this point, I have the beginning of a working hypothesis about the couple.
I can tell they lack a sense of the relationship as a "safe harbor" for vulnerable
feelings and don't trust that they can safely accommodate conflict without a loss
of trust. I don't yet have a clear idea about their underlying attachment styles and
relationship positions, per EFT, but I can see that there are vulnerable emotions of
hurt, sadness, guilt/shame, and longing underneath the surface of their angry, snip-
ing conflicts.*

*I also have a strong sense that this move, and the different ways they feel validated
and invalidated by their current environment, is part of what has fed their discon-
nection over the past couple of years. Having broached topics of race, gender, sexual*

orientation, and gender identity, we have the beginnings of an intersectional understanding of their relationship to build on in future conversations.

Finally, though I have more history to gather, including what they see as their strengths as a couple, I can see that they can still be a little vulnerable with each other, at least with my assistance, and they seem fairly responsive to my input and challenges.

I'm feeling cautiously hopeful about the couple, though there is a lot of work yet to do.

Notes

1   I will use the abbreviations "**LGB**" and "**LGBT**" throughout this chapter. When I leave out the T, it is to make clear that the literature in question is addressing only sexual minorities and/or same-gender couples, without considering gender minorities specifically.

2   "**Transgender**" refers to people whose gender assigned at birth does not match their internal experience of their gender identity. As "trans" means "opposite to," "cis" means "aligned with." Thus, gender activists coined the term "**cisgender**" to mean people whose gender assigned at birth does match their internal experience of their gender identity—in other words, "not transgender."

3   The term "queer," used in a pejorative sense in generations past, has been re-claimed in more recent decades as an umbrella term encompassing sexual and gender minority people—LGBT, as well as those who do not fit or identify comfortably with those labels. It often has a political connotation of solidarity with others who are also sexual and/or gender minorities. There is still something of a generational divide in use of the term, though some older LGBT people have readily adopted it while some younger people are still troubled by it. Clinicians are generally advised to ask clients what label(s) or term(s) they prefer for themselves; heterosexual and cisgender therapists should be particularly cautious about assuming "queer" will be a comfortable term for their clients.

4   Bias and stigma against bisexuals, e.g. "bisexuals always cheat" or "bisexuals can't make up their mind/are just going through a phase."

5   **Cissexism**: the assumption that everyone's gender identity matches their gender assigned at birth. Also the belief that there are only two genders (male and female) into which all people can be clearly and definitively categorized, based on looking at their genitals. **Transphobia/trans-negativity**: bias and stigma against gender minorities. For a detailed exploration of these concepts, and a discussion of the preference for "cissexism" rather than "cisgenderism" in this conversation, see Serano (2013, 2016).

6   Schüssler Fiorenza suggested that the term "patriarchy"—"father rule"—was inadequate, because "for instance, black men do not have control over white [men and women] and some women (slave mistresses) have power over subaltern women and men (slaves)" (p. 212–213). "Kyriarchy," from the Greek for "lord/master rule," implies a more complex system of "intersecting structures of domination" (p. 211).

7   My adaptation of the Diller et al. (1996) diagram is anchored by kyriarchical values specific to present-day North America. While "Western" values along many axes have shaped the kyriarchy of non-Western countries—e.g. the value placed on light skin in countries where "Whites" are a minority group—no doubt some dimensions would look quite different from the perspective of other countries or regions, or at other points in time.

8 **Heteronormativity**: a worldview that views heterosexuality as the normal or preferred sexual orientation.
9 **Microaggression**: a casual slight that denigrates or reinforces the devalued status of a member of a marginalized group.
10 Transmisogyny: devaluation of transgender women due both to transphobia and misogyny, the assumption that female/feminine people and things are inferior to male/masculine people and things. An intersectional concept—see Serano (2016).
11 Resistance: refusing to take on cultural norms that devalue your identity and experience; substituting your own voice and norms instead.
12 Subversion: turning dominant norms or expectations to your own ends; undermining them by making them your own in some way.
13 Testosterone—like many transgender men, David takes a small dose of testosterone via a trans-dermal patch. Testosterone can cause increased libido.
14 Top surgery: mastectomy, or removal of the breasts, an important step in transition for some transgender men, especially those who had naturally large breasts, as it makes them less likely to be incorrectly identified as female by others.
15 Read: identify. Also "clock."

References

Adamczyk, A., Boyd, K. A., & Hayes, B. E. (2016). Place matters: Contextualizing the roles of religion and race for understanding Americans' attitudes about homosexuality. *Social Science Research*, 57, 1–16.

Addison, S. M., & Coolhart, D. (2015). Expanding the therapy paradigm with queer couples: A relational intersectional lens. *Family Process*, 54(3), 435–453.

Anderson, H. (1997). *Conversation, language, and possibilities: A postmodern approach to therapy.* New York, NY: BasicBooks.

Bertrand, M., Kamenica, E., & Pan, J. (2015). Gender identity and relative income within households. *The Quarterly Journal of Economics*, 130(2), 571–614.

Blumer, M. L., Green, M. S., Knowles, S. J., & Williams, A. (2012). Shedding light on thirteen years of darkness: Content analysis of articles pertaining to transgender issues in marriage/couple and family therapy journals. *Journal of Marital and Family Therapy*, 38, 244–256.

Bornstein, K. (2006). *Hello, cruel world: 101 alternatives to suicide for teens, freaks, and other outlaws.* New York, NY: Seven Stories Press.

Bradford, M. (2015). Affirmative bisexual couple therapy. In J. J. Bigner & J. L. Wetchler (Eds.), *Handbook of LGBT-affirmative couple and family therapy* (pp. 57–68). New York, NY: Routledge.

Buxton, A. P. (2004). Paths and pitfalls: How heterosexual spouses cope when their husbands or wives come out. In J. J. Bigner & J. L. Wetchler (Eds.), *Relationship therapy with same-sex couples* (pp. 95–109). New York, NY: Haworth Press.

Cardemil, E., & Battle, C. (2003). Guess who's coming to therapy? Getting comfortable with conversations about race and ethnicity in therapy. *Professional Psychology: Research and Practice*, 34, 278–286.

Cho, S., Crenshaw, K. W., & McCall, L. (2013). Toward a field of intersectionality studies: Theory, applications, and praxis. *Signs*, 38(4), 785–810.

Clark, W., & Serovich, J. M. (1997). Twenty years and still in the dark? Content analysis of articles pertaining to gay, lesbian, and bisexual issues in marriage and family therapy journals. *Journal of Marital and Family Therapy*, 23(3), 239–253.

Collins, J. F. (2004). The intersection of race and bisexuality: A critical overview of the literature and past, present, and future directions of the 'Borderlands.' *Journal of Bisexuality*, *4* (1/2), 99–116.

Connolly, C. M. (2004). Clinical issues with same-sex couples: A review of the literature. In J. J. Bigner & J. L. Wetchler (Eds.), *Relationship therapy with same-sex couples* (pp. 3–12). New York, NY: Haworth Press.

Crenshaw, K. W. (1989). Demarginalizing the intersection of race and sex: A black feminist critique of antidiscrimination doctrine, feminist theory and antiracist politics. *University of Chicago Legal Forum*, *1989*, 139–67.

Davies, D. (2000). Towards a model of gay affirmative therapy. In D. Davies & C. Neal, (Eds.), *Pink therapy: A guide for counselors and therapists working with lesbian, gay and bisexual clients* (pp. 24–40). Philadelphia, PA: Open University Press.

Day-Vines, N. L., Bryan, J., & Griffin, D. (2013). The Broaching Attitudes and Behavior Survey (BABS): An exploratory assessment of its dimensionality. *Journal of Multicultural Counseling and Development*, *41*(4), 210–223.

Day-Vines, N. L., & Holcomb-McCoy, C. (2013). Broaching the subjects of race, ethnicity, and culture as a tool for addressing diversity in Counselor Education classes. In J. D. West, D. L. Bubenzer, J. A. Cox, & J. M. McGlothlin (Eds.), *Teaching in Counselor Education: Engaging students in learning* (pp. 151–166). Alexandria, VA: Association for Counselor Education & Supervision.

Day-Vines, N. L., Wood, S. M., Grothaus, T., Craigen, L., Holman, A., Dotson-Blake, K., & Douglass, M. J. (2007). Broaching the subjects of race, ethnicity, and culture during the counseling process. *Journal of Counseling & Development*, *85*(4), 401–409.

DiAngelo, R. (2011). White fragility. *International Journal of Critical Pedagogy*, *3*(3), 54–70.

Diller, A., Houston, B., Morgan, K. P., & Ayim, M. (1996). *The gender question in education: Theory; pedagogy & politics*. Boulder, CO: Westview Press.

Falicov, C. J. (2014). Psychotherapy and supervision as cultural encounters: The MECA framework. In C. A. Falender, E. P. Shafransky, & C. J. Falicov (Eds.), *Multiculturalism and diversity in clinical supervision: A competency based approach*. Washington, DC: American Psychological Association.

Foucault, M. (1984). Nietzsche, genealogy, history. In P. Rabinow (Ed.), *The Foucault reader* (p. 76–100). New York, NY: Pantheon.

Glass, V. Q., & Few-Demo, A. L. (2013). Complexities of informal social support arrangements for black lesbian couples. *Family Relations*, *62*(5), 714–726.

GLSEN (2013a). *School Climate in Maine (State Snapshot)*. New York: GLSEN. Retrieved February 12, 2016 from www.glsen.org/article/state-state-research.

GLSEN (2013b). *School Climate in Texas (State Snapshot)*. New York: GLSEN. Retrieved February 12, 2016 from www.glsen.org/article/state-state-research.

Green, R. J. (2012). Gay and lesbian family life: Risk, resilience, and rising expectations. In F. Walsh (Ed.), *Normal family processes* (pp. 172–195). New York, NY: Guilford Press.

Green, R. J. & Mitchell, V. (2015). Gay, lesbian, and bisexual issues in couple therapy. In A. S. Gurman, J. L. Lebow, & D. K. Snyder (Eds.), *Clinical handbook of couple therapy* (pp. 489–511). New York, NY: Guilford.

Green, R. J., Rubio, R. J., Bergman, K., & Katzuny, K. E. (August 7, 2015). *Gay fathers by surrogacy: Prejudice, parenting, and well-being of female and male children*. Paper presented at the American Psychological Association Convention, Toronto, Ontario, Canada.

Greenhalgh, S. (2015). *Fat-talk nation: The human costs of America's war on fat*. Ithaca, NY: Cornell University Press.

Hardy, K. V., & Laszloffy, T. A. (2002). Couple therapy using a multicultural perspective. In A. Gurman & N. Jacobson (Eds.), *Clinical handbook of couple therapy* (pp. 569–593). New York, NY: Guilford.

Hartwell, E. E., Serovich, J. M., Grafsky, E. L., & Kerr Z. Y. (2012). Coming out of the dark: Content analysis of articles pertaining to gay, lesbian, and bisexual issues in couple and family therapy journals. *Journal of Marital and Family Therapy, 38*(s1), 227–243.

Higginbotham, E. B. (1993). *Righteous discontent: The women's movement in the Black Baptist Church, 1880–1920.* Cambridge, MA: Harvard University Press.

Hook, J. N., Davis, D. E., Owen, J., Worthington, E. L., & Utsey, S. O. (2013). Cultural humility: Measuring openness to culturally diverse clients. *Journal of Counseling Psychology, 60*(3), 353–366.

Hudak, J., & Giammattei, S. V. (2014). Doing family: Decentering heteronormativity in "marriage" and "family" therapy. *Critical Topics in Family Therapy: AFTA SpringerBriefs in Family Therapy,* 105–115.

Killian, K. D. (2003). Homogamy outlaws. *Journal of Couple & Relationship Therapy, 2*(2–3), 3–21.

Knox, S., Burkard, A. W., Johnson, A. J., Suzuki, L. A., & Ponterotto, J. G. (2003). African American and European American therapists' experiences of addressing race in cross-racial psychotherapy dyads. *Journal of Counseling Psychology, 50,* 466–481. doi:10.1037/0022-0167.50.4.466.

Lev, A. I. (2004). *Transgender emergence: Therapeutic guidelines for working with gender-variant people and their families.* New York, NY: Haworth Press.

Lev, A. I., & Sennott, S. (2015). Transsexual desire in differently gendered bodies. In J. J. Bigner & J. L. Wetchler (Eds.), *Handbook of LGBT-affirmative couple and family therapy* (pp. 113–128). New York, NY: Routledge.

Madsen, P. W., & Green, R. (2012). Gay adolescent males' effective coping with discrimination: A qualitative study. *Journal of LGBT Issues in Counseling, 6*(2), 139–155.

Malpas, J. (2006). From otherness to alliance. *Journal of GLBT Family Studies, 2*(3–4), 183–206.

Malpas, J. (2015). Can couples change gender? Couple therapy with transgender people and their partners. In J. J. Bigner & J. L. Wetchler (Eds.), *Handbook of LGBT-affirmative couple and family therapy* (pp. 69–85). New York, NY: Routledge.

McDowell, T. (2015). *Applying critical social theories to family therapy practice.* New York, NY: Springer International.

Meyer, I. H. (2003). Prejudice, social stress, and mental health in lesbian, gay, and bisexual populations: Conceptual issues and research evidence. *Psychological Bulletin, 129*(5), 674–697.

Mulick, P. S., & Wright, L. W., Jr. (2002). Examining the existence of biphobia in the heterosexual and homosexual populations. *Journal of Bisexuality, 2*(4), 45–64.

Ortega, R., & Coulborn Faller, K. (2011). Cultural humility for child welfare professionals: A paradigm shift. *Child Welfare, 90*(5), 27–49.

Owen, J., Tao, K. W., Imel, Z. E., Wampold, B. E., & Rodolfa, E. (2014). Addressing racial and ethnic microaggressions in therapy. *Professional Psychology: Research and Practice, 45*(4), 283–290.

Petford, B. (2005). Therapy from the fence: Therapists who self-identify as bisexual and their approach to therapy. *Journal of Bisexuality, 5*(4), 19–33.

Reynoso, A., & Friend, C. (2015). Child maltreatment and child welfare. In E. Schott & E. L. Weiss (Eds.), *Transformative social work practice* (pp. 183–200). Thousand Oaks, CA: SAGE Publications.

Riggs, D. W. (2015). Ethical issues in LGBT couple and family therapy. In J. J. Bigner & J. L. Wetchler (Eds.), *Handbook of LGBT-affirmative couple and family therapy* (pp. 421–432). New York, NY: Routledge.

Rutter, P. (2015). Sex therapy for gay male couples: Affirming strengths and stemming challenges. In J. J. Bigner & J. L. Wetchler (Eds.), *Handbook of LGBT-affirmative couple and family therapy* (pp. 89–98). New York, NY: Routledge.

Schüssler Fiorenza, E. (2001). *Wisdom ways: Introducing feminist Biblical interpretation.* Maryknoll, NY: Orbis Books.

Seacat, J. D., Dougal, S. C., & Roy, D. (2014). A daily diary assessment of female weight stigmatization. *Journal of Health Psychology, 21*(2), 228–240.

Serano, J. (2013). *Excluded: Making feminism and queer movements more inclusive.* Berkeley, CA: Seal Press.

Serano, J. (2016). *Whipping girl: A transsexual woman on sexism and the scapegoating of femininity* (2nd ed.). Berkeley, CA: Seal Press.

Singh, A. A., & Harper, A. (2015). Intercultural issues in LGBTQQ couple and family therapy. In J. J. Bigner & J. L. Wetchler (Eds.), *Handbook of LGBT-affirmative couple and family therapy* (pp. 283–298). New York, NY: Routledge.

Stone Carlson, T., & McGeorge, C. R. (2015). LGB-affirmative training strategies for Couple and Family Therapist faculty: Preparing heterosexual students to work with LGB clients. In J. J. Bigner & J. L. Wetchler (Eds.), *Handbook of LGBT-affirmative couple and family therapy* (pp. 395–408). New York, NY: Routledge.

Tervalon, M., & Murray-García, J. (1998). Cultural humility versus cultural competence: A critical distinction in defining physician training outcomes in multicultural education. *Journal of Health Care for the Poor and Underserved, 9*(2), 117–125.

Thompson, C. E., & Jenal, S. T. (1994). Interracial and intraracial quasi-counseling interactions when counselors avoid discussing race. *Journal of Counseling Psychology, 41*(4), 484–491.

Watts-Jones, T. D. (2010). Location of self: Opening the door to dialogue on intersectionality in the therapy process. *Family Process, 49*(3), 405–420.

Wyatt, R. C. (2008, June). Kenneth V. Hardy on multiculturalism and psychotherapy. Retrieved March 8, 2016 from www.psychotherapy.net/interview/kenneth-hardy.

INDEX